Access2000

for Busy People

BLUEPRINT *for Busy People*

Create and print mailing labels for addresses, badges, and more.

Select your label stock for a perfect fit.

Create a sheet of labels as easily as a report.

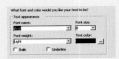

Choose the font, font size, and color.

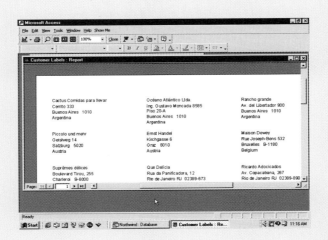

Design the layout of the label using table fields and text.

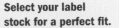

Click Finish and you're done.

Choose the fields for sorting the completed labels.

Publish your database to your Web site.

Add any form or table to your Web site.

Just export the form or report from the Database window.

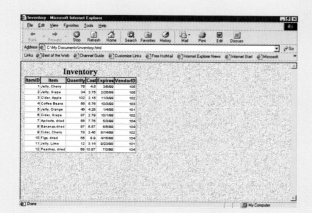

Choose a static HTML page or dynamic page that reflects the current data.

Create high-impact onscreen presentations and reports with charts and graphs.

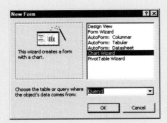

Graph data in a form for onscreen presentations or as a report for printing or faxing.

A variety of charting options lets you pick the best way to display your data.

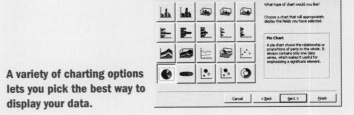

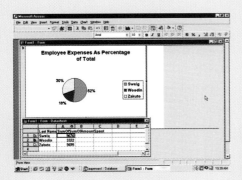

Adding data is as easy as creating a spreadsheet.

Create titles and subtitles, and customize the chart to suit your own tastes.

Customize the way Access works and looks.

There are dozens of settings that you can customize to control how Access looks and works.

Formatting tools are onscreen in a handy toolbar.

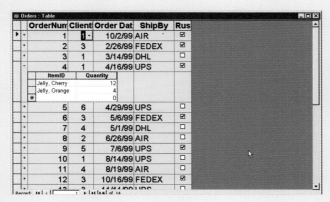

Adjust how tables appear onscreen, selecting colors, effects, and column sizes.

Create your own toolbars...

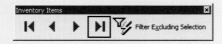

...and then customize how they appear.

Customize toolbars and menus...and create your own.

Create data access pages for use in Access as well as the Internet.

Access wizards takes you step-by-step.

You can customize every aspect of the Web page.

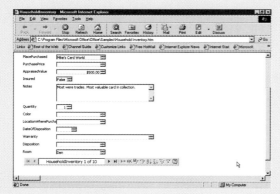

Work with the same form in Access or on the Internet.

Create Web pages with multiple forms from related tables.

Add backgrounds, headlines, and even sound.

Analyze and report information on the fly.

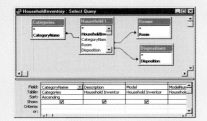

Get data quick from multiple related tables.

Create cross-tabulations to see trends and forecasts.

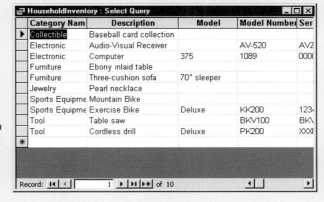

Use queries to create quick reports that analyze information to help decision making.

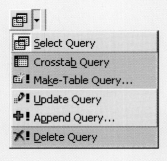

Use queries to make new tables, change tables, or add and delete information.

Access information using SQL commands and syntax.

BLUEPRINT *for Busy People*

Create invoices and other business documents.

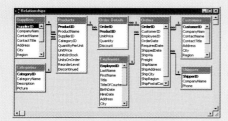

Relate tables to merge data
from multiple sources.

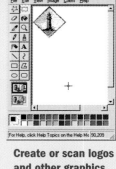

Create or scan logos
and other graphics.

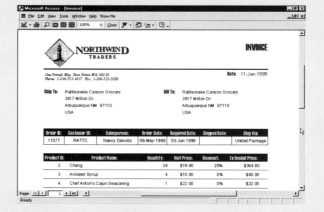

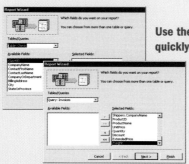

Use the Report Wizard to
quickly create the invoice.

Add page numbers to organize
long reports, and the date to
keep track of information.

Take advantage of built-in templates for complete databases.

Access includes a variety of complete databases.

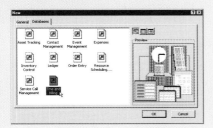

Use templates to create a complete database with tables, forms, reports, and data access pages—just add your own information.

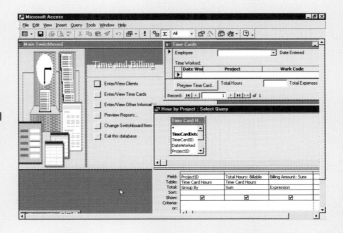

Use the Switchboard as a central database interface.

Store company or personal information for consistent reports and forms.

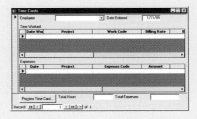

Harness the power of sophisticated multiple-table forms for viewing, adding, and changing information.

To Izzy, Joe, Lori, Lou, and Rich—the team of medical super-heroes who finally conquered the Lyme spirochete within me. Thank you.

About the Author

Alan Neibauer (Huntington Valley, PA) is the best-selling author of *Corel WordPerfect Suite 8: The Official Guide*, *Access 97 for Busy People*, *Microsoft Word for Windows 95 Made Easy*, and the soon-to-be-published *Office 2000 Made Easy* and *WordPerfect Office 2000: The Official Guide*. Since 1985, he has published over 30 popular books on both hardware and software. Neibauer has spent over 14 years teaching computer science at the high school and college level, and is also a popular corporate trainer in Microsoft Access and other Office Applications.

Access2000

for Busy People

The Book to Use When There's No Time to Lose!

Alan Neibauer

OSBORNE

Osborne/McGraw-Hill

Berkeley / New York / St. Louis / San Francisco / Auckland / Bogotá
Hamburg / London / Madrid / Mexico City / Milan / Montreal / New Delhi
Panama City / Paris / São Paulo / Singapore / Sydney / Tokyo / Toronto

A Division of The McGraw·Hill Companies

Osborne/**McGraw-Hill**
2600 Tenth Street
Berkeley, California 94710
U.S.A.

For information on translations or book distributors outside the U.S.A., or to arrange bulk purchase discounts for sales promotions, premiums, or fund-raisers, please contact Osborne/**McGraw-Hill** at the above address.

Access 2000 for Busy People

1234567890 DOC DOC 90198765432109

ISBN 0-07-211983-7

Publisher   Brandon A. Nordin
Associate Publisher and Editor-in-Chief   Scott Rogers
Acquisitions Editor   Joanne Cuthbertson
Project Editor   Mark Karmendy
Editorial Assistant   Stephane Thomas
Technical Editor   Mark Hall
Copy Editor   Claire Splan
Indexer   Rebecca Plunkett
Computer Designers   Michelle Galicia, Roberta Steele
Graphic Artists   Robert Hansen, Beth Young, Brian Wells
Series Designer   Jil Weil
Cover Design   Damore Johann Design, Inc.
Cover Illustration/Chapter Opener Illustration   Robert deMichiell

This book was composed with Corel VENTURA.

CONTENTS

Acknowledgments

My thanks to everyone who helped make this book, and series, a reality. Thanks to acquisitions editor Joanne Cuthbertson, project editor Mark Karmendy, copyeditor Claire Splan, and technical editor Mark Hall. Special thanks to acquisitions assistant Stephane Thomas, for keeping me afloat in a sea of chapters and figures.

I also want to thank Microsoft's beta support team and the hundreds of beta testers who shared their ideas and knowledge over the Office 2000 newsgroup.

Thanks to Donut Boy and Huntingdon Valley Spice for fun interludes during this hectic period.

Finally, thanks to Barbara, my confidant, caretaker, financial advisor, wife, and best friend. For 32 years she has amused, surprised, pleased, and loved me. I promise I will match my socks one day.

Introduction

Finding just the right book for your needs is not always easy, especially facing the hundreds of competing titles in the bookstore. Still, it is an important task. Suppose you're looking for a book on Access, which isn't much of a stretch since you're reading this now. What goes through your mind? If you are busy, like most of us, you might be thinking, "How much time can I really afford learning this program?" After all, you have Access so you can start using, not reading, about it.

A lot of books, unfortunately, are written to impress or entertain you. That's not necessarily a bad thing if you're cuddling by the fire with a spine-tingling thriller, or feeding your brain cells with Umberto Eco's latest foray into antiquity. But no one buys a computer book for its literary value. A computer book has one purpose, and one purpose only—to get you productive as quickly and as painlessly as possible. It should be easy to read, pleasing to the eye, and down to the point.

To make my point, that's why we've published this Busy People series. It is expressly for people who want to get a job done, and who don't have any time to waste. People who want to know how to get something done in as little time as possible, but who won't be satisfied with sketchy information and half-hearted examples.

I Know You're in a Hurry, So...

Enough of the required introduction. If you haven't yet installed Access onto your computer, boot up your computer and insert the Access 2000 CD, or the Microsoft Office Professional 2000 CD, whichever you have. Follow the instructions on the screen to install the program. When you're done, keep the CD handy—you may need it later to add or remove parts of Access to set up features that were not installed or to clear extra space from your disk drive.

When you've got Access installed, and you know your way somewhat around Windows, then you're ready to start. Because you are busy, I suggest starting at the beginning. In the first chapter of this book, you'll learn how to create databases—and pretty sophisticated ones at that—in less time than the average coffee break. I call these Almost Instant Databases. The next several chapters show you how to use these databases, so you can enter, edit, and sort information; select specific information when you need it; and print forms and reports. If you are busy, these Almost Instant Databases can satisfy most of your database needs, and make you a hero or heroine around the office.

After that we really take off. The remaining chapters show you how to create custom databases, almost instantly as well, and put together a complete database package with custom forms and reports, ad hoc queries, and even share information between Access and other Windows programs.

Things You Might Want to Know About This Book

Like Access, this book is designed to make your life easier. You can go through it chapter by chapter, creating your own databases, forms, and reports using our examples as a guide. You can also use this book as a reference. Trying to do something right now? Just go directly to the section in the book, find out how to do it, and then just do it. We've even added special elements to make sure you don't waste any time.

Blueprints

At the beginning of this book you'll find eight blueprints. The blueprints show you how to harness the power of Access by using some of the templates that come with this program. A template creates a complete database, including tables, forms, reports, and queries—even sample information. Use the blueprints to get your creative juices flowing so that you can get a working database in just a few clicks of the mouse.

FAST FORWARDs

Each chapter begins with a section called *FAST FORWARD*. FAST FORWARDS are step-by-step directions, with illustrations, that quickly guide you through the tasks explained in the chapter. Sometimes that's all you'll need to read to perform an Access function. But if you need more, you'll find page references right there so you can just flip to the section in the chapter that discusses the subject in detail.

EXPERT ADVICE

The ***EXPERT ADVICE*** boxes suggest timesaving tips, techniques, and worthwhile addictions. Force yourself to develop some good habits now, when it's still possible! These notes, marked by the lecturing professor, also give you the big picture and help you plan ahead.

Margin note

Throughout the book, cross-references and other minor asides appear in the margins.

Look for these in the margin.

SHORTCUTs

SHORTCUTs are designed for the busy person—when there's a way to do something that may not be as full-featured as the material in the text, but is *faster*. These will show up in the margin, identified by the leaping businessman.

CAUTIONs

Sometimes it's too easy to plunge ahead and fall down a rabbit hole, resulting in hours of extra work just to get you back to where you were before you went astray. The terrified face that appears in a *CAUTION* will warn you before you commit time-consuming mistakes.

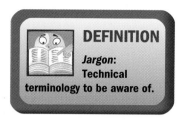

DEFINITIONs

Usually, I'll explain computer or Access processing jargon in the text, wherever the technobabble first occurs. But if you encounter words you don't recognize, look for this dictionary searcher in the margin. *DEFINITIONs* point out important terms you reasonably might not know the meaning of. When necessary, they're strict and a little technical, but most of the time they're informal and conversational.

Let's Do It!

Ready? Let's dig into Access 2000 before the next millennium!

Incidentally, I'm always happy to hear your reactions to this or any of my other books. You can reach me through the publisher or on the Net at:

ComputerAuthor@hotmail.com

CHAPTER 1

Almost Instant Databases

INCLUDES

- Learning about Access
- Starting Access
- Creating a database using a Database Wizard
- Understanding the Access screen
- Learning about databases
- Learning about the Database window
- Using the switchboard
- Opening a database

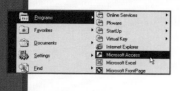

Start Access ➥ pp. 5–8
1. Click the Start button in the taskbar.
2. Point to Programs.
3. Click on Microsoft Access.

Create a Database ➥ pp. 8–13
1. Start Access.
2. Click on Access Database Wizards, Pages, and Projects.
3. Click OK.
4. Click on the Databases tab.
5. Double-click on the desired template.
6. Enter the database name and click Create.
7. Follow the instructions on the screen, clicking Next to advance through the dialog boxes.
8. Click Finish.

Display Parts of the Database ➥ pp. 14–19
1. Display the Database window.
2. Click on the category to see lists of database objects:
   - Tables
   - Queries
   - Forms
   - Reports
   - Pages
   - Macros
   - Modules
3. Double-click the object to be opened or displayed.

Add a Database Object to a Group ➥ p. 17
1. Display the Database window.
2. Enlarge the Database window, if necessary, to display the objects and groups.
3. Click on the object that contains the item you want to move to the group.
4. Drag the item to the group name.

Open a Database ➡ pp. 24–25

- When starting Access, double-click on the database listed at the bottom of the Startup dialog box.
- When Access is already open, click the Open Database button, and double-click on the database in the Open dialog box.

Close a Database ➡ p. 25

- Choose Close from the File menu, or
- Click the Close box on the right side of the Database window.

Unless you're a control freak, you don't have to design every database from the ground up. To get you up and running quickly, this chapter introduces you to the Database Wizard, a nifty tool that lets you create a complete, sophisticated database with a few clicks of the mouse. You get a complete database, even with sample information if you want it. To start with, it may not have every feature that you need, but you will learn how to easily add tables, forms, reports, and other elements later on. The idea is that the wizard will let you create and start using a database—for all of that important work you have to do—in a short time. Then as you become more familiar with Access, you can modify and expand the database to perform all of the functions for which you purchased Access.

DEFINITION

Wizard:
A series of dialog boxes that guide you through the process of completing a task.

Anatomy of a Database

DEFINITION

Database:
A repository of information.

Table:
A collection of information relating to a specific category of information.

Record:
A collection of information about one object in the table.

Field:
A specific category of information in each record.

Before we dive in, let's review a few important concepts and terms. There aren't too many of them, but it's important to spend a few minutes getting oriented. Let's start with the term *database*.

A database is a place where you store information. You can consider a box of three-by-five index cards to be a database. So, too, can you consider a filing cabinet full of folders and papers a database. In fact, let's do that. Picture a database as a large filing cabinet holding all of your company's records. Put all of those records on a computer, and have a program to find, edit, and print information, and you have a database. Simple.

Now look at the labels on the filing cabinet drawers. One label might say employee records, another client information, another invoices, and another inventory. In database-speak we call each of these drawers a *table*.

For example, the Clients table contains the information we need about our clients. The Invoice table contains information about invoices. The tables are separate but do they have anything in common? Sure. They all contain information about your company, so they are all in the same database.

Now open a cabinet drawer. In the invoice drawer you'll see a series of invoices. Each invoice contains the information about one order. This is what database geeks call a *record*. What does each record in the client drawer contain? The name, address, and other information about a client.

OK, now look at a sheet of paper containing that client's information. Each piece of information—such as the name or phone number—is called a *field*. And finally, each field is simply made up of individual letters, numbers, or punctuation marks.

So let's review the parts of a database by working backward, from the smallest entity to the largest:

- Individual characters make up a *field*—a single piece of information.
- The fields are categories of information collected in *records*—the information about one client, invoice, or whatever.
- The records are contained in *tables*, which store the information about all of the clients, invoices, or whatever.
- Tables are contained in *databases*.
- Databases are stored on your disk.

Starting Access

Before you can start Access, you need to start your computer and Windows. Once Windows is running, start Access as follows:

1. Click the Start button in the taskbar.

2. Point to Programs.

3. Click on Microsoft Access.

If Access is not listed on the Programs menu, then one of two things has occurred. Either you did not yet install Access on your system, or Access is contained in a group within the Programs option.

Look for a listing such as MSOffice or Office. Point to it and see if Access is there. If it is, click it. Otherwise, you'll have to install Access: gather together your Office CD or Access disks and follow the setup instructions in Appendix A. Then come back, please.

When you start Access for the very first time, your cute little Office Assistant will ask if you want some help. Click on the button labeled Start Using Microsoft Access to see the dialog box shown in Figure 1.1. This dialog box will automatically appear now whenever you start Access to let you open or create a database.

In the background, behind the Startup dialog box, is the Access screen, shown labeled, without the dialog box blocking your view, in Figure 1.2. At the top of the screen are the title bar, menu bar, and toolbar. The menu bar contains options for performing Access functions. The toolbar contains buttons for performing the most typical Access functions. To use the toolbar, just point to the button for the function you want to perform and click. If you're not sure what function a button performs, don't worry. When you point to a button, Access displays a ToolTip—a small box showing the button's

If you create a blank database, you'll have to create tables, forms, reports, and pages yourself.

The Database Wizard takes you step-by-step through creating a complete database.

Use this option to open an existing database. Recently used databases will be listed in this dialog box.

Double-click to open a sample database.

Figure 1.1: This dialog box appears whenever you start Access—use it to start a new database or open an existing one

name. The buttons in the toolbar will change depending on what you are doing in Access, and some of the buttons may be dimmed. You'll learn how to use the toolbar throughout this book, but take a look at it now so you can see how it changes.

At the bottom of the screen is the status bar. Here Access tells you something about the state of your system. On the left of the status bar, for example, it will report the current view, the type of function you are performing, or the function of the toolbar button you are pointing to with the mouse. If the status bar says Form View, for example, then you are looking at a form. On the right are status boxes, telling you if your CAPS LOCK, NUM LOCK, or SCROLL LOCK keys are on, or if you are inserting or overtyping (replacing) characters as you type. In the

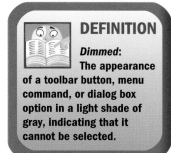

DEFINITION

Dimmed: The appearance of a toolbar button, menu command, or dialog box option in a light shade of gray, indicating that it cannot be selected.

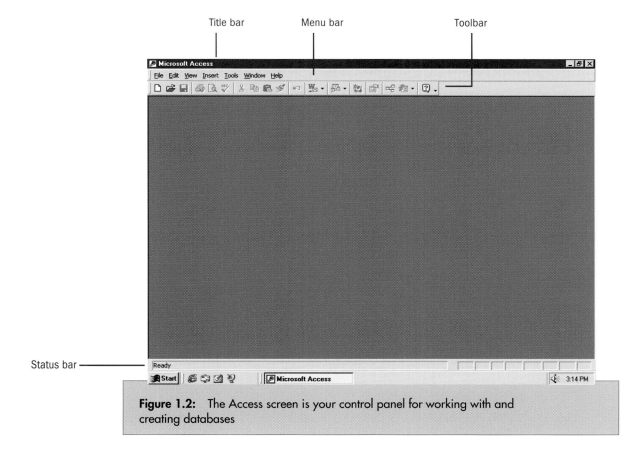

Figure 1.2: The Access screen is your control panel for working with and creating databases

space between the toolbar and the status bar, you see your database and the various parts of it.

Almost Instant Databases

To see how easy it is to create a database, let's create a database right now. We'll create a database to track employee expenses, which will please your accountant, the IRS, and your bottom line. It will have four related tables, and it will be complete with seven forms and three reports. There'll even be a menu that lets you perform the most typical functions. All of this with just a few clicks! No more theory and technobabble—let's just jump right in.

Let's start the Database Wizard and create the database. The Startup dialog box should be on your screen, so let's go.

1. Click the Access Database Wizards, Pages, And Projects option button. This tells Access that you want it to create a database for you.

2. Click OK. The New dialog box will appear with two tabs, General and Databases. (You would use the General tab to start a blank database, which would require you to design the tables yourself.)

3. Click on the Databases tab to see the page shown in Figure 1.3. In this dialog box, you select one of several existing database types. They include many of the common functions that people use databases for.

If you do not see a database that seems perfect for your needs, look for one that comes close. You can then modify it to suit your needs.

4. Point to Expenses and double-click. The File New Database box appears. In this box, you give the database a name and you tell Access where on your disk you want to save it. By default, Access saves databases in the My Documents directory. Access will give the database a name based on the type you've chosen, such as Friends1 or Contact Management1.

EXPERT ADVICE

When you need to create a database, try the Database Wizard first—it can save you a lot of time. Once a Database Wizard creates the database for you, you can add additional tables, forms, reports, and other elements as you need them.

Use the Databases tab to select
from predesigned databases.

Use these tools to display items by
icon, in a list, or in detail.

Use the General
tab to create a
blank database.

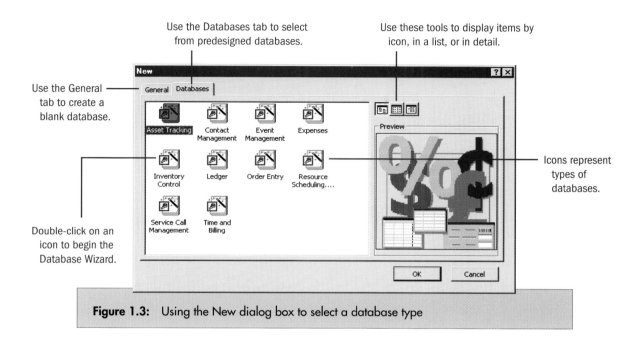

Icons represent
types of
databases.

Double-click on an
icon to begin the
Database Wizard.

Figure 1.3: Using the New dialog box to select a database type

5. Type **Office Expenses** and then click Create.

Access does a few chores, and after a few moments the first
wizard dialog box appears as shown in Figure 1.4. This box

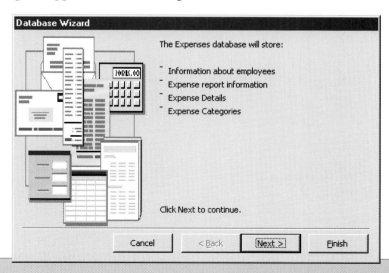

Figure 1.4: The wizard tells you what information the database will store

shows you the type of information that the database will store. At the bottom of the wizard dialog box are four buttons: Cancel, Back, Next, and Finish.

- Click on Cancel to stop the wizard.
- Click on Back to go to the previous wizard dialog box.
- Click on Next to move to the next dialog box.
- Click on Finish to complete the wizard using the default values for the remaining dialog box.

   6. Click Finish—you're done. Access now creates your database.

Depending on your computer, this can take several minutes, or longer, so be patient. First, you'll see a blank Database window on the screen (you'll learn more about this later) and then Access creates the tables, forms, and reports, and other elements that make up the database. When the database is created, the Main Switchboard form will appear, as shown in Figure 1.5.

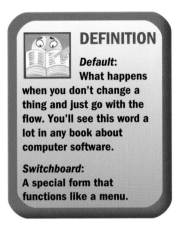

DEFINITION

***Default*:**
What happens when you don't change a thing and just go with the flow. You'll see this word a lot in any book about computer software.

***Switchboard*:**
A special form that functions like a menu.

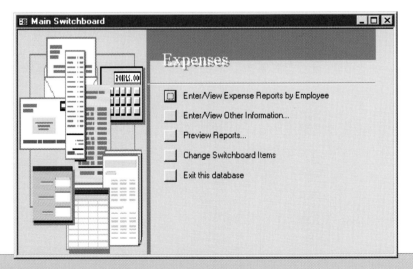

Figure 1.5:   Main Switchboard form

A Quick Tour of the Almost Instant Database

There are quite a few parts to an Access database, so let's take a minute to orient ourselves in this new terrain.

What you're looking at now is the Main Switchboard. Access provides switchboards for the databases it creates with the wizard, but they will not automatically appear in databases you create yourself. Switchboards make it easy to perform tasks in a database, so you should get to know them. In front of each item in the switchboard is a button, like this:

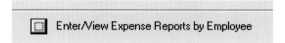

To perform the function listed, click the button.

Access Forms

Click the button next to Enter/View Expense Reports By Employee, the first option on the switchboard menu. Access displays a form, as shown in Figure 1.6. (If you used the Database Wizard before and selected design elements, your form may look a little different than ours.)

DEFINITION

Form:
An electronic version of a paper form that you use to enter information into the database, to change the information, and to view it on the screen.

Forms are a great way to work with a database. Not only can you use it to enter, edit, and review information, but you can also print a copy of the form for reference. In most cases, the fields in a form correspond to the fields in an underlying table. However, you can also have calculated fields—categories of information calculated from the values in other fields. These are not part of any table, they just appear on the form.

The form contains labels and text boxes. The labels let you know what to type in the text box. Because there is no data in the table yet, the form is blank. The form in Figure 1.6 is actually a special type of form that is two forms in one. On the top will be information about an employee; on the bottom will be a list of that employee's expenses. The form gets its information from two different tables. Notice that

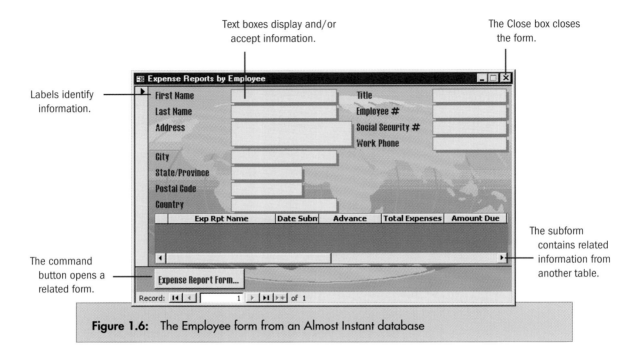

Text boxes display and/or accept information.

The Close box closes the form.

Labels identify information.

The command button opens a related form.

The subform contains related information from another table.

Figure 1.6: The Employee form from an Almost Instant database

when this form is displayed, fewer buttons on the toolbar are dimmed. This means that you can use more of the buttons (in other words, perform more functions) than when the Main Switchboard form was on the screen.

Now click the form's Close box to return to the switchboard.

Clicking the Close box on the right of the Access title bar will close Access. If you click there by mistake, just start Access again and select the Office Expenses database in the Startup dialog box.

Access Reports

You can print forms, but they are primarily designed to be used onscreen. When you want a hard copy, use a report. A report is used for printing information from the database. You can even perform calculations in reports for some statistical analysis, or to summarize large amounts of data.

To see a report, click Preview Reports, the third item on the Main Switchboard menu. A new switchboard menu appears with three options—two types of reports that you can print, and the option to return to the Main Switchboard.

Click the first option—Preview The Expense Rpt Summary By Category Report. A box appears asking for the starting and ending dates, so you can print expenses that occurred between two dates. Since there's no information in this database, you can't enter the dates or preview the report, so click the Close box to return to the switchboard, then click Return To Main Switchboard. Had there been information in the database, the report would have appeared as shown in Figure 1.7. Notice the different toolbar.

A special function displays starting and ending dates.

The report header identifies the report.

A formula in the report footer calculates and displays column totals.

The page header repeats column headings on each page.

Details from the database

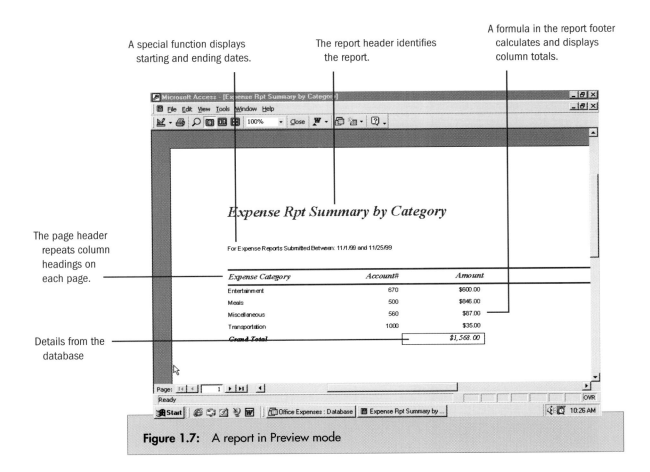

Figure 1.7: A report in Preview mode

EXPERT ADVICE

Switch between open windows by clicking on any portion of a background window to bring it into the foreground. If you cannot see a window in the background, switch to it using the Window menu.

The Database Window

Forms, reports, and other objects are parts of the database. You can access some of the parts through switchboards, but to access all of the parts you will have to use the *Database window*, the main interface to an Access database. Let's look at the Database window now.

So far, you've closed one window before opening another. This time, click the Database Window button. Access displays the main Database window, as shown in Figure 1.8, moving the switchboard into the background. If you close the switchboard by mistake, you'll see the Database window minimized at the bottom of the Access

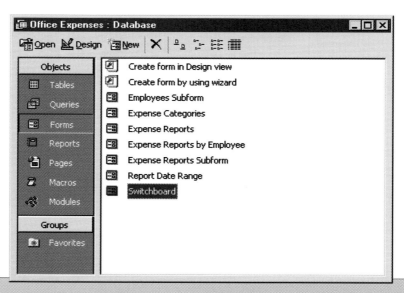

Figure 1.8: The Database window

screen. Click the Restore button to display the Database window. No matter what type of window you have open in Access, you can always click the Database Window button to see the main Database window.

The Database window represents the open database. On the left of the Database window is a list of database objects. Clicking Tables, Queries, Forms, Reports, Pages, Macros, or Modules from the list shows the objects on the right. For example, to see a list of tables in the database, click Tables in the Objects list. To see a list of forms, click Forms.

In addition to the list of items, the Database window also contains *new object shortcuts*, commands to create new tables, forms, reports, and so on, such as the command Create Table in Design View. You can use these commands to create new objects or the command buttons on the top of the Database window. When you are looking at the Tables, Queries, or Forms pages, the following buttons will be available:

- **Open**   To display the item you select in the Database window.
- **Design**   To modify the item selected in the Database window.
- **New**   To create a new object.

Open is replaced by the Preview button when viewing the Reports page, and by Run when viewing the Macros and Modules pages.

Now click each of the objects to see what items have been created for this database.

Datasheets

Forms and Reports are two ways that you can look at the information in a table. When you use a form you see one or more records at a time, depending on the form's design. When you want to see as many records as can fit on your screen at one time, look at the table as a datasheet.

You access datasheets from the Tables page of the Database window, so let's look at a datasheet now. Click on Tables on the left of the Database window to see the list of tables.

Click Employees in the list of tables, and then click Open.

The table appears like a spreadsheet—a series of rows and columns—as shown in Figure 1.9. There's no data in this table so

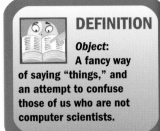

DEFINITION

Object: A fancy way of saying "things," and an attempt to confuse those of us who are not computer scientists.

DEFINITION

Datasheet: The display of table information in rows and columns. The column headings are the field names, and each row is another record.

The Switchboard Items table is a special table that stores the options shown in switchboards. You can add items to this table to add items to the switchboard form.

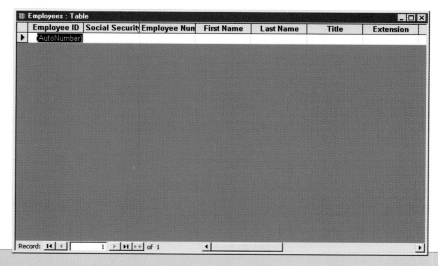

Figure 1.9: Table in Datasheet view

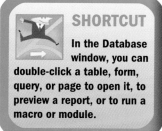

SHORTCUT

In the Database window, you can double-click a table, form, query, or page to open it, to preview a report, or to run a macro or module.

there's only one blank row under the field names. The notation (AutoNumber) means that Access will automatically number the records as you enter them, inserting the number in the Employee ID field.

Choose File | Close to close the datasheet and return to the Database window.

Other Parts of a Database

All Almost Instant databases come complete with forms, reports, datasheets, and a Global Code Module already created for you. They won't have any queries, macros, or custom modules—the other three parts that can make up a database. You have to create those yourself.

A *query* is a question you ask to find information in the table. Who hasn't paid their bill in over 30 days? is a query, and an important one if you plan on staying in business. What the question really tells Access is, show me the records of clients who have unpaid invoices dated over 30 days ago. Each time you ask the question, you may get a different answer, depending on the status of your receivables at the time. When you save the query in Access, you are saving the question, not the answer. You can then run the query to get the latest information.

A *page* (fully known as a *Data Access Page*) is a form that you can use either within Access or with a Web browser. You can place Access pages on a Web server so they are available to persons on the Internet or your company intranet; these persons can then view and edit the data in your database.

A *macro* lets you perform a series of Access tasks by issuing just one command. A *module* is similar, but much more complicated, and requires some computer programming knowledge. Macros and modules are for advanced users.

Groups are convenient places to collect items. For example, suppose you have a large database with many forms and queries but you usually use the same form and query every day. To access the form you'd have to switch from the Tables to the Forms objects list and then find the form you want to use. Then to use the query, you need to change to the Queries object list and find it. Rather than having to switch and search, you can add the form and query to a group, then access them both from the same list. To see the list of groups, click the Groups button below the Objects list. There is one built-in group, called Favorites, that comes with every database. To add an item to Favorites, click the object in the Objects list and then drag the item to the Favorites icon in the Groups list. You can also create new groups by right-clicking anywhere in the left of the Database window and selecting New Group from the menu that appears.

Learning About Relationships

In general, you won't want to put all of your information in one table. It's like the old adage about putting all of your eggs in one basket. For one reason, the more fields and information you put in a table, the more difficult it is to work with. Most of the time, you will divide the information into more than one table, and then tell Access how the tables relate to each other.

For example, suppose you're still using paper forms to record your company's information. If you have more information than can fit on one page, you use a second or third sheet of paper to complete a form. So, while one piece of paper contains address information on client X, another piece of paper contains credit information. When you want to look at address information, you just need the first page. When you want credit information you just need the second. The two pages are related, however, because they both discuss client X. How do you know? You look at the top of both pages and you make sure they both have the same client name, or client number, or some other piece of information that links the two together.

The same should be true with your computer database. You divide the information into more than one table. You then relate the tables to each other, using one or more fields to match the records in one table with the records in the other.

In a database, you can create several types of relationships. In what's called a *one-to-one relationship*—a true monogamy—every record in one table is related to just one record in the other table. So for each client address record, there is just one client credit record.

You can also have a polygamous relationship, called *one-to-many*. This means that a record in one table can be related to one *or more* records in another table. For example, you certainly hope that each client places more than one order. So a client record, in the client table, can be related to more than one record in the order table. How does the database keep track? Because the client name or number in the client record matches the client name or number in the order record. Note that the one-to-many relationship works in only one direction. An order can only be from one client, so each order in the order table is connected to only one client record.

You can see how tables are related from the Database window. Click the Relationships button, which is the third button from the right on the toolbar. Access opens the Relationships window, shown in Figure 1.10.

The figure shows that there is a one-to-many relationship between the Employees and Expense Reports tables linked on the EmployeeID field, and between the Expense Reports and Expense Details tables on the ExpenseReportID field. The line between the Expense Details and the Expense Categories tables (on the ExpenseCategoryID field) indicates a one-to-one relationship; there is no infinity symbol on either end of the line. This means that each expense detail record can only relate to one expense category. The small arrow on one end of the line

Information is often divided into several tables because it makes it easier and more efficient to process.

CAUTION

There is also a relationship called *many-to-many* that requires three tables. It is quite complex, so let's not worry about it for now, OK?

The line from one table to another shows the field that is used to relate the tables, and the type of relationship.

The "1" indicates the "one" side of the relationship.

Each box represents a table, listing its fields.

The infinity symbol indicates the "many" side—that each employee can have one or more expense reports, and that each expense report can include one or more expenses.

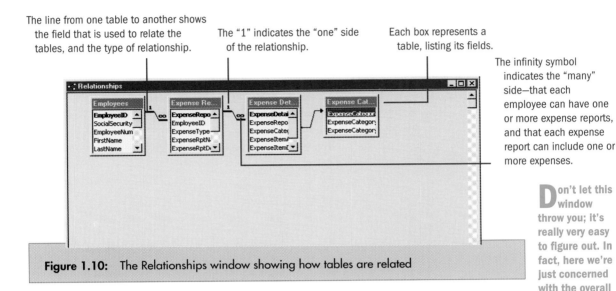

Figure 1.10: The Relationships window showing how tables are related

Don't let this window throw you; it's really very easy to figure out. In fact, here we're just concerned with the overall meaning of the window, so if you don't feel you're ready to handle it, just skip ahead to the next section.

means that it is a special relationship called an *outer join* in which queries will select all matching records from the Expense Details table whether or not there is a matching record in Expense Categories.

That's enough for now. Click the Close box in the Relationships window to return to the Database window.

Creating a Custom Almost Instant Database

When you created the Office Expenses database, you clicked Finish in the first Database Wizard dialog box. Access created the database using all of the default values. This means that it selected which fields to include in the tables and the style of forms and reports. If you don't feel comfortable being so passive, you can make other choices yourself by displaying additional wizard dialog boxes.

Access automatically closes and saves the open database when you create or open another. You cannot have more than one database open at a time, but you can copy information between databases.

EXPERT ADVICE

If you are satisfied with the default database options, just click Finish when the first wizard dialog box appears.

Let's create another database now, this time working through each of the Database Wizard boxes, so you can see what choices you have in creating an Almost Instant database.

1. Click the New Database button in the toolbar, or choose File | New Database.
2. Click on the Databases tab, and then double-click Contact Management. The File New Database dialog box appears where you enter the database name.
3. Type **Contacts** and then click Create. The first wizard box appears listing the type of information that will be stored in this database.
4. Click Next, instead of Finish, to display the next dialog box, shown in Figure 1.11.

The second wizard box shows you the tables that are included with the database (on the left) and the fields that are included in the tables (on the right). You can also select from optional fields that Access does not include by default, and you can select to have Access fill the database with sample data—not because you don't have enough

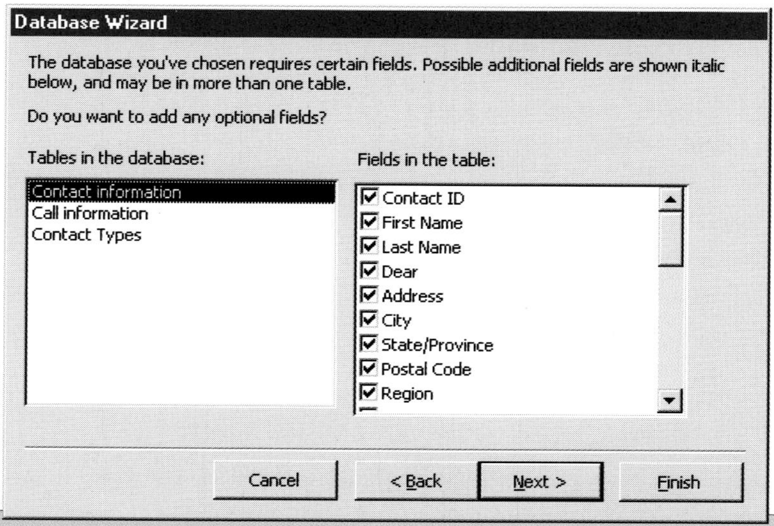

Figure 1.11: The Database Wizard showing tables and fields

contacts on your own, but so you can practice using the database with phony information.

Because the Contact information table is selected on the left, the fields in that table are shown on the right. The check mark next to the field name means that it will be included in the table.

1. Scroll down the Fields in the table list. Below the Work Extension field you'll see Home Phone. It is in italics and the check box is not checked. This means that it is an optional field—that you can have the Database Wizard include it if you want.

2. Click on the check box next to the Home Phone field to select the field, inserting a check mark in the box so Access will now include it in the table.

3. Scroll the list some more and click on the check box next to the optional Birthdate field to include it in the table.

4. Click on the Call Information and Contact Type tables to see their fields.

5. Click Next. This next wizard screen, shown in Figure 1.12, lets you choose a design to use for the forms when you are working

I f you change your mind about including an optional field, click on it again to remove the check mark. You can only remove the check mark from optional fields.

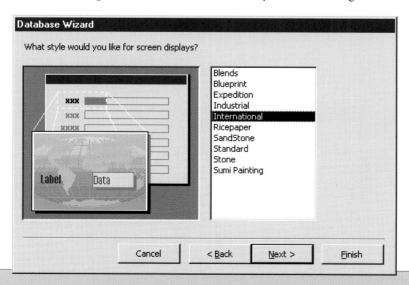

Figure 1.12: The Database Wizard screen for designing a form

with the database. The names of the styles are on the right. When you click a style, the panel on the left will illustrate its appearance. The word "Label" indicates how the name of the field will appear; the word "Data" indicates how the information that you type will appear.

6. Click each of the types to see how they will appear.

7. Click Blends, or another setting that you like, and then click Next. The next wizard screen (Figure 1.13) shows styles for printed reports. Click each of the styles on the right to see how it appears on the left.

8. Click Corporate—let's use the default style to see how it looks—and then click Next. This next dialog box (Figure 1.14) lets you enter the title for the database to use on the switchboard, and asks if you want to include a picture on the main screen and in reports. If you select to include a picture,

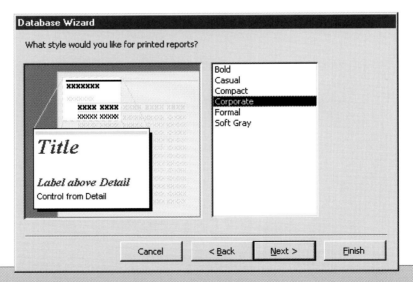

Figure 1.13:   The Database Wizard screen for report design

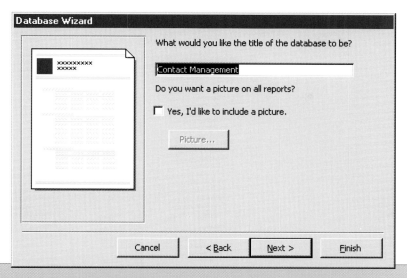

Figure 1.14:   The Database Wizard lets you choose a title and picture

you'll need to find it using the Picture button, so leave this option alone for now.

9. The text in the box is selected, so type **Contacts** and then click Next. The final dialog box has only two options. If you select Yes, Start The Database (selected by default), Access will display the switchboard when the wizard ends.

10. Click the Yes, Start The Database option to deselect it. This will prevent the switchboard from displaying.

11. Click Finish. After Access creates the database, the Office Assistant displays a message telling you so.

12. Click OK.

The Database window looks the same as the one you saw previously; only the listed objects are different.

Click on the database objects to see the names of the tables, forms, and reports created as part of the database. Open one or two of the forms to see how they appear.

The Help option will show you how to work with the database. You have this book, so you don't need to select Help.

The Wizard Remembers

Once you select a look for forms and reports in the Database Wizard, the same styles will automatically be selected when you run the wizard again. If you now create a database by selecting Finish in the first wizard dialog box, for example, the new database will use the Clouds style for forms and the Corporate style for reports. To change the styles, you must select others from the wizard dialog box.

But the wizard also forgets. The wizard does not remember if you've selected optional fields. The next time you create a database using the same template, the optional fields will not be selected by default.

Opening a Database

As you saw, Access closes the open database when you create another. In fact, you can't have more than one database open at a time. If you want to return to the previous database, you have to open it again.

You can open a database when you first start Access, or any time after. When you start Access, databases that you've created will be listed in the dialog box that appears. Double-click the database name, or select it and then choose Open. If you want to open a database directly into the Database window, rather than the switchboard, hold down the SHIFT key as you open it. To see databases that are not listed in the box, click More Files.

Once you start Access, you can open a database using the File menu or the toolbar. Click on the File menu. At the bottom of the file menu, you'll see the names of the last four databases that you worked on. To open one of the databases, just click its name.

To open any database—even one not listed on the File menu—choose File | Open Database, or click on the Open Database button, if it appears in the toolbar, to display the open dialog box shown in Figure 1.15. Do that now.

Now double-click the name of the database you want to open, Office Expenses. Access opens the database and automatically displays the switchboard form. Click Exit This Database to close the database.

In general, to close a database, choose File | Close, or click the Close box on the right side of the Database window. You do not have to save it first; Access takes care of saving most things for you, or prompts you if any objects need to be saved.

You've done enough for one session. To exit Access, choose File | Exit, or click the Close box on the right side of the Access title bar. If you've made any changes to a database that were not saved, a dialog box will appear asking if you want to save the changes. This is Access's way of protecting you from your own mistakes.

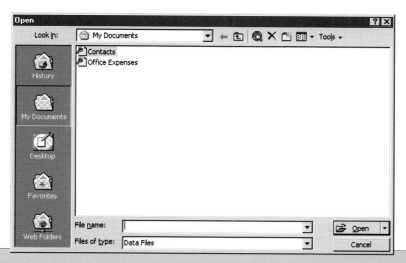

Figure 1.15: Open a database using this dialog box

Summary

Let's suspend the guided tour for a moment and give you a chance to catch your breath. In this chapter, you learned how to create a complete database in just a few mouse clicks and keystrokes. Almost Instant databases contain tables, forms, and reports—the basic building blocks of even the most sophisticated databases. If you want, try it out yourself by selecting other database templates and seeing the Almost Instant databases that you can create.

Then when you're ready, in Chapter 2 you'll learn how to use the Almost Instant databases that you've created so you can start your own database projects.

CHAPTER 2

Using Forms and Data Access Pages

INCLUDES

- Adding records with a form
- Changing information with a form
- Deleting records
- Sorting records
- Filtering information
- Using Data Access Pages

Record: |◄ ◄ | 3 | ► ►| ►* | of 3

Navigate Through Forms ➡ p. 31

- Click First Record.
- Click Previous Record.
- Click in Go To Record box (F5), type **record number**, and press ENTER.
- Click Next Record.
- Click Last Record.

Add a Record ➡ p. 32

- Click New Record.
- Choose Insert | New Record or press ENTER in last field of the last record in some forms.

Cancel Changes ➡ p. 38

Click Undo Current Field/Record to restore current field or entire record.

Delete a Record ➡ pp. 38–39

1. Display record onscreen.
2. Click Delete Record button.

Sort Records ➡ pp. 39–40

1. Click in field containing data to sort by.
2. Click either the Sort Ascending or Sort Descending button.

Filter by Selection ➡ pp. 41–42

1. Click in field containing data to use for filter.
2. Click Filter By Selection button.

Filter for Specific Text ➥ pp. 42–43

1. Right-click in field that you want to use for the filter.
2. Click in the Filter For text box.
3. Type the text you want to use for the filter.
4. Press ENTER.

Filter by Excluding ➥ p. 43

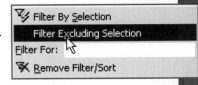

1. Right-click in the field containing data to exclude from the filter.
2. Select Filter Excluding Selection.

Filter by Form ➥ pp. 44–45

1. Click the Filter By Form button.
2. Enter or select the field contents to use for filter.
3. Click on OR and set OR operations.
4. Click Apply Filter.

Remove a Filter ➥ pp. 46–47

- Select Records | Remove Filter/Sort.
- Click Remove Filter button.

Navigate a Data Access Page ➥ pp. 48–49

1. Open the data access page in Access or your Web browser.
2. Use the toolbar to change, sort, add, and delete records.

Now that you've created your Almost Instant database in Chapter 1, it's about time you actually use it. There are three things that you'll want to do most often: add, find, and edit information. Almost Instant databases let you work with information in either a datasheet or a form. Datasheets are useful because they display many records at a time. But because we're used to holding pieces of paper in our hands, forms more closely resemble the way we work with information in the real world. Think of a form as a security blanket to use before graduating into the cold, hard world of databases. So instead of changing our work habits to deal with information in a datasheet, we'll start by working with something more familiar.

Don't skip this chapter, even if you don't plan on using Database Wizard forms. You can use the same techniques explained in this chapter to change, sort, filter, and delete records both on forms that you create yourself, and in Datasheet view as well.

A Tour de Form

Start Access and open the Contacts database as you learned in Chapter 1. Access will display the switchboard. Click Enter/View Other Information to see a second switchboard. Click Enter/View Contact Types to display the form shown in Figure 2.1. If you change any information on the form or add new records using a form, you are actually changing the contents of the table. So the form is more than just a pretty face. It is a way to work with the table in a nicely designed layout.

The insertion point—the blinking line—is in the Contact Type field because you cannot enter or change the information in the Contact Type ID box. This is one of those AutoNumber fields that you saw in Chapter 1. Access will number the first record you enter as 1 (one), the second record as 2 (two), and so on.

If your own database doesn't have a switchboard, click on Forms in the Database window, and then double-click on the form you want to open.

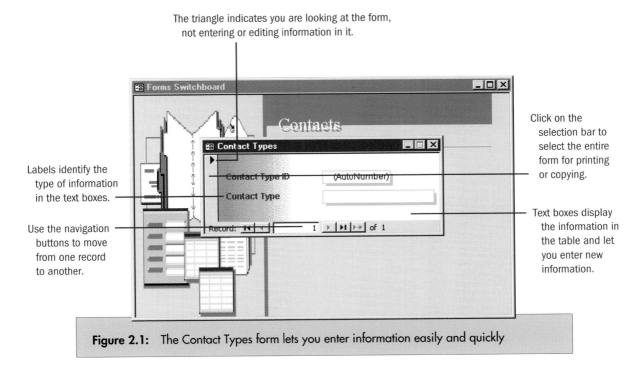

The triangle indicates you are looking at the form, not entering or editing information in it.

Labels identify the type of information in the text boxes.

Use the navigation buttons to move from one record to another.

Click on the selection bar to select the entire form for printing or copying.

Text boxes display the information in the table and let you enter new information.

Figure 2.1: The Contact Types form lets you enter information easily and quickly

The navigation buttons at the bottom of the form let you move from record to record:

Button	Name
◀◀	First Record
◀	Previous Record
1	Go To Record
▶	Next Record
▶◀	Last Record
▶*	New Record

To use the Go To Record box, click in the box with the mouse or press F5, replace the number there with the record number you want to display, and then press ENTER.

The Previous Record button is dimmed because there is no previous record—you're looking at the first record in the table so you cannot go to any previous record. Click Next Record. The form now shows the information for the second record in the table.

Adding Records with a Form

Since a blank form is on your screen, complete the record by typing **Buyer**. As soon as you start typing, Access inserts the next ID number in the Contact Type ID field. This is the first record, so the number 1 appears. Notice that it also replaces the triangle in the selection bar with the pencil icon, indicating that you are making changes to the underlying table.

You can add a new record by displaying a blank form and filling it out, just like you would with paper forms. To add a new record, press ENTER after the last field on the form, or click the New Record button. Do that now. You'll see two New Record buttons, one on the toolbar and the other next to the record navigation buttons. Click either one. Access dims both the Next Record button, because there isn't any next record, and the New Record button, because you're already in that mode.

The Contact Type ID field contains the AutoNumber indicator and the insertion point is in the Contact Type field. Type **Seller**. Now press ENTER. Because you were already in the last field, Access displays another blank form. Moving to any other record saves the current one; you do not have to perform any action yourself to save the table or the database.

Type **Friend** and then click the New Record button to display another blank form. Type **Relative.** Now click the Close button on the right side of the form's title bar to return to the switchboard.

Working with Complex Forms

Not all forms are created equal. While the Contact Type form is pretty simple, with just two fields, other Almost Instant database forms can be much more complex. As an example, click Return to

You can also press CTRL-= (equal sign) to add a new record, or click Next Record if you are at the end of the table.

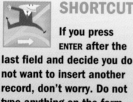

SHORTCUT

If you press ENTER after the last field and decide you do not want to insert another record, don't worry. Do not type anything on the form—just go to another record or close the form. Access does not save blank records with the table.

Main Switchboard, and then click Enter/View Contacts to see the form shown in Figure 2.2. The information in the form represents the contents of the Contacts table and there are buttons on the bottom that run macros. For example, clicking on Calls will show a list of phone calls made by the contact, in an even more complex form. Since the form is blank, no calls will appear if you click on the button. But if the database did have information, the form might appear as shown in Figure 2.3. Clicking on Dial will dial your phone. Clicking on Page 1 or Page 2 changes pages of this two-page form.

The Contacts form contains a number of text boxes, divided into two pages. Before adding information to the table, practice moving around the form. At this point, you are viewing the form, not changing it. The contents of the current field are highlighted, or appear as light text on a dark background.. To move forward from field to field, press TAB, ENTER, or the RIGHT ARROW or DOWN ARROW keys. Move backward by pressing SHIFT-TAB, LEFT, or the UP ARROW key. You can also click in a text box.

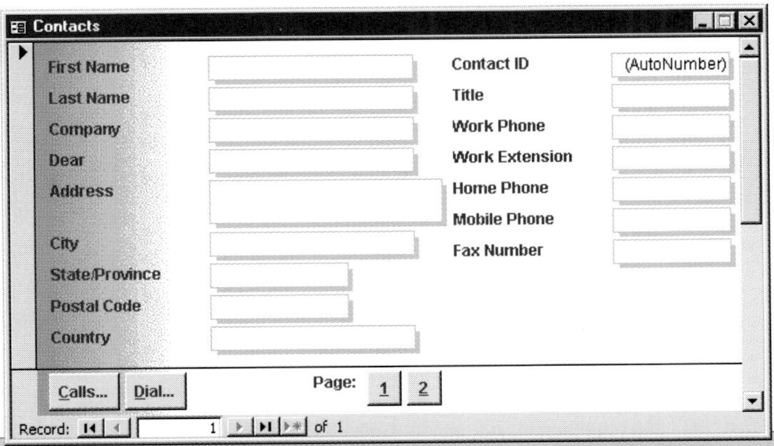

If clicking Page 2 does not display the entire second page of the form, use the scroll bar to scroll the second page into view.

Figure 2.2: A more sophisticated Contacts form

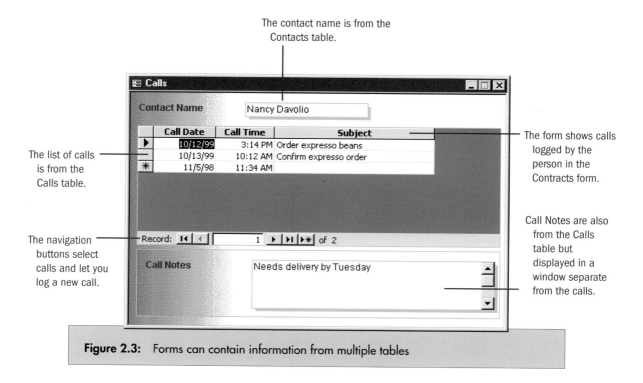

Figure 2.3:   Forms can contain information from multiple tables

Now make sure you are in the first text box for the First Name field, and then follow these steps:

1. Type **Nancy** and then press ENTER to reach the Last Name field.

2. Type **Davolio** in the Last Name field and press ENTER.

3. Type **Cascade Coffee Roasters** in the Company field and press ENTER.

4. Type **Nancy** in the Dear field.

5. Press ENTER to reach the Address field. The text box is larger than the others in the form, indicating that it can contain more then one line of text.

6. Type **507 20th Ave. E.** and then press CTRL-ENTER to type the next line in the field. If you pressed ENTER by itself, the insertion point would move to the next field.

7. Type **Apt. 2A** and then press ENTER to move out of the Address field and into the City field.

8. Type **Seattle** in the City field, and then press ENTER.

9. Type **WA** in the State/Province field.

Ensuring Valid Data with Input Masks

Now press ENTER or TAB to move to the Postal Code field and then type **9**, the first number of the ZIP code. When you start to type in the field, Access displays a mask indicating the format of the field.

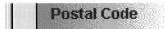 

This mask shows that the ZIP code is formatted to appear with a hyphen after the first five characters. This means that you don't have to type the hyphen yourself—Access has already inserted it for you. But there's more to the mask than that. A mask can also determine the number and types of characters that you can enter.

Type **812** and then press ENTER before completing the code. Access shows a warning message that you did not enter the correct format. Click OK to clear the message box and then type **2** to complete the five characters of the ZIP code. The insertion point jumps to the other side of the hyphen. Now press ENTER to move to the Country field. A message does not appear because the last four numbers of the Postal Code input mask are optional. Type **USA** in the Country field, and **Sales Rep** in the Title field.

In the Work Phone field, start by pressing **2**. When you start typing the phone number, Access displays the field input mask. This tells you to enter a three-digit area code, three numbers for the exchange, and the four final numbers. Access will insert the parentheses and the hyphen—you do not have to type them yourself. Complete the phone number by typing **065559857**. Now complete the fields by entering **(206) 555-3487** as the Home Phone, **(206) 555-8888** as the Mobile Phone, and **(206) 555-9858** as the Fax Number.

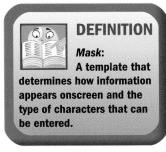

DEFINITION

Mask: A template that determines how information appears onscreen and the type of characters that can be entered.

If you try to leave a field and Access complains that you haven't entered correct data, re-enter it in the correct format or delete the contents altogether.

If you press ENTER after typing the Fax number, the insertion point moves to the first field on the page. To start the second page of the form, click on the Page 2 button. You'll see that the contact name is already filled in for you. Access combines the first name and last name you already entered to display the full name. Actually, this field is only displayed on the form; it is not saved with the table. After all, why should it be? The first and last names are already stored and Access can combine them to display the full name whenever it needs to. You won't be able to edit the information in the Contact Name box directly. To change the contact name, you must edit the First Name and Last Name fields on the first page of the form.

EXPERT ADVICE

Never waste space in a table by including fields that can be derived or calculated from other fields.

Picking Values with Lists

Look at the Contact Type field. It has a drop-down list arrow. Click on the arrow to see a lookup list—the contact types that are stored in the Contact Types table. A lookup list makes it easy to enter information into a field, and it ensures that you do not enter a contact type that does not really exist. Click on Seller and then press ENTER to reach the Email Name field. Type **nancy@roasters.com** and press ENTER twice to reach the Birthdate field. Type **11**—the date mask appears. Complete the date by typing **2245**—Access will move the day and year to the proper positions in the field—and then press ENTER to move to the Notes field.

Press SHIFT-ENTER if you want to save the record before you leave it.

Leave the Notes field blank for now, and click on either of the New Record buttons to display a new blank form. The form appears with the insertion point in the Notes field. The insertion point remains in the current field when you move from record to record. Click the

Page 1 button to move to the first page of the form, and then enter the information shown here:

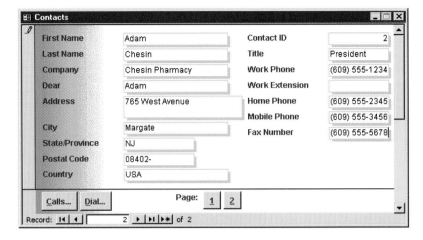

SHORTCUT

Entering a field with some of the same information as in the previous record? Press CTRL-' (apostrophe) to automatically insert it.

If you want, you can leave the second page of the form blank or enter some information of your own.

Changing Information in a Form

The world is always changing, and so is the information in a database. Contacts move or change their phone numbers, prices go up and down, inventory is always changing. Changing the information in your database is just as easy as entering it. In fact, it's easier because you only have to update the fields that changed.

To change information in a field, just go to its text box and type. When you move into a box using the keyboard (with the TAB or ENTER keys, for example), the entire field will be selected. Pressing any other key will delete the contents so you can enter something else. To just edit the contents, without deleting it all first, press F2 to enter edit mode, or click in the field with the mouse. Then change the information just as you would edit text in a word processing program.

- Press BACKSPACE or DEL to erase characters.

- Press INS to change between insert and overtype mode. If the characters "OVR" appear in the status bar, new characters you type will erase those already there; otherwise, they will be inserted between existing characters.
- Use the mouse to drag over characters that you want to select to delete or cut and copy to other locations using the Cut, Copy, and Paste buttons, or the Edit menu options.

To see how this works, change some information in the first record.

1. Click the First Record button to move to the record for Nancy Davolio.
2. Click in the Company Name field and replace the word "Roasters" with **Incorporated**.
3. Now click in the City field, and replace the word "Seattle" with **Wallace**.

Remember, a record is saved when you move to a new record, or when you close the form. Since you did neither of these, the changes you just made are not yet saved on the disk. So if you change your mind about the changes, you can still do something about it. To undo your actions, you use the Undo button. This button serves a dual purpose:

SHORTCUT

Press ESC once to undo the current field; press ESC twice to undo the record.

- If you did not yet move out of the field you just changed, click on the button to undo the change.
- If you already moved out of the field, click on the button to return the entire record to its original contents.

Deleting Records

Sometimes information changes so much that you no longer need it in the database. Club members drop out, inventory goes out of stock, or you drop an item from your collection. When you no longer need a record in the database, you should delete it. This saves you the trouble of scrolling past outdated records, and it saves space on your hard disk.

To delete an entire record, click the Delete Record button in the toolbar. A dialog box will appear, warning you that the record will be deleted. Click Yes to actually delete the record. You can also delete a record by selecting it—clicking on the selection bar or choosing Edit | Select Record—and then either pressing DEL or choosing Edit | Cut. To delete every record, choose Edit | Select All Records and then press DEL.

SHORTCUT

Press CTRL- -
(hyphen) to
delete the current record.

Sorting Records

The form determines the way your information is displayed, but not its order. Seeing records in a particular order can help you find and analyze information. If you're a teacher, for example, wouldn't it be helpful to list students in grade order? It would certainly save you money to print a mailing list in ZIP-code order to take advantage of bulk-rate postage. And, it would be easier to locate items if they appeared in alphabetical order.

The order that records appear in as you move from one to the other depends on how the table was created. If the table has a primary key, then they will appear in primary key order. (Let's save time and be informal, and just call it the key from now on, OK?) For example, in the Contacts table, the key is the Contact ID field—the number that Access enters as you create new records. As you move from record to record, the number in the Go To Record box will match the Contact ID number. Because the ID is the key, it just so happens that the ID and Go To Record number are the same. The ID, however, is solely based on the order in which you entered the records—probably in the order that clients signed on.

When you want to display the records in some other order, you sort them. Sorting does not change the physical order in which the records are stored on your disk, only the order in which they are displayed on the screen. And sorting does not change the key.

Access does not recycle AutoNumber numbers. For example, if you delete the last 10 of 20 records, Access uses the number 21 for the next record you add, even though the last one that exists is 10.

DEFINITION

Key:
A field or combination of fields used to determine the order of records in the table. A key makes it easier and faster to find records, and to perform many other database functions. You'll learn all about primary keys later.

Sorting also works sort of the same (excuse me, I couldn't help it) in Datasheet view.

The fastest way to sort the information is to use the Sort Ascending and Sort Descending buttons in the toolbar, or to select Sort Ascending or Sort Descending from the shortcut menu that appears when you right-click in a field. First, place the insertion point in the field you want to sort by. If you want to display records by the client's last name, for example, click in the Last Name field. To sort by ZIP code, click in the Postal Code field. Then click on either Sort Ascending or Sort Descending, depending on the order that you want.

Let's try it now.

1. If the first record is not already displayed, click the First Record button. The record number and the Contact ID read 1.

2. Now click on the Last Name field and then on the Sort Ascending button.

That's it, the records are sorted. The record for Chesin now comes first, as you can see by the number 1 in the record counter. But notice that the Contact ID says 2, which is the actual contents of the field. That's fine. It just means that you are viewing the records in some other order than their key.

Since you cannot click on the Contact ID field on the form, you cannot sort records on that field. It doesn't matter because that is the key field. To return the records to their original order, select Records | Remove Filter/Sort. Do that now. The record number and the Contact ID fields will now match.

If you want to sort on more than one field, you must use the Advanced Sort feature. I'll show you how in Chapter 4.

Filtering Records

DEFINITION
Filter: Something that keeps something else out; or one or more conditions that a record must meet in order to be displayed.

While sorting changes the order in which records are displayed, scrolling through the table will still display all of the records. There are plenty of times, however, when you're only interested in certain ones—such as clients who owe you a lot of money, or customers who have not ordered this year. To display specific records, you must apply a filter.

When you make coffee, the paper filter lets the coffee through to the pot while keeping back the grounds. It determines what makes it into the pot. An Access filter determines which records make it to the screen. A filter does not delete records from the database. Those not meeting the conditions will not be displayed, but they are still part of the database. There are three ways to filter records: by selecting, by form, or with an advanced filter that you'll learn about in Chapter 3. All three methods work the same way with both forms and datasheets; I just couldn't fit everything into this chapter, and advanced filters introduce a special feature called the *grid*.

Now to make this part of the chapter more interesting, start by adding the following record:

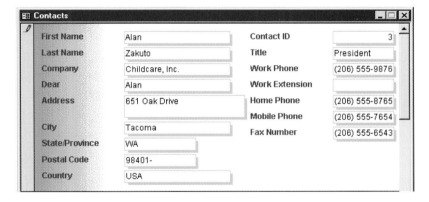

Again, you can leave the second page of the form blank or enter some information of your own.

Finally, enter some information of your own to the table—use the names and addresses of friends or relatives, or just make something up. Enter enough records so you feel comfortable working with the form.

Filter by Selection

In the filter by selection method, you select a field already containing the information you want to use for the condition. For example, if you want to display contacts in Washington, click on any of the State fields for a Washington contact. To display all contacts who are buyers, click on the Contact Type field for a buyer. Once you've selected the field, click the Filter By Selection button.

Try it now. Click on the State/Province field of the displayed record, and then click the Filter By Selection button. The record counter shows you the number of records that meet the criteria, and it will remind you that you are looking at a filtered view of the table, as shown here:

Now, as you move from record to record, only those meeting the filter condition will appear—a subset of the entire table. You will only see contacts in the same state as the selected record. If you now select another field for the filter, only those from the subset will be considered. This way, you can filter on the contents of more than one field (but just one field at a time).

To apply a new filter to the entire table, you must first remove the filter. In the toolbar, you'll see this button pressed down.

When pressed down, it is called Remove Filter; when not pressed, it is called Apply Filter. Click on that button now, or choose Records | Remove Filter/Sort. With the filter removed, all of the records will again be visible.

SHORTCUT
To apply the same filter again, click Apply Filter.

Filter For

The problem with filter by selection is that you must first find one record with the information you want to use for the filter. If you are looking for a contact in Margate, for instance, you must find one first. One way to avoid searching the database for a field that contains the information is to use the Filter For feature. Here's how.

1. Right-click in the field that will contain the information you want to use for the filter. The text box itself does not have to contain the information you want to filter on. For example, if you want to locate contacts with the last name of Smith, right-click on the Last Name field of any record.

2. In the shortcut menu, click the Filter For option. This places the insertion point in the option's text box as shown here:

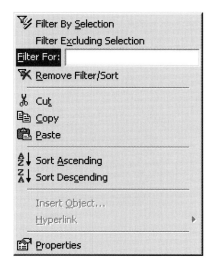

3. Type the text you want to use for the filter, then press ENTER to apply the filter.

Filter Excluding Selection

Filter by selection excludes all records that do not match the contents of the selected field. But what if you want to see all records except those that meet a condition, such as the records for all clients who are not in Washington? To exclude specific records from the filter, use the Filter Excluding Selection command.

To do this, click in a field containing the information that you want to use to exclude records—just the opposite of filter by selection. Then right-click in the field and choose Filter Excluding Selection from the shortcut menu that appears.

Filter by Form

The Filter For option saves you from having to first find a record with the information you want to use for the filter. But if you want to filter on the contents of more than one field—say contacts in Margate, New Jersey, but not Margate, England—you must perform each filter separately.

Filter by form solves this problem. When you filter by form, Access displays a blank form, except for any conditions you last used for a filter. If you just filtered the records in New Jersey state, for example, NJ will appear in the State/Province field.

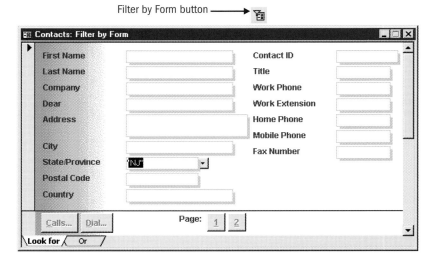

Try to create a filter now. Click the Filter By Form button, and then follow the steps shown in Figure 2.4.

You can enter conditions in as many fields as you want, meaning you can filter on multiple fields in one operation. Follow along.

SHORTCUT

If you want to remove the criteria and start over, click the Clear Grid button.

1. Click the Filter By Form button again. The form appears with the criteria you've already entered.

2. Click in the City field.

3. Pull down the list and select Tacoma.

4. Now click the Apply Filter button. Only contacts in Tacoma, Washington will be included in the subset.

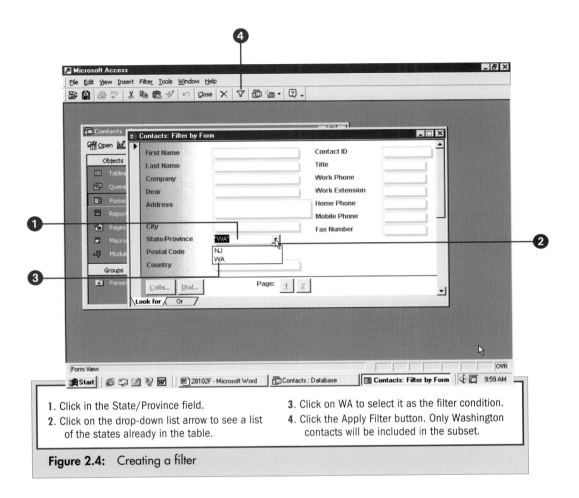

1. Click in the State/Province field.
2. Click on the drop-down list arrow to see a list of the states already in the table.
3. Click on WA to select it as the filter condition.
4. Click the Apply Filter button. Only Washington contacts will be included in the subset.

Figure 2.4: Creating a filter

Creating an OR Condition

Click Filter By Form once more and look at the bottom of the form—at the OR tab. When you enter information in more than one field, Access treats it as an AND operation. This means that the record must match all of the conditions in the form—both Tacoma in the City field and WA in the State field. What if you wanted to list contacts in either Tacoma or any city in New Jersey? This is called an OR operation. To add an OR condition, you need to use another form.

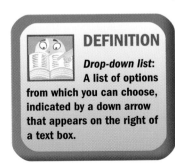

DEFINITION

Drop-down list:
A list of options from which you can choose, indicated by a down arrow that appears on the right of a text box.

1. Click on the OR tab at the bottom of the form. A blank form appears—and another dimmed OR tab.

2. Click in the State/Province field, pull down the list, and select NJ.

3. Apply the filter.

The subset now includes contacts in Tacoma, Washington and in any city in New Jersey.

You cannot type an OR condition in one field, as in WA or NJ. You must use an OR page for the second condition.

You can have more than one OR condition. Just click on the dimmed OR tab to display another form. If you have the spare time, keep on clicking the dimmed OR tab to see just how many conditions you can have. I got to 25 and then gave up.

Removing the filter redisplays all of the records. However, it does not erase the criteria from the filter form. The next time you open the form—even after closing and reopening the database—the last used criteria will appear in the filter form. Try this out. Click the Remove Filter button so the table is no longer filtered. Now click the Filter By Form button. The criteria are still there in the City and State/Province fields, as shown in Figure 2.5. To erase the filter criteria, click the Clear Grid button, also indicated in Figure 2.5.

When you enter a value into a field box, or select one from the list, Access looks for an exact match. If you type CA in the State/Province field, for example, the record must contain CA to be included in the filtered set. You can also search for less exact matches using wildcards and comparison operators. This is pretty much the usual Windows stuff. In fields that contain text, use the wildcards ? and *. The question mark represents any one character, so if you enter ?A in the State/Province field, records containing "PA," "CA," and "MA" will be in the set, as well as any other with one letter followed by the letter "A." The asterisk represents any number of characters. If you enter **Sm***, for example, you'll get records containing any text starting with the letters "SM" and followed by any other characters, such as "Smith," "Smyth," and "Smoot."

Unless you clear the grid, the last applied filter is stored with the table as something called a *property*. Store that away until you read Chapter 7.

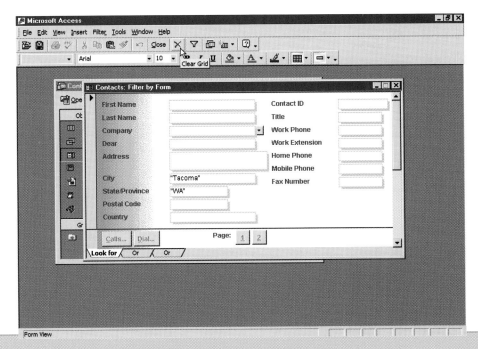

Figure 2.5: Criteria remain even after removing the filter

In fields that contain numbers, use these comparison operators:

<	Less than
>	Greater than
<=	Less than or equal to
>=	Greater than or equal to
<>	Not equal to

For example, entering <5 in the Client ID field will include only the first four clients in the filtered set.

To end your session, click the Close button in the Filter by Form window. You can now work with your form, return to the Database window, or exit Access.

Using Data Access Pages

A data access page is similar to a form, but it can be used to access your database from a Web browser as well as within Access itself. In fact, unlike a form that is saved as part of the Access database file, data access pages are stored individually on your disk with the HTM file extension. If you open the data access page from the desktop, rather than from within Access, Windows starts your Web browser and opens the data access page in it.

A typical data access page, opened in Access, is shown in Figure 2.6. Like a form, it displays fields in text boxes in which you can view, edit, and add information. At the bottom of the page is a special toolbar containing the familiar buttons to navigate, add records, and delete records, as well as buttons to save and undo record changes, sort the table, and create and apply a filter.

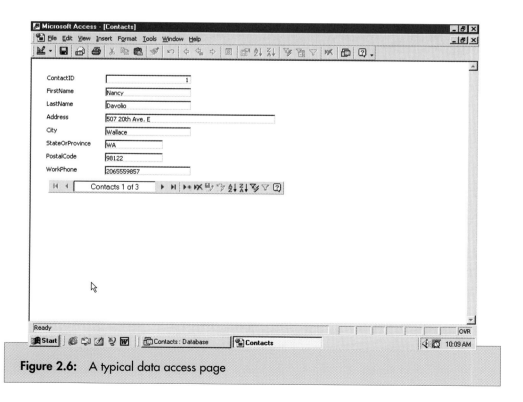

Figure 2.6: A typical data access page

When you open a data access page you are actually looking at a Web page. Right-clicking on the page displays your browser's shortcut menu rather then Access's shortcut menu.

Summary

Forms are a great way to work with your tables. A form appears onscreen like a paper form, with information neatly arranged in an easy-to-use order. Just remember that when you add, edit, or delete information on a form, you are also making the same changes to the database itself. The form just gives you a way to look at your information, even if it comes from more than one table. You can also sort and filter your information using a form, so you can customize how the records appear. Couldn't be any easier.

Of course, sometimes you may want to see more than one record onscreen at a time. In this case, you are less interested in the arrangement of fields or in fancy backgrounds. To see multiple records, you can display your information in rows and columns, in what Access calls the Datasheet view, which just happens to be the topic of Chapter 3.

Using Datasheets—Almost Instant and Otherwise

INCLUDES

- Displaying a table as a datasheet
- Selecting records and fields
- Changing column width
- Changing row height
- Moving, hiding, and freezing columns
- Changing the font
- Formatting cells and gridlines
- Performing an advanced filter and sort

Display a Table in Datasheet View ➡ pp. 55–56

Double-click on the table in the Tables page of the Database window.

Show Records from Related Tables ➡ pp. 58–59

- Click the plus sign to show related records.
- Click the minus sign to hide related records.

Select Fields, Records, and Columns ➡ pp. 59–60

- To select a record, click the record selector.
- To select consecutive records, drag over the record selectors, or select the first record and then SHIFT-click on the last record.
- To select a column, click the field selector button.
- To select consecutive columns, drag over the field names, or click the field name on the first column and then SHIFT-click the field name for the last column.
- To select a record's field, click on the gridline to the left of the field (the mouse pointer will look like a white cross). Drag over to select multiple fields.

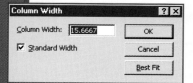

Change the Width of Columns ➡ pp. 60–61

Drag the right boundary of the column's field name, double-click on the right boundary of the field name, or follow these steps:

1. Click anywhere in the column that you want to adjust, or select multiple columns.
2. Choose Format | Column Width.
3. Do one of the following:
    - Click Best Fit.
    - Enter the width in characters and then click OK.
    - Select Standard Width and then click OK.

Change the Height of Rows ➡ pp. 62–63

Drag the line below the record selector for the row whose height you want to adjust, or follow these steps:

1. Click on the row.
2. Choose Format | Row Height.
3. Select Standard Height or enter the height in points, and then click OK.

Hide and Unhide Columns ➡ pp. 63–64

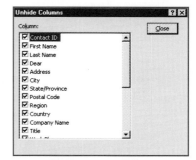

- To hide a column, click anywhere in the column that you want to hide; then choose Format | Hide Columns.
- To unhide columns, choose Format | Unhide Columns, click on the empty check boxes next to hidden field names, and then close the dialog box.

Freeze Columns ➡ pp. 64–65

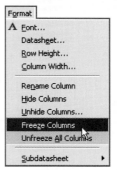

1. Click in any field in the column.
2. Choose Format | Freeze Columns.

To unfreeze columns, choose Format | Unfreeze All Columns.

Change the Order of Columns ➡ p. 65

1. Select the column that you want to move by clicking its field name, or drag across the field names to select multiple columns.
2. Point to the selected column's field name.
3. Drag the selected column to the position ahead of the column that you want to follow the selected column.

Change the Datasheet Font ➡ pp. 65–66

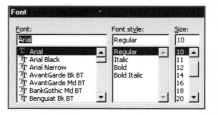

Choose Format | Font and select a font, style, size, and color.

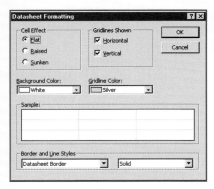

Format the Datasheet ➥ pp. 66–67

1. Choose Format | Datasheet.
2. Enable or disable the horizontal and vertical gridlines.
3. Select a gridline color.
4. Select a cell background color.
5. Select flat, raised, or sunken effect.
6. Click OK.

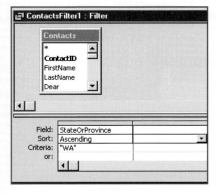

Save a Modified Datasheet Layout ➥ p. 69

- Click the Save button, or
- Close the datasheet and select Yes (from the message that appears) to confirm that you want to save the changes.

Switch from Form to Datasheet View ➥ pp. 69–70

When the form is displayed, pull down the Form View button menu and select Datasheet View.

Perform an Advanced Filter and Sort ➥ pp. 71–74

1. Display the datasheet or form for the table.
2. Select Records | Filter | Advanced Filter/Sort.
3. Double-click the fields from the field list to insert them into the Grid.
4. Select Sort options.
5. Enter criteria for filtering.
6. Click Apply Filter, or choose Filter | Apply Filter/Sort.

Forms are nice to look at and easy to use. And while they are great for entering information, you can't get an overall look at your data. Sometimes I like to see what's already in my table as I enter a new record or edit an existing one. That's when I use the datasheet, which can display many records at once. Glancing through the table in a datasheet often gives me ideas, helping me fill out the record I'm working on. It's a great time-saver for us busy folks, so I'm sure you'll find the datasheet useful for the same reasons—even if it doesn't look as pretty as a form.

Displaying a Datasheet

To display a datasheet, just open a table from the Database window. It's as quick as that. Try it now.

1. Start Access and open the Contacts database as you learned to do in Chapter 2.

2. Click the Database Window button in the toolbar to display the Database window. Remember, you can hold down the SHIFT key when opening a database, bypassing the switchboard, so the Database window appears automatically.

3. Click on Tables in the Objects list to see the tables that are part of the database.

4. Now click on the Contacts table and select Open. You can also double-click on a table name to open it, or right-click on the table name and choose Open from the shortcut menu that appears.

What you're looking at is called a datasheet. (See Figure 3.1.)

 DEFINITION

Datasheet: A representation of the information in a table organized in rows and columns. Field names are the column headings, and each row represents a record.

You can't click on a hyperlink field to edit it because you'll jump to the link instead. See Chapter 7 for more information.

 EXPERT ADVICE

Don't fight it. You should learn how to work with datasheets, even if you prefer forms. As you work with queries and other database functions, you won't be able to avoid datasheets entirely, so it pays to be comfortable with them.

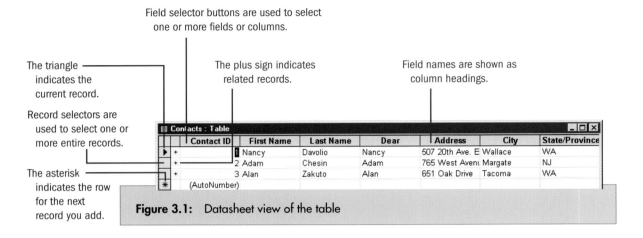

Field selector buttons are used to select one or more fields or columns.

The triangle indicates the current record.

The plus sign indicates related records.

Field names are shown as column headings.

Record selectors are used to select one or more entire records.

The asterisk indicates the row for the next record you add.

Figure 3.1:   Datasheet view of the table

Navigating Tables

Now for some standard Windows stuff. If you can't see all of the fields on the screen, there'll be a scroll bar on the bottom next to the record navigation buttons. (That's one of the problems with datasheets—you can't see too many fields at a time.) There'll also be a scroll bar down the right side of the window if there are more records than can be displayed on one screen. To move around the datasheet, just click where you want to add or edit information, scrolling as needed. If you're not into using your mouse, you can move through the datasheet using the keystrokes listed in the table following. It's up to you, but I usually find a combination of mouse and keyboard to be best. I use keys like TAB, HOME, END, and the arrows to travel around consecutive fields and rows, but the mouse when I'm moving about at random.

You can't click on a hyperlink field to edit it because you'll jump to the link instead. See Chapter 7 for more information.

PG UP	Up one window of records
PG DN	Down one window of records
CTRL-PG UP	Left one page of fields
CTRL-PG DN	Right one page of fields
TAB	To the next field
SHIFT-TAB	To the previous field
HOME	To the first field in the current record
END	To the last field in the current record

UP ARROW	To the same field in the previous record
DOWN ARROW	To the same field in the next record
CTRL-UP ARROW	To the same field in the first record
CTRL-DOWN ARROW	To the same field in the last record
CTRL-HOME	To the first field in the first record
CTRL-END	To the last field in the last record

Entering Records in a Datasheet

The plus signs in the records of the Contacts table won't do you any good because there are no related records in the Calls tables. So before seeing how related records appear in a datasheet, let's enter some information into the Calls table.

Click the Close button on the Contacts datasheet, and then double-click Calls in the Database window. Click in the Contact ID field. Access displays the down arrow indicating a lookup field. Click the arrow to see a list of people in the Contact's table:

Call ID	Contact ID	Call Date	Call Time	Subject	Notes
(AutoNumber)					
	Chesin,Adam				
	Davolio,Nancy				
	Zakuto,Alan				

Click the first name in the list to add the name to the field, then press TAB to reach the Call Date field. Type **10/12/99**—Access displays the date input mask—and then press TAB. Type **12:31 PM** in the input mask that appears, and press TAB. Type **Buy flavored coffee**. Leave the Notes field blank and click the New Record button. Now enter the following records into the table and then close it. (The columns were widened here so you can see the full text—you'll learn how to do that soon yourself!)

Calls : Table

	CallID	Contact ID	Call Date	Call Time	Subject	Notes
	1	Chesin,Adam	10/12/99	12:31 PM	Buy flavored coffee	
	2	Davolio,Nancy	10/12/99	3:14 PM	Order expresso beans	
	3	Davolio,Nancy	10/13/99	10:12 AM	Confirm expresso order	
	4	Zakuto,Alan	10/13/99	1:23 PM	Order coffee filters	
	5	Chesin,Adam	10/18/99	11:32 AM	New coffee prices	
▶	6	Zakuto,Alan	10/22/99	4:15 PM	Confirm filter delivery	
*	(AutoNumber)					

Displaying Subdatasheets

In Chapter 2 you learned that forms could display information from more than one table. So can datasheets. If the table you're looking at in a datasheet has related records from another table, you'll see the plus sign in the first column. Click the plus sign to expand the record, displaying the related information in what Access calls a *subdatasheet*. The plus sign changes to a minus sign. Click the minus sign when you no longer want to see related records.

In Figure 3.2, for example, two records from the Clients database are expanded to show the calls from the Calls table. There is a one-to-many relationship between the tables so a customer can have one or more orders.

Unlike multiple-table forms, which have a separate set of navigation buttons for each table displayed, there is only one set of navigation buttons in the datasheet, no matter how many tables are displayed. When you click in a table, the record counter in the navigation buttons reflects that table, and the buttons affect that table.

To add a new call for a contact, for example, click the plus sign next to the contact's name to expand the record, showing calls. Then click in the blank row of the bottom of the calls to enter a new one.

You can quickly expand a datasheet to show all of its subdatasheets by choosing Format | Subdatasheet | Expand All. Choose Format | Subdatasheet | Collapse All to hide the subdatasheets. Choose Format | Subdatasheet | Remove if you no longer want to be able to access

If you remove the subdatasheets, you can later reinstate them using table properties. See Chapter 6.

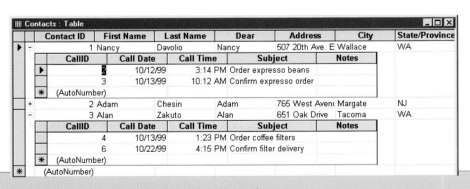

Figure 3.2: Subdatasheet showing related records

subdatasheets for this table. If you select Remove, however, you'll be asked if you want to save the table layout when you close the datasheet.

Déjà Vu

Now look at the toolbar and the record navigation buttons. They are exactly the same as in Form view. In fact, all of the techniques for moving between records, and for adding, sorting, filtering, and deleting records, work exactly the same in either view. To paraphrase one of our former Presidents—let me make this perfectly clear (thanks for the quote, Mr. Nixon). To recap:

- *To add a new record,* either click the New Record button, or move into the blank row and enter the data.

- *To enter or edit information,* move to the field and type, just as you learned for a form.

- *Sort the datasheet* by clicking in the column you want to sort by, and then clicking Sort Ascending or Sort Descending.

- *Filter the datasheet* by selection, excluding selection, or by form exactly as you learned in Chapter 2. When you click Filter By Form, Access displays a blank datasheet, in which you enter the filter information. You'll also be able to select information from a drop-down list, just as you can from a form.

- *To delete a record,* click any of its fields and then click the Delete Record button. To delete several records, select them first. You can also select the row, or rows, and then press the DEL key on the keyboard.

- All of the same *shortcut keys* work: CTRL-+ to add a record; CTRL to delete a record; ESC to undo; CTRL-' to copy the cell contents from the previous record; SHIFT-ENTER to save the record; and F2 to edit a record.

If you feel like entering new records without seeing existing ones, choose Records | Data Entry. To see the entire datasheet again, choose Records | Remove Filter/Sort.

Selecting Fields and Records

Working with information is a two-step dance—you first select what you want to deal with, and then you do something with it.

Use the same techniques to select entire columns. Just point to the field name so the mouse pointer appears like a black down arrow.

SHORTCUT

Select consecutive fields in a row, such as City and State, to filter and sort on multiple fields at one time using an AND condition. Select fields in consecutive rows to filter and sort using an OR condition.

To select a record, point to the record selector next to the record so the mouse pointer appears as a black right-pointing arrow and then click—the entire record will become highlighted. To select several consecutive records, select the first record; then hold down the SHIFT key and click on the last record in the group you've chosen to select. You can also drag to select: point to the first record selector so the pointer appears like the arrow, hold down the mouse button and drag down to the last record to be included in the selection. To select every record, select Edit | Select All Records. You can also select all of the records by pressing CTRL-A or by clicking on the record selector button to the left of the first field name.

You can also select entire fields when you want to delete their contents or use them for filters and sorts. Point to the line to the left of the field so the pointer appears like a large plus sign and then click. All of the text in the field will be selected, as well as any blank space following the text. To select more than one field—even if they are in different records—drag the plus sign pointer, or select the first field in the group and then SHIFT-click on the last field.

Getting the Most from Your Columns

Column width can be a real dilemma—it's either feast or famine. Sometimes you can't see all of the information in a field, as in the Address field. Sometimes there looks like there is wasted space, with a lot of blank spaces, as in the Dear and State/Province fields.

To change the column to any other size, even narrower than the column heading, drag the line with the mouse. Drag to the left to make the column narrower or to the right to make it wider. A quick and handy solution, however, is Best Fit. Best Fit makes a column just as wide as its largest entry (including the field name), and it's quick—just double-click on the line to the right of the field name (the right boundary of the field selector). For example, to see the full address, double-click on the right boundary line of the Address field. Access will widen the column. If you now apply Best Fit to the Dear column, however, Access will narrow the column to minimize the amount of blank space following the short field entries.

If you want to set the column width to an exact number of characters, then click anywhere in the column you want to adjust (or select several columns to adjust them all at the same time), then choose Format | Column Width to see this dialog box:

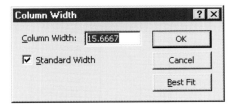

The Column Width command will be dimmed if you have any cells selected. Just click the mouse in the column to make the option selectable.

You can enter a new column width in characters, return to the standard width, or have Access adjust the column for you with the Best Fit option.

By the way, don't bother trying Best Fit on the State/Province field to eliminate the spaces after the state abbreviations. The Best Fit option will not make a column narrower than the field name itself. You can make the column narrower by dragging, but then you won't see the complete field name. The choice is yours, but I'd always rather see more columns on the screen, even if some field names are not fully displayed. After all, it doesn't take much of a genius to guess what the two-letter abbreviations represent.

It's usually a waste of time to widen all of your columns to Best Fit, anyway. There will be some columns that you won't use that often in Datasheet view, like the Address field.

If you want to enter a lot of information in a column but do not want to widen it, use the Zoom Box. The Zoom Box is a like a mini-word processor that saves you the trouble of widening a column you do not use that often, which saves you some scrolling time. Move

---

EXPERT ADVICE

Because you cannot cancel layout changes with the Undo command, save your table layout after each change that you find successful. If you really mess things up, you can always close the datasheet without saving it, and then reopen the previously saved version.

to the field you want to enter, edit, or view, and press SHIFT-F2 to display the Zoom Box.

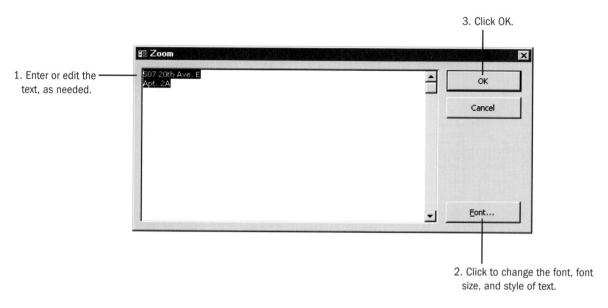

1. Enter or edit the text, as needed.

3. Click OK.

2. Click to change the font, font size, and style of text.

As you type in the Zoom Box, text will wrap when it reaches the right margin, and there'll be a scroll bar to scroll through a really long field. To end a line manually and start another, press CTRL-ENTER; pressing ENTER by itself will close the Zoom Box.

Displaying More Information in Rows

If you don't want to widen a column to see a long field, you can try increasing the height of the rows. To me, it's the only reason to change row height. Of course, while this displays more information in the same column space, you'll see fewer records onscreen at a time. Life's just full of decisions. You can't change the height of an individual row, only all of them at the same time. Still, it's a good alternative to using the Zoom

Box. It can also be faster, since the Zoom Box only displays one field at a time (and you have to open and close it each time you want to see another field). By increasing the height of rows, you see the full contents of several records at a time. And because you deepen every row with just one action, it's pretty fast.

To change row height by dragging, point to a line between any row selector and drag—up for shorter rows, down for taller ones. When you release the mouse, all of the rows will be set at the new height. To set a specific height, or quickly return to the default, choose Format | Row Height. In the dialog box that appears, enter the row height in points (there are 72 of them to the inch) or click Standard Height, and then click OK.

Displaying Important Fields

One other way to see more fields on the screen is to hide columns that you're not interested in at the moment. For example, in the Contacts database there are no entries in the Region field. If you do not plan on using a field for the time being, you can keep it from being displayed. You can hide as many columns as you want. So if you want to scan the datasheet for names and telephone numbers, for example, you can hide all but those two fields.

Hiding doesn't delete the field and its information; it just prevents it from being displayed. Deleting a column actually erases the information from the database.

Here's how hiding works. Click anywhere in the column that you want to hide, and then select Format | Hide Columns. The column will no longer appear onscreen but it is still part of the table. The information is there, and you can get it back just as easily as you hid it. To unhide columns, choose Format | Unhide Columns. Access will display a list of the fields with check marks next to those that are

The standard height is always slightly larger than the font size used for the text, so if you make your rows too narrow by mistake, just select Standard Height to adjust them automatically.

displayed. The check boxes of hidden columns will be empty. To unhide a column, click on its check box and then click Close.

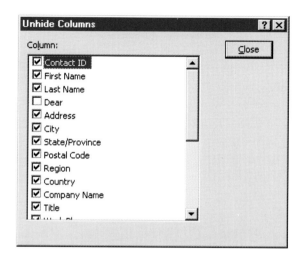

SHORTCUT

If you want to hide multiple columns, don't bother selecting them first. Just select Format | Unhide Columns, and click on the check boxes of those columns you want to hide.

Freezing Columns for Easy Reference

DEFINITION

Freeze: To fix the position of a column on the far left of the datasheet, so it remains there when you scroll other columns into view.

Scrolling to see fields can be a pain, but having to scroll back and forth is torture. It's hard to avoid. In most databases, the first field or so identifies the record—usually a number, name, or some other piece of information that tells what the record is all about. As you scroll more columns into view, the identifying fields scroll off the left edge of the screen. So when you are typing the Work Phone for the Contacts table, for example, you won't be able to see the ID or name for the record you are adding.

The solution is to freeze the identifying columns so you'll always know which record you are working with. Freezing is a great time-saver, and I mean a lot of time, when you're either adding or editing records. Trust me. To freeze a column, click in any field within it (or select multiple columns when you want to freeze more than one), and then select Format | Freeze Columns. Access moves the columns to the left of the screen—if they were not there before—and selects them. Click the mouse to unselect the columns. The frozen columns will be separated from the rest by a solid black line. Now as you scroll, the frozen columns will remain in view.

To unfreeze the columns, select Format | Unfreeze All Columns. The column is no longer frozen. Quick and easy, but there's a catch. The unfrozen (or is it unfreezed?) columns stay right there at the far left of the table, even if they were not there originally. If you want to move the columns back to their original position, read on.

SHORTCUT
The Column Width, Hide Columns, and Freeze Columns commands are also available in the shortcut menu when you right-click on a selected column.

Changing the Order of Columns

You can change the order of fields in the datasheet to make it more convenient to enter or edit information, or to select consecutive fields for sorting or filtering. For example, if you want to sort on the State and Contact type fields, you can place them together so you can select and sort on both at one time. Changing the order of columns does not change the actual table itself—just its layout in the datasheet. Remember, the datasheet is not the table; just one way of looking at it.

To change the order of fields, select the column that you want to move by clicking its field selector. Select multiple columns by SHIFT-clicking or by dragging across the field names all at the same time. Point to the field name—in any of the selected columns—so the pointer appears like an arrow, and then hold down the mouse button. If you did it correctly, you'll see a small rectangle below the mouse pointer and a vertical line to the left of the column. Drag the mouse to where you want to move the column and then release the mouse button.

Changing the Datasheet Font

Now you're ready for the fancy stuff. You can change the way your datasheet looks by choosing a new text font. The default font is Arial 10-point Normal. Your selections affect the entire table. Sorry, Microsoft doesn't trust us to format individual cells, columns, or rows. When a datasheet is displayed, choose Format | Font to see the dialog

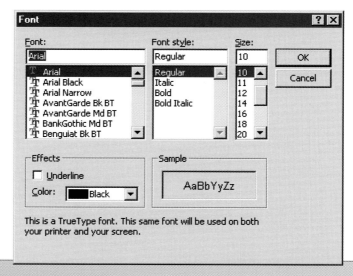

Figure 3.3: Font dialog box

box shown in Figure 3.3. Select the font, its size and style of characters, whether you want it underlined, and its color. For some fonts you can also choose a script to select characters other than the Roman (or Western) alphabet. Some options are Greek, Turkish, and Hebrew.

Changing the Appearance of Cells

While you'll probably be printing information out in a form or report, datasheets are good for viewing a number of records on the screen. If you are using the datasheet to give a presentation, even if for just one important person, then you can format its appearance for a more professional look.

EXPERT ADVICE

As you select options, keep an eye on the Sample or Preview section. Make sure the sample looks right before accepting the settings.

To format the datasheet, choose Format | Datasheet to display the Datasheet Formatting dialog box, then follow these steps:

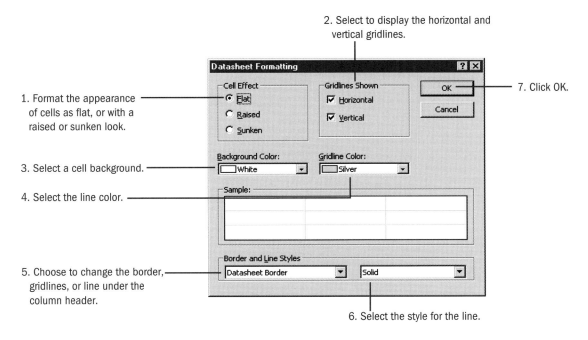

2. Select to display the horizontal and vertical gridlines.

1. Format the appearance of cells as flat, or with a raised or sunken look.

3. Select a cell background.

4. Select the line color.

5. Choose to change the border, gridlines, or line under the column header.

6. Select the style for the line.

7. Click OK.

The Border and Line Styles lists let you change the lines used for the datasheet border, horizontal and vertical gridlines, and the line under the column headings. There are nine types of lines that you can choose for each, as shown here:

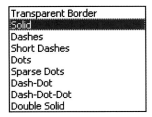

Some color and effect combinations can really look terrible and can even make your table unreadable. If you select a combination that looks like a cheap tie, return to the defaults by clicking on the same Cell Effect option in the dialog box. Access will automatically restore the default settings for that effect.

Using the Formatting Toolbar

As an alternative to the Font and Datasheet Formatting dialog boxes, you can use the Formatting toolbar. While it may seem easier to use a toolbar, I think the sample panels in the dialog boxes give them the edge. Changes to the layout cannot be undone with the Undo button or the Edit | Undo command. With the dialog boxes, you can look at the sample panel to see how your choices will affect the cells. So, you can always continue selecting until it looks right, or select Cancel in the dialog box to scrap the whole thing. There's no preview using the toolbar. If you change your mind about a selection, you must select something else from the same toolbar list. Of course, you can always display the Cells Effects dialog box and click on the effect to reset it to the default, but then you're using the dialog box anyway.

If the Formatting toolbar is not displayed, right-click the toolbar that is displayed to see this menu:

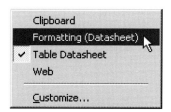

From the shortcut menu, click Formatting (Datasheet) to see the toolbar shown here:

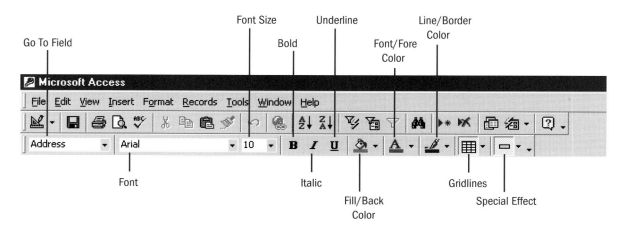

Use the Go To Field list, which shows the name of the current field, to move from column to column. Pull down the list and select the field you want to move to. The other buttons and lists in the toolbar change the appearance of the entire table, just like their corresponding options in the dialog boxes. The toolbar will automatically be removed when you leave Datasheet view, but it will reappear when you look at another datasheet. To remove the toolbar yourself, right-click on any toolbar and then click Formatting (Datasheet) again.

Some Things to Avoid at this Stage of the Game

As you go boldly forth into the exploration of Access, you'll see some options on menus—regular or shortcut—that you should avoid for now. It's not that you won't need them. It's just that choosing them could create problems that you're not quite ready yet to handle, especially if you're taking advantage of forms and reports in an Almost Instant database that you created with the Database Wizard. So for now, avoid renaming, deleting, and inserting columns. These options actually affect the table, not just the appearance of the datasheet.

Saving Your New Layout

When you add or modify records, Access saves your changes automatically. After making any changes to the datasheet layout, you must save the table before you close it. If you don't, your changes will not be there when you next open it. After adjusting the datasheet, click the Save button in the toolbar.

If you do not save the datasheet, Access will display a message asking if you want to save it when you close the datasheet. Select Yes to save the changes, or No to cancel them. Close the datasheet now, saving any changes that you've made if you like how they appear.

Switching Between Form and Datasheet View

When you're looking at a form, you can quickly switch to Datasheet view without going through the Database window. It's not the same datasheet that you see when you open a table, but it's a datasheet nonetheless.

When you open a form, you are in Form view, looking at your information through a form. To change views, use the View button and drop-down arrow on the far left of the toolbar. The picture on the button represents the view you will switch to when you click on the button:

	Design View	Allows you to change the appearance of the form, as you will learn in Chapter 13.
	Form View	Displays the form.

For even more views, click the down arrow next to the button and select a view from this list:

Not all views will be available at all times. If you pull down the list and select Datasheet View, you'll see a datasheet. Is it the same datasheet you used before—by opening the table? Not at all. When you switch to Datasheet view from a form, the datasheet has just the fields that appear in the form, and they're in the same order in which they appear on the form, not as in the original table. So the fields in this datasheet are in a different order than they were when you opened the datasheet from the Database window, and any layout changes that you applied do not appear. Still, it's a datasheet, and you can work with the information just as you did when you were working with the table's datasheet. To switch out of Datasheet view, click the down arrow and select Form View.

Now close the form to return to the Database window.

Getting More Control with Filters

Choices, choices, and even more choices. In Chapter 2 you learned how to filter records by selection and by form. There's yet another way to filter that actually gives you more control over the process. It's called Advanced Filter/Sort. This command lets you filter and sort in one operation, on more than one field at a time, and using a wide range of criteria to select records.

You can use the Advanced Filter/Sort command when either a datasheet or form is displayed; however, you'll notice the results more immediately in a datasheet.

Selecting Records with the Grid

The Advanced Filter/Sort command lets you select records using criteria and sort the records at the same time. To illustrate how the feature works, we'll be using the Calls table from the Contacts database. This table contains records of calls—I'm not sure if they are calls in or out, but it really doesn't matter. Our filter will display a list of calls concerning coffee, sorted by contact, but showing the most recent call for each first. It seems like quite a job, but it is easy with the Grid.

The Grid looks exactly the same if you display it from a form.

1. Open the Calls table.

2. Select Records | Filter | Advanced Filter/Sort to see the Grid, shown in Figure 3.4. You use the Grid to determine the fields and criteria that you want to use for the filter.

3. Double-click the fields you want to use for criteria or sorting. When you double-click on a field, Access inserts it into the first empty cell in the Field row of the Grid. You can also drag the field to the first empty cell in the Field row, or click in the first empty cell and then select the field from the drop-down list that appears. (To remove a field from the Grid, click on the gray bar above the field name and press DEL.) For example,

The current table is shown here
with the fields listed.

Use the Criteria row
to select records.

Each field that you want to use for sorting
or filtering must appear in the Field row.

Select a sort order, if
desired, for each field.

Use the Or row for
more complex
filters.

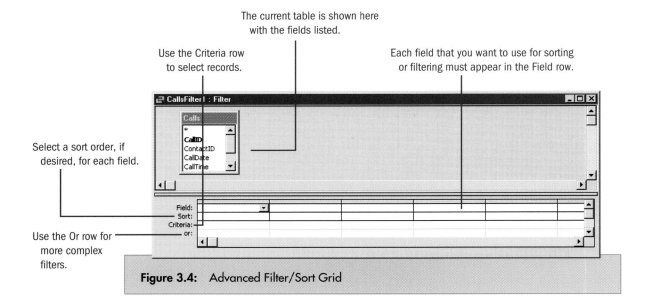

Figure 3.4:   Advanced Filter/Sort Grid

here's my filter for the Calls table after I've inserted the
Subject, ContactID, and CallDate fields.

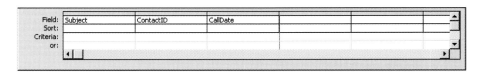

Remember, each asterisk
means "any other
characters." So in this case, it
means any record that contains
the characters "coffee," no
matter where they appear in
the field.

4. Click in the criteria row for a field that you want to use to
select records, and enter a criteria just as you learned for Filter
By Form in Chapter 2. Sorry, you cannot select a value from a
drop-down list. In this example, I entered ***coffee*** to display
calls that contain the word "coffee." Access automatically
entered the word "Like" and the quotation marks when I
pressed ENTER:

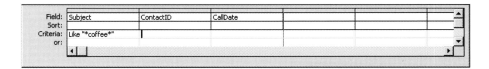

5. To sort on a field, click on the Sort cell for the field, pull down the list that appears and choose Ascending, Descending, and [not sorted]. In my example, I'm sorting by the ContactID in Ascending order, and by the CallDate in Descending order, as shown here:

Field:	Subject	ContactID	CallDate			
Sort:		Ascending	Descending			
Criteria:	Like "*coffee*"					
or:						

6. Click the Apply Filter button. The datasheet appears with only those records meeting the criteria and sorted just as you want.

Applying a filter to a table—by selection, by form, or advanced—is treated as a change to the table layout. When you close the table, a dialog box will appear asking if you want to save the changes. If you choose to save the changes, the filter will be saved, and you can reapply it when you next open the table.

To return from the filtered datasheet to the Grid, pull down the Window menu and choose the filter. It will be listed like CallsFilter1: Filter, referencing the table name.

Creating Complex Filters and Sorts

As you learned in Chapter 2, criteria can be simple or they can be complex using AND or OR operations. The same goes for advanced filters and sorts. Access treats criteria in more than one field—in the Criteria row of the Grid—as an AND operation. You can create OR conditions in a field or across fields using the OR row in the Grid.

To create an OR condition in the Subject field, enter criteria such as ***espresso* or *flavored***. If you want to list only calls made in November and December of 1999, use criteria such as **Between 11/1/99 and 12/31/99**. Access will automatically surround the dates with # symbols, as in **Between #11/1/99# and #12/31/99#**. This is Access' way of identifying the entries as a date, not as two division operations.

SHORTCUT

Because complex criteria can be long, use the Zoom Box when entering criteria. (Press SHIFT-F2 to display the Zoom Box.) This saves you from having to scroll back and forth to see the entire entry.

You can also create an OR operation for a field, and even for different fields, using the OR row. For example, to list calls that had to do with espresso and all calls on a certain date, regardless of their subject, enter ***espresso*** in the criteria row under Subject, and enter the date in question in the OR row for the CallDate field.

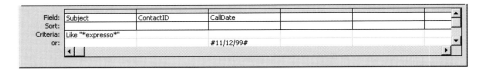

Summary

A form and datasheet are two ways of looking at the information in a database. Both let you display selected fields and records, and both let you apply filters and sorts. As you learned in this chapter, the datasheet lets you see more than one record at a time, but you may have to scroll to see all of the fields. How do you choose which to use? Just pick the one that's best for the job at hand.

So you've got a lot of information in that database of yours. In Chapter 4, you'll learn quick ways to find and replace information, streamline data entry, correct your spelling, and print forms, reports, and datasheets.

Finding, Correcting, and Printing Information

INCLUDES

- Finding and replacing information
- Streamlining data entry with AutoCorrect
- Checking your spelling
- Printing and previewing forms, reports, and datasheets

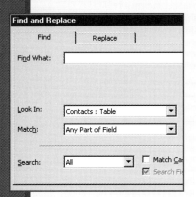

Find Information in the Table ➡ pp. 78–81

1. Click in the field containing information you want to find.
2. Click the Find button.
3. Type text you want to locate.
4. Select Find options.
5. Click Find Next until done.
6. Click Close when you are finished.

Replace Information Automatically ➡ pp. 81–82

1. Click in the field containing information you want to replace.
2. Choose Replace from the Edit menu.
3. Type text you want to replace in the Find What box and press TAB.
4. Type the text you want to insert in the Replace With box.
5. Select search and match options.
6. Click on Replace All, or click on Find Next and then Replace if desired.
7. Click Close when you are finished.

Create AutoCorrect Entries ➡ pp. 82–84

1. Choose AutoCorrect from the Tools menu.
2. Enter a word the way you misspell it, or an abbreviation you want to use to represent a word or phrase.
3. Press TAB.
4. Enter the correct spelling of the word, or of the full text to replace the abbreviation.
5. Click Add.
6. Click OK.

Check Your Spelling ➧ pp. 85–88

1. Select text, field, or records to check.
2. Click the Spelling button.
3. Select appropriate dialog box options for each word.

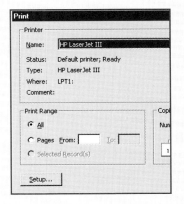

Preview Forms, Reports, and Datasheets ➧ pp. 88–90

1. Select the object in the Database window or open it onscreen.
2. Click the Print Preview button.
3. Click the Close button on the Print Preview toolbar when done.

Set Page Layout Options ➧ pp. 90–92

1. Open the object you want to layout.
2. Choose Page Setup from the File menu.
3. Set the Margins, Page, and Columns options (Columns options are not available when working with the datasheet).
4. Click OK.

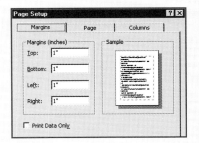

Print Forms, Reports, Datasheets, and Data Access Pages ➧ pp. 93–94

1. Select the object in the Database window or open it onscreen.
2. Click the Print button, or choose Print from File menu and select Print options.

You've covered a lot of material in the past three chapters, but there are still lots of ways to enhance the way you work with forms and datasheets. There are faster ways to find information in your database than using the navigation keys, and better ways to change information, especially when making the same change to more than one record. And I'm sure you'll want to print information in datasheets, forms, or reports so you don't have to carry your computer everywhere you go!

Finding Information

If you're anxious to print something and cant wait for the section on printing in this chapter, just open what you want to print and click on the Print button in the toolbar. Feel better?

I don't know about you, but I get really annoyed when I can't find something. My keys, my wallet, my car in the parking lot. You could get just as annoyed if you're trying to find a particular something in a large table.

To find a specific record in a table, you can always use the Next and Previous buttons to scroll through the table one record at a time. This isn't a bad idea if you have a small table, or if you're not exactly sure what record you're looking for. But if you know what you're looking for—just not exactly where it is—then viewing every record is a serious waste of time. Rather than scan the table yourself, let Access do it with the Find command, which works the same whether you're looking for information in a form or datasheet.

First, you have to know a piece of information contained in the record. For example, you're looking for a contact whose last name is Taylor, or for all contacts in Washington state, or for any contact containing the word Chocolate in the record.

EXPERT ADVICE

If you really do want to scan through records yourself, use a datasheet rather than a form. More records on the screen at a time, less scrolling.

If you know which field contains the information, start by placing the insertion point in that field, in any of the records, in either the datasheet or the form. So if you want to look for contacts in Washington, click in the State field of any record, even if the state in that record is not Washington. If you don't know which field it's in—or don't care—the insertion point can be in any field. Then, click on the Find button in the toolbar—that's the button that looks like the binoculars—to see this dialog box, shown after you click the More>> button to display additional options:

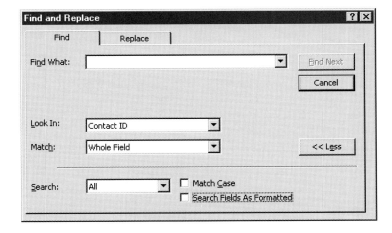

The Look In list of the dialog box indicates that Access will look for information in the current field. That's fine. If you want to search all of the fields, pull down the Look In list and choose the name of the table. In the Find What box, you type what you're looking for. Next, decide how much of the table you want to search. Pull down the Search list (you have to click on the More>> button to display it—and then the button changes to <<Less) and select one of the following:

SHORTCUT You can also display the dialog box by right-clicking in the column heading and selecting Find from the shortcut menu that appears.

- *Up* to look through records from the current one to the first;
- *Down* to look through records from the current one to the end of the table; or
- *All* to look through all of the records.

The Match option determines where in the field the text must be. Your choices are Any Part of Field, Whole Field, and Start of Field.

When set at Whole Field, Access only locates a record if the entire field is the same as the Find What entry. For example, if you type Chesin and search the Company field for a match on the Whole Field, Access won't find Chesin Pharmacy—the whole field contains more than just the name Chesin. However, if you select Any Part of Field, Access will locate records that contain the Find What characters, regardless of where they are within the field. The purpose of the Start of Field option should be obvious.

The other two check boxes let you further control the search. Selecting Match Case means that the field must match the exact way you type the Find What text; uppercase for uppercase, lowercase for lowercase. Search Fields As Formatted is an interesting option. You can tell Access that you want some types of information to appear on the screen in a certain way, even though it is not actually stored on disk the same way. The best example is a date. Using techniques that you'll learn in Chapter 6, you can tell Access to display a date in a special format, say 10/22/45. When Access actually saves the date on the disk, it saves it as a code that takes up as few characters as possible. You don't have to worry about that. When you do not search for a date as formatted, you can enter the Find What text in any other date format that Access understands. So searching for October 22, 1945 will locate a record containing 10/22/45. If you select this option, however, you must type the date as it appears onscreen to locate it.

Let's try the Find operation now using the Contacts table in your Contacts database. Suppose you want to locate contacts in the 206 area code, in any of the fields containing telephone numbers.

1. Open the Contacts database while holding down the SHIFT key to bypass the switchboard, then open the Contacts table in Datasheet view.

2. Scroll the table and click in the Work Phone field of the first record.

3. Press HOME to make sure the insertion point is at the very start of the field. Otherwise, the Find operation might miss checking the characters to the left of the insertion point.

> **Y**ou can only use Search Fields As Formatted if the Look In option is set for the field rather than the entire table, and if Match Case is not selected.

4. Click the Find button.

5. Type (**206**) in the Find What box.

6. Since (206) is not the entire phone number, pull down the Match list and select either Start of Field or Any Part of Field.

7. Click More>>.

8. Click to select the Search Fields As Formatted option.

9. Click Find Next. Access moves to the first matching record, which is the current one in this case, and highlights the located text, (206).

10. Click Find Next. Access locates the next occurrence of (206).

11. Now let's change the option to look for any phone number in that area code. Pull down the Look In list and choose Contacts: Table. This means the search includes the entire table.

12. Click Find Next again. Access moves to the Home Phone field of the same record.

Continue clicking Find Next until you feel comfortable with the Find command, and then close the Find box.

Replacing Information Automatically

Many times you search for information because you want to change it. So, it is a two-step process, find and then replace. There's an easier way to find and replace information, particularly when you want to make the same change in a number of records.

If you want to replace text in a particular field, then click in the field before you begin, either in a form or a datasheet. If you want to replace text no matter where it is, you can start in any field. Then select Replace from the Edit menu and use the dialog box as shown in Figure 4.1. Yes, Virginia, it is just the other tab of the Find box and contains most of the same options.

Replace in Access works just like the replace function in many word processing programs, such as Word for Windows. The only difference is that you can choose to replace text in any field, or in a specific field by placing the insertion point in it first.

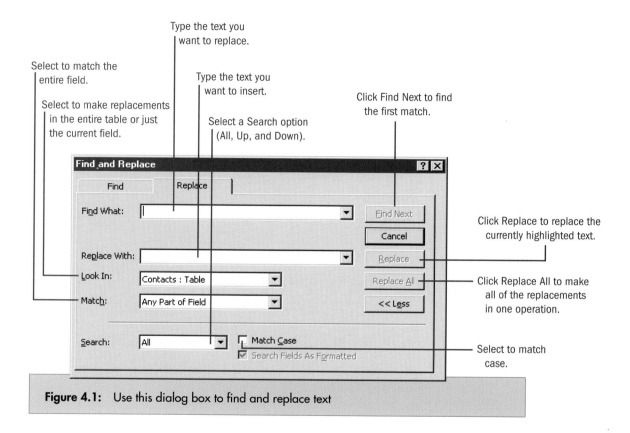

Figure 4.1:   Use this dialog box to find and replace text

Streamlining Data Entry with AutoCorrect

AutoCorrect is one of those great features that works so well, you sometimes don't even know it's there. In fact, it might have helped you already, without you even knowing it. AutoCorrect corrects mistakes automatically—that much is obvious by the name. If you mistakenly—or otherwise—capitalize the first two letters of a word, for example, AutoCorrect changes the second uppercase character to lowercase. If you forget to start the name of a day with an uppercase letter, AutoCorrect will make the change for you, too.

AutoCorrect will also correct a whole bunch of common misspellings—such as replacing acheive with achieve, and yuor with your. But because most information in a database will usually be nouns—names, places, people, and things—and numbers, the built-in replacements of AutoCorrect may not be used that often. The real power of AutoCorrect, at least in Access, is that you can add AutoCorrect entries to correct your own common misspellings or to quickly insert text when you type an abbreviation for it. You can create an AutoCorrect entry by following these steps:

1. Choose AutoCorrect from the Tools menu.

2. Enter a word the way you misspell it, or an abbreviation you want to store.

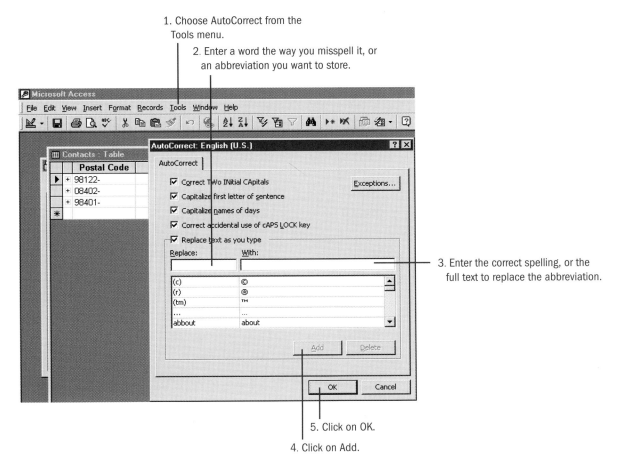

3. Enter the correct spelling, or the full text to replace the abbreviation.

5. Click on OK.

4. Click on Add.

Now whenever you misspell the word or type the abbreviation, Access will make the correction for you.

To see how AutoCorrect works, pull down the Tools menu and click on AutoCorrect to see the AutoCorrect dialog box. You can turn off each of the AutoCorrect options if you don't want them to be performed. For example, if you want to type day names with lowercase letters—although I can't think of a reason—then click on Capitalize Names Of Day to remove the check mark. To turn off the automatic replacement feature, deselect Replace Text As You Type. You can also click on Exceptions to specify words that begin with two capital letters, or to designate abbreviations ending with periods, so that the first word following the abbreviation will not automatically be capitalized.

When AutoCorrect is turned on, it will make the replacements shown in the list box. Scroll the list to see the predefined entries. You create your own AutoCorrect entries using the Replace and With text boxes. For example, suppose you commonly misspell the word acid as asid. To have Access correct the mistake for you, type **asid** in the Replace box and **acid** in the With box. Then click on Add and then OK. Now when you type asid and press SPACEBAR, ENTER, or TAB, or type a punctuation mark—any of which triggers AutoCorrect—Access will change it to acid.

Now think about it. If Access replaces text as you type, why not use it to streamline your work? Getting tired of typing Los Angeles for all of your clients in the City of Angels? Type an abbreviation such as LA in the Replace box, and the full name in the With box. When you type LA in a field, Access automatically replaces it with Los Angeles, saving you quite a few keystrokes.

Use the Delete button to remove the selected entry from the list. Be careful—you can delete the default entries that Access provides as well as your own.

EXPERT ADVICE

AutoCorrect is a common tool in Office 2000, so AutoCorrect entries that you create in one Office 2000 program will be available to the others. Create AutoCorrect entries to help you enter names, places, and things that you frequently enter in the table.

Checking Your Spelling

Before printing your database forms or reports, especially if you're distributing them to VIPs, it's always a good idea to make sure that everything is spelled correctly.

The spelling feature works a lot like the one in Microsoft Word. It compares each word in the selected records against those in its dictionary. To begin checking your spelling, place the insertion point where you want to start the process. To skip checking the first four records, for example, click in the first field of record five. You can also select what you want to check—the contents of a field, the entire record, or all of the records—by choosing Select All Records from the Edit menu. Then click on the Spelling button in the toolbar (or press F7). When Access finds a word that is not in its dictionary, it displays the dialog box shown in Figure 4.2. The Not In Dictionary text box shows the word the way it is spelled in your table. If there are some suggested spellings in the Suggestions list box, the Change To box shows the selected word in the list. If Access cannot find any suggested spellings, the notation, (No Suggestions) will appear in the list. You now have several options, depending on whether the word is spelled correctly or incorrectly.

If you've used the spelling checker in Word for Windows, then save some time by skipping this section. The only difference in Access is that you can select to ignore specific fields.

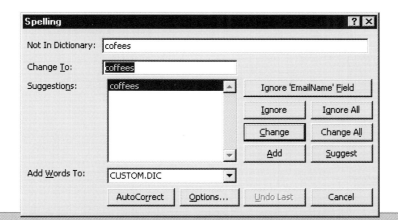

Figure 4.2: Use the Spelling feature to avoid embarrassments

Click on the Ignore Field button when you want Access to ignore the entries in the named field for the remainder of the records. For example, since you know the E-Mail Name field will contain some strange combinations of characters, click on Ignore 'E-MailName' Field.

When the Word Is Spelled Incorrectly

If you see the correct spelling in the list, double-click on it or select it, and then choose either Change or Change All. Access inserts the correctly spelled word and then searches for the next error. When you choose Change, Access will report the next occurrence as a possible error so you can again select from the list. When you choose Change All, Access will automatically replace other occurrences of the same misspelling. Change All is useful when you know you've misspelled the same word, in the same way, several times in the same table.

If you do not see the correct spelling, or if no suggestions are listed, type another spelling for the word in the Change To box, and then click on either the Change button or the Suggest button, which becomes visible when you begin typing your new word. If you select Change, Access looks in the dictionary for the new word; if it isn't there, Access will ask whether you want to use the replacement anyway and continue, or look up your replacement for possible alternatives. If you select Suggest, Access looks up the word you typed and displays alternative spellings for it.

The Change All option only affects the current spelling checker operation. If Access locates the same misspelling when checking another table or form, it will again report it as an error. When you know it's a word that you frequently misspell, click on the correct spelling in the list, or type it in the Change To box, and then click on the AutoCorrect button. Access will make the replacement in your document and create an AutoCorrect entry. Now whenever you type the incorrectly spelled word, AutoCorrect will replace it with the correct spelling.

When the Word Is Spelled Correctly

If the word is indeed spelled correctly, click on either Ignore or Ignore All. Access leaves the word as you typed it and continues the spelling

---

If you forget a space between words, as in MicrosoftAccess, the combination will be reported as not in the dictionary. Just edit or retype the words, with the space, in the Change To box and select Change.

check. When you choose Ignore, Access will stop at the next occurrence and report it as a possible error. When you choose Ignore All, Access skips over all occurrences of the word in the table.

The Add option inserts the word into the custom dictionary so the same word will not be reported as misspelled in other tables. This custom dictionary is used by all Office programs, so any additions you make will be effective in all Office 2000 applications.

More Spelling Choices

Now let's look at some other options in the Spelling dialog box.

If you select Change or Ignore by mistake, click on the Undo Last button to return to the previous word. If you've just changed the word, the original spelling will appear. Until you take some action in the Spelling dialog box, the Undo Last button will be dimmed.

To delete a word from the table, clear the contents of the Change To box. The Change and Change All buttons will change to Delete and Delete All. Select Delete to erase the single occurrence of the word; select Delete All to erase them all.

If Access encounters two of the same correctly spelled words in a row, such as do do, the second occurrence of the word is highlighted and the Not In Dictionary box will be labeled Repeated Word. The Change To box will be empty. Choose Delete to erase the duplicate, or choose Ignore to leave it alone. To replace the word with another, type the replacement in the Change To box—the Delete button will become Change so you can make the replacement.

Customizing Spelling

By default, the spelling checker ignores words in all uppercase characters and words that contain numbers. To change these and some other spelling settings, click on Options in the Spelling dialog box, then choose the options as shown in Figure 4.3.

A message box will appear reporting when you've checked all of the selected text. Click OK to remove the box and to close the Spelling dialog box.

CAUTION

Undo Last does not work with the Delete All command, and there is no way to undo it, so think twice before clicking on the Delete All button.

Access ignores common pairs of duplicate words, such as had had and that that, so check your work carefully to make sure a mistake does not slip through.

SHORTCUT

If you have a slower computer, there may be some delay as Access looks up suggested words. If you usually type the replacement word yourself, deselect the Always Suggest option. If you do want Access to find alternative spellings when checking a document, click on the Suggest button in the Spelling dialog box.

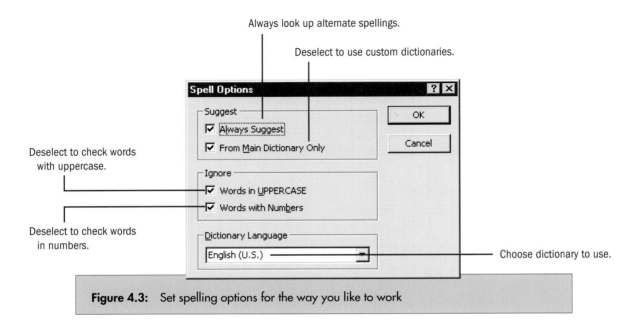

Figure 4.3:   Set spelling options for the way you like to work

Previewing Forms, Reports, and Datasheets

Reports are always previewed; there's no Open option for them anyway. That's because you cannot open a report to change its contents—only changing the database does that.

Because a data access page is really a Web page, you cannot use the preview command in Access to see how it will appear when printed. Instead, click on the page in the Database window or open the page, and then choose Web Page Preview from the File menu. Access opens your Web browser and displays the page.

Paper may be cheap, but your time isn't. There aren't many things as frustrating as waiting for a long report or a series of forms to print, only to discover you've printed the wrong thing, or you just don't like the way it looks printed. When it happens to me, my office floor becomes like the bottom of a birdcage, littered with discarded pages.

Before printing a form, report, or datasheet, you should check how the printout will appear using Print Preview. Now in some ways, Print Preview is a carryover from those ancient days, when dinosaurs roamed the earth. Something called dBASE (yes, it is spelled oddly) was worshipped as a deity, and every character displayed on the computer was the same size and font. Print Preview switched to a special graphics mode that displayed how a document would actually appear when printed, more or less.

With Windows, what you see on the screen is what gets printed. But Preview does have some special features, so it is not entirely a throwback to appease DOS Neanderthals. For example, you can see how much information prints on a page—how many forms or rows of the datasheet, for example—so you can make adjustments to the page layout before wasting your time and paper. You can preview a form or datasheet directly from the Database window without opening it first.

To preview a datasheet or form, for example, click on its name in the Database window, and then click on the Print Preview button on the toolbar, or choose Print Preview from the File menu. The Access screen changes to the Preview mode, as shown in Figure 4.4. Now you see how your information will appear when printed, and how much of the page it takes up. When you preview a datasheet, Access automatically prints its name and the date at the top of the page, and the page number at the bottom. Here's what the Preview toolbar buttons are used for:

	View	Lets you change to another view, such as design, form, or datasheet.
	Print	Prints the object displayed in the Preview window.
	Zoom	Toggles between enlarged and reduced display.
	One Page	Shows one page at a time.
	Two Pages	Shows two pages at a time
	Multiple Pages	Lets you select to display up to 20 pages.
Fit	Zoom	Lets you change the displayed magnification, or fit the page to the screen.
Close	Close	Closes the Preview window, not the database.
	Office Links	Lets you use the object for a Word Mail Merge, or publish the object in Word, or insert into an Excel table.
	Database Window	Switches to the Database window, without closing the preview.
	New Object	Lets you create a new table, query, form, report, macro, or module without returning to the Database window.
	Office Assistant	Offers help on common tasks, and lets you search for help.

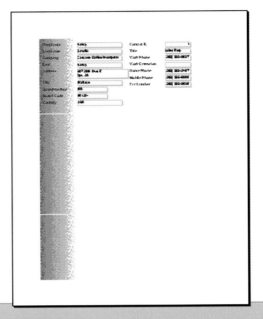

Figure 4.4: Forms in preview mode

SHORTCUT
You can select other magnifications from the Zoom list on the toolbar, from 200 percent to 10 percent. The Fit option displays the full page.

If the preview image is too small for you to see how the object will really look, point the mouse on the simulated page so the pointer appears like a magnifying lens, and then click. Access enlarges the display to 100 percent, the same size as it will be when printed. Click the mouse again to reduce the display to see the whole page.

Click on Close when you're done looking at the preview.

Changing Page Layout

If you do not like how your printout appears in Preview, then you're not going to like how it prints. Most printout problems are caused by the page layout— the margins, page size, or other settings. So before printing, or even after, if you have to print it over, set the page layout how you want it.

SHORTCUT
You can also set the Margins and Columns options for forms and reports, and the Margins options for tables, by selecting Setup in the Print dialog box.

Each object in the database—whether it is a form, report, or datasheet—can have its own page layout settings. You can use one set of margins for one report, a different set for another. Either open the object you want to set the layout for, or click on its name in the Database window. Then choose Page Setup from the File menu.

The Page Setup dialog box has three tabs—Margins, Page, and Columns—as shown in Figure 4.5. The Margins tab lets you change the page margins and whether you want to print just the data from the form, or the data, labels, and any other text or graphics.

In the Page tab of the dialog box, you select the orientation, the page size, and source, and set a printer to be used for the current object. The settings in the Page Setup dialog box affect just the selected object in the Database window, and they are saved along with the database.

The options in the Columns tab, shown in Figure 4.6, control the layout of forms or report sections.

The Page Setup option will be dimmed when the Pages and Tables page of the Database window is displayed. To set up a page for a table, open the table first. The box will not contain a Columns tab. The Setup command is not available for data access pages.

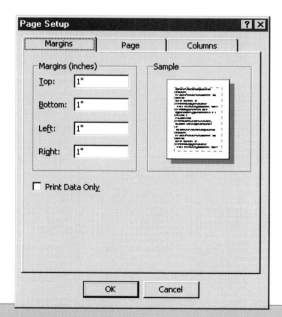

Figure 4.5: Margins tab of the Page Setup dialog box

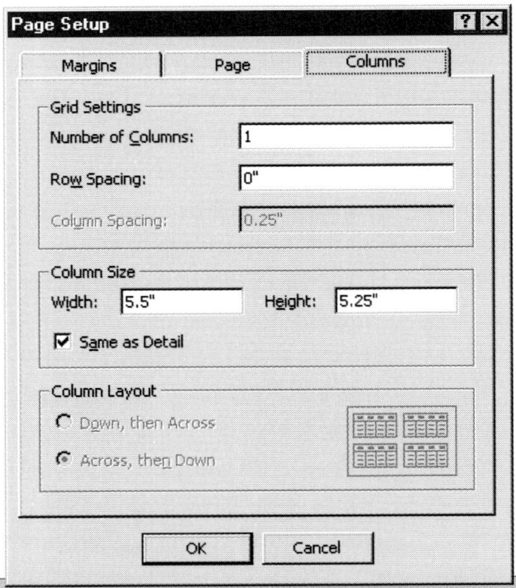

Figure 4.6: Columns tab of the Page Setup dialog box

The Grid Settings area controls how many forms print across the page, if more than one can fit, and their spacing. Column Size sets the size of the columns when printing multiple-column reports or labels. When Same As Detail is checked, the form will print the same size as was designed, and how it appears onscreen. If you enter a smaller size, some of the form will not appear on the printout.

The Column Layout section determines the order of the forms and report sections. If you select Down, Then Across, Access first fits as many records as it can down the left side of the page, then continues with more records to their right. When you select Across, Then Down, Access fits as many across the top of the page, and then continues the others in rows below them.

When you are finished with the Page Setup options, click OK to accept your changes, or click Cancel to close the box without implementing any changes.

EXPERT ADVICE

While you do not have to open a table or form to print it, it takes just a few seconds to open it and confirm it is really the object you want to print.

Printing Forms, Reports, and Datasheets

Viewing information on the screen is nice, but if you don't have a laptop, does it mean you have to lug around your desktop when you want to see that information? Talk about exercise. Fortunately, anything on the Access screen can also be printed—forms, datasheets, reports, and data access pages.

Printing is a snap. First, select the object you want to print (form, table, report, data access page) in the Database window, open the object, or display it in preview. Then, just click on the Print button in the toolbar. Access will send all of the information to your printer.

If you want to print specific records or pages, or otherwise control the printing process, then select Print from the File menu or press CTRL-P. Access will display the dialog box shown in Figure 4.7. This dialog box is pretty much straight Windows stuff.

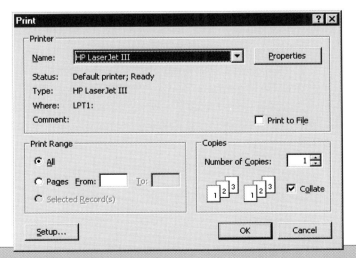

The Print dialog box is different for data access pages—it's the Print dialog box from your Web browser.

Figure 4.7: Print dialog box

Still the wrong printer? Click on the Start button, point to Settings, and click on Printers. Then use the Add Printer program to install and set up your printer. You might need your original setup disk or CD so make sure they are handy when you add additional printers.

The Printer section shows which printer will be used. Wrong printer? Pull down the Name list and select the correct one. Use the Properties button to fine-tune the printer setup, and use the Print To File option to output the print job to a file on your disk that you can print later or e-mail.

The Print Range section determines how many records will print. All prints them all. Pages prints just those pages designated in the From and To boxes. Selected Record(s) prints just the selected records.

The Copies section determines...well, you know (the number of copies to print). Collate is useful when printing more than one copy. When selected, each complete set of pages prints separately. When not selected, you get multiple copies of the first page, then multiple copies of the second page, and so on.

When everything is set the way you want it, click OK.

Summary

We covered a lot in this chapter, so take a moment to review. By using the Find and Replace commands you can easily locate or change information. Use AutoCorrect to streamline data entry, and use Spelling to avoid embarrassing mistakes. Choose Page Setup options to customize your printouts, and try Print Preview to make sure you get exactly what you want.

So what's next? Put the pink sofa over there, and then move the chair to the other side of the fireplace. No, maybe on the other side. We all like to decorate and customize our surroundings, to make things just more livable. It's no different with Access. In Chapter 5, you'll learn how to customize the way Access works, so it works the way you like it.

Stuff to Do Once to Make Your Life Easier

INCLUDES

- Setting Access options
- Moving and displaying toolbars
- Creating custom toolbars

FAST FORWARD

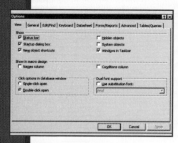

Set Access Options → pp. 98–105

1. Open a database.
2. Choose Tools | Options.
3. Click on each tab and select the appropriate options.
4. Click OK to close the dialog box and implement the changes.

Change a Toolbar's Appearance → pp. 105–107

1. Right-click on a toolbar.
2. Click Customize.
3. Click Options.
4. Select the appropriate options.
5. Close the dialog box.

Move a Toolbar → p. 107

- Point to the blank area around any button and drag the toolbar.
- Resize the toolbar as desired.

Display/Hide Toolbars → pp. 108–109

Open the object that displays the toolbar, or follow these steps:

1. Right-click on a toolbar.
2. Click the toolbar listed in the shortcut menu.
3. If the toolbar you want to open is not listed, click Customize.
4. Click on the Toolbars tab.
5. Click the check box for the toolbar you want to display or hide.
6. Close the dialog box.

Add Buttons to a Toolbar ➥ p. 109

1. Display the toolbar.
2. Right-click on the toolbar.
3. Click Customize.
4. Click on the Commands tab.
5. Select the category of the function you want the button to perform.
6. Drag the button to its position in the toolbar.
7. Close the dialog box.

Create a New Toolbar ➥ pp. 110–113

1. Right-click on a toolbar.
2. Click Customize.
3. Click on the Toolbars tab.
4. Click New.
5. In the New Toolbar dialog box type the toolbar name and select OK.
6. Click on the Commands tab.
7. Select the category of the function you want the button to perform.
8. Drag the button to the toolbar.
9. Close the dialog box.

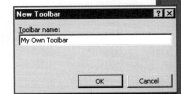

Default settings are great if they give you what you want and need. If they don't, why suffer the capriciousness of Microsoft? You can change things so Access looks and works the way you want it to. In fact, you can change many of the default settings, even create custom toolbars, and then go on your merry way without even thinking about it again. How badly can you screw things up? Not at all. You can always change the settings back again. So go for it; do your own thing!

Setting Database Options

DEFINITION

Options: Settings that Microsoft has determined you can be trusted to change, which can customize the way a program works and how you interact with it.

Access lets you change a number of default settings to customize the way you like to work. The command you use is called Options, which is appropriate because the choices are up to you. You can leave everything set as is, or you can pick and choose which settings you want to change. Microsoft gives us eight pages of options that we can change, a lot of which are for really advanced users, network or workgroup administers, and those who love to live on the edge. However, there are options that almost everyone can choose to make Access more comfortable. I'll just mention a few that I think you might want to consider, but don't be afraid to look at some of the other options—just be careful.

Open any one of your databases—the Options command will be dimmed in the Tools menu when you do not have a database open. Choose Tools | Options to display the Options dialog box, click on the tab for the options you want to set, and then have fun. Use the View tab, for example, to select what Access elements are displayed on the screen, as shown in Figure 5.1.

EXPERT ADVICE

For more information about a setting, click on the What's This? button and then on the setting in the dialog box. Read the information that appears, then click the mouse to continue working.

Turn on/off the status bar.

Select to display hidden objects in the Database window.

Select to display tables that Access uses to manage the database.

Select to show the Startup dialog box when you start Access.

Show commands to create new objects in the Database window.

Select to display macro names when creating macros.

Select how many clicks are needed to open objects.

Show each open object in the taskbar.

Select to display condition names when creating macros.

Use multiple fonts for displaying multiple languages.

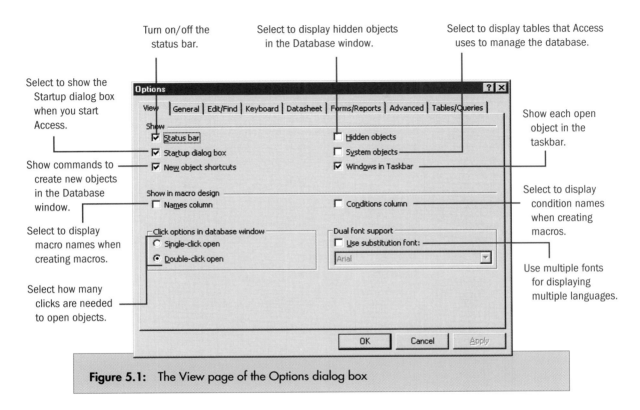

Figure 5.1: The View page of the Options dialog box

The options in the Tables/Queries, Forms/Reports, and Advanced pages are used for special purposes. They won't make a lot of sense to you until you learn how to create your own tables, queries, and other objects, so I won't waste your time with them now. For example, the options in the Tables/Queries page determine the default settings of tables and queries. You can change the settings each time you create a table or query, or you can set your own default settings for every new table or query using this dialog box. They'll mean something to you after you read Chapter 6, so come back and visit these options later.

Glance over these other pages on your screen, and file these options away in your gray matter until later.

Customizing the Default Layout

Use the General tab of the Options dialog box (see Figure 5.2) to control some overall ways that Access works. This is a good place to start.

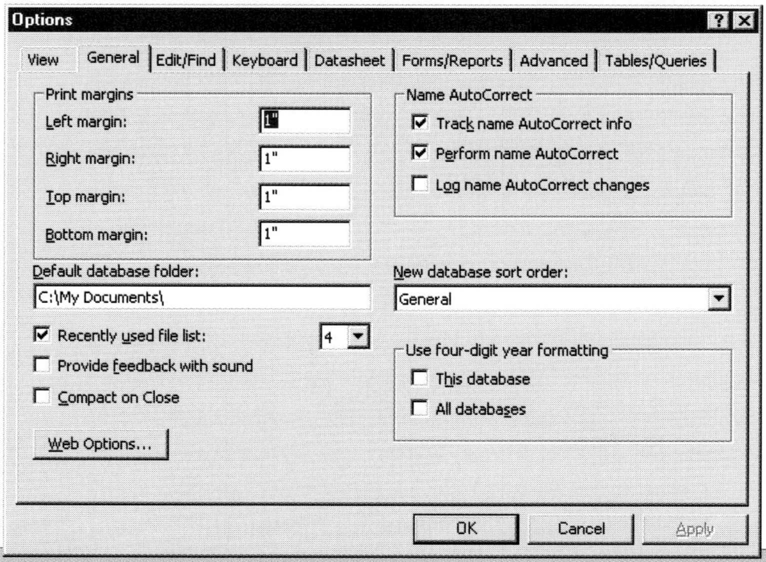

Figure 5.2: General options

If you don't like the default one-inch margins for printed forms, reports, and datasheets, for example, enter new margins here. Your settings affect all new forms and reports, and all existing datasheets. To change the margins of an existing form or report, you need to select it in the Database window and use the Page Setup dialog box.

The Default Database Folder setting determines the location where Access saves and expects to find your databases. You can use the default that's shown in your Options box or change it to suit your needs. You may want to save all of your databases in a folder separate from Word documents and Excel worksheets to help organize your work or make backups easier.

The Recently Used File List option controls whether your recently used databases are listed at the bottom of the File menu. You can turn this option on and off, and set the number of files that are displayed.

The Provide Feedback With Sound option lets you play sound effects on certain Access and other Office 2000 events, such as when you move or close a toolbar, or when a process is completed. This can be really annoying if you work in a crowded office—with beeps, whistles, and other sounds going off all around you—but it adds something to those long work sessions when you're alone. Deselect the option to turn off the sounds in Access as well as other Office 2000 applications. You can control which sounds play at a specific event using the Sounds program in the control panel. All of the events are listed in the Office 2000 section of the dialog box.

Use the Compact On Close setting to remove wasted space whenever you close the database. This wasted space is accumulated when you edit and delete information in the database. You can set when to compact the database based on the percentage of space that will be saved.

The Name AutoCorrect section of the dialog box offers a feature new to Access 2000. When you create forms and reports, Access knows where to place information based on the field names. For example, it takes information from the City field in a table and places it where you designate the City field to appear. In previous versions of Access, if you modified the table and changed the name of the field to Town, Access would not place the information where you told it to insert the City field—because the City field no longer exists. You would have to modify the forms and reports as well, inserting the Town field where the City field was located.

When the Track Name AutoCorrect Info check box is selected, Access 2000 keeps track of where your field names appear. When the Perform Name AutoCorrect check box is also selected, Access automatically changes the names of fields in forms, reports, and other objects when they are changed in the table. The Log Name AutoCorrect Changes option saves a record of the changes to a table named AutoCorrect Log.

The Web Options button displays a dialog box to customize the way links appear when creating documents for the World Wide Web. A hyperlink is text you click to move to a site on the Internet. By default, hyperlink text will be underlined, and when you point to the link its address will appear on the status bar. Until you click the text, it will appear in blue, the Hyperlink Color setting. Once you click the link, it changes to purple to indicate that you've already followed, or jumped to, the location. You can change the Hyperlink Color and Followed Hyperlink Color, turn off the underlining, or choose not to show their addresses in the status bar.

Streamlining Find and Replace

Now look at the Edit/Find page (see Figure 5.3). These options are a little esoteric, but they are useful if you use the Find and Replace features a lot, or if you use Filter By Form. If you don't, it's okay to skip this section.

The Default Find/Replace options determine the default settings in the Find and Replace dialog boxes. You can change any of the settings once you display the Find or Replace dialog box, but this is how they'll start:

- Fast Search searches just the current field and matches on the whole field. Looking for "Smith," for example, will not match with "Asmithson."
- General Search looks through every field and finds a match regardless of where the characters are located. So, looking for "Smith" will locate the characters in "Asmithson."

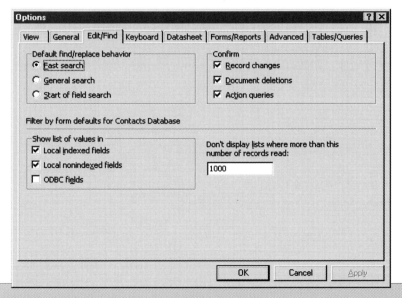

Figure 5.3: Edit/Find options

- Start Of Field Search matches the beginning characters of the current field. So a search for "Smith" will find a match with "Smithson," but not with "Asmithson."

The Confirm options determine if a warning box will appear, asking you to confirm certain actions. I'd leave them selected to play it safe, unless you want to play a dirty trick on some unsuspecting user. Really think twice before you turn off the Confirm options.

If you recall, when you perform a Filter By Form, you can pull down a list to select the field contents you want to filter on. The list always shows unique values, no matter how many times a specific value is repeated. It is a great way to look for records because you don't have to worry about typing a value in a text box, or wasting your time looking for information that doesn't exist. With the small databases I've been using as examples, the list appears almost instantaneously. That's the up side of Filter By Form. The down side? If you're working with a large database, it can take Access quite some time to create and display the pull-down list.

The Filter By Form Defaults section at the bottom of the Edit/Find dialog box controls what appears in the list. By default, records in external databases are not shown because it can take a lot of time to add them to the list. If you want to see the items in external databases, select the ODBC Fields option. It also takes more time to display items in non-indexed fields, so deselect that option if you're always in a hurry. The more records that have to be read, the longer it takes to build the list, especially for non-indexed fields. By default (there's that word again!), Access won't bother showing the list if there are more than 1,000 records. Change this value in the text box in this section to accommodate your own needs.

Unlike most settings in the Options dialog box which affect all Access databases, those in the Filter By Form Defaults section affect only the currently open database.

Streamlining Keyboard Entry

The Keyboard tab (see Figure 5.4) can be your best friend if you use the TAB, ENTER, or arrow keys to move around the datasheet or form. So take your time and consider these options carefully.

The options in the Move After Enter section determine what happens when you press the ENTER key. You can select to have Access

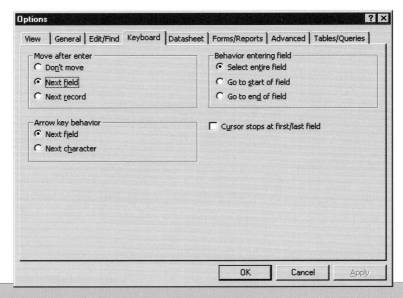

Figure 5.4:   Keyboard options

SHORTCUT

If you are entering a series of information into the same field of every record, as you would when completing a field that you just added to the table, set the option to Next Record.

stay where it is, move to the next field, or move to the next record. The default setting is Next Field, so after you enter information into a field, you just press ENTER to move to the next field, or from the last field to the first field of the next record.

The Arrow Key Behavior options determine what happens when you press the arrow key when a field is selected. Normally, when a field is selected, pressing an arrow key moves to the next field—in the direction of the arrow. If you change the setting to Next Character, pressing an arrow key deselects the field and remains there so you can edit the contents.

The Behavior Entering Field options determine what happens when you press TAB, ENTER, or an arrow key to move to a field. The default is Select Entire Field. If you want to go to a field and then start editing immediately, you can change this to either Go To Start Of Field or Go To End Of Field. When you move into a field, the insertion point will move to that position so you can start typing or editing.

Finally, the Cursor Stops At First/Last Field option determines what happens when you reach the first or the last field. When this option is not selected, pressing the RIGHT ARROW key when the last field is selected will move to the next record, or to the previous record when you press the LEFT ARROW from the first field. If you select this option, Access won't move off the field to the next record.

Customizing Your Datasheets

The Datasheet page lets you set the default appearance for datasheets. It offers the same choices as the Font and Cells Effects dialog boxes that we looked at in previous chapters (that's why I'm not even showing it to you here), as well as the chance to set the default column width. Use this box if you have a special combination of effects that you want to use for every datasheet. Please see Chapter 3 if the Font and Cells Effects boxes have slipped your mind (I won't be insulted).

SHORTCUT
If you have a lot of editing to do, change to either Go To Start Of Field or Go To End Of Field. This saves you the trouble of pressing F2 to switch to editing mode for each field.

Ah! The Wonder of Toolbars

You've already used many of the buttons in the toolbar, and you might have also displayed the Formatting (Datasheet) toolbar in Chapter 4. You also know that the toolbar will change when you do certain functions. The toolbar shown when you're looking at the Database window, for example, is not the same when you're looking at a form or previewing an object.

Access has 25 different toolbars (that's a lot of buttons), many of which most of us will never get to use. I've talked about a lot of the buttons throughout the first several chapters in this book, and I'll cover many more as we continue. However, Microsoft's standard selections may not match your personal needs as closely as you'd like. In this section, I'll offer some suggestions for keeping the most handy buttons within reach.

Setting Menu and Toolbar Options

First, take a quick look at how you can change the appearance of the toolbar, as well as how the pull-down menus appear. Right-click on a toolbar, click Customize, and then click Options to see choices for customizing the toolbars and menus. (You can also choose View |

Toolbars, click Customize, and then click Options.) Select options from the dialog box, as shown in Figure 5.5.

Access 2000 offers personalized menus. It starts by displaying a basic set of commands on its menus and lists the commands you use most often at the top. If you don't see the command you want to perform, just pause on the menu or click the down arrows at the bottom of it. Access expands the menu to show additional items. If you choose an item from the expanded menu, Access figures you'll be using it again and displays it on the unexpanded menu automatically. If you want to reset the menus so they no longer include these items, click Reset My Usage Data, and then select Yes to the message that appears.

Turn off the Show Full Menus After A Short Delay check box if you do not want menus to expand automatically. Turn off the Menus

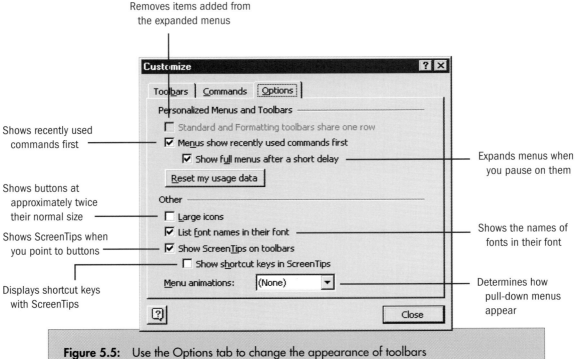

Figure 5.5: Use the Options tab to change the appearance of toolbars

Show Recently Used Commands First option if you do not want menus organized in this manner.

The Menu Animations option, by the way, controls the way menus appear when you click the menu bar. By default, a menu just pops up when you click a menu item. You can also choose to have menus slide down like a window shade, unfold at an angle, or appear using random angles.

Making Toolbars Handier

The toolbars appear across the top of the window beneath the menu bar. If you think a toolbar will be more convenient somewhere else, then you can move it by dragging. Access will remember the position of the toolbar when you exit, so the toolbar will be in the new location the next time it is displayed.

To move a toolbar, point to the blank area around any of the buttons and then drag the toolbar to a new position. As you drag, an outline of the bar moves with the mouse, showing the position and size it will be when you release the button. If you drag the toolbar to the left or right edge of the Access widow, it will become vertical with all of its buttons in a column. Some toolbars even change their buttons when docked on the left or right of the screen. If you drag it to the bottom of the window, or back under the menu bar, all of the buttons will be aligned horizontally. Move the toolbar anywhere else and it will appear in a window. When the toolbar appears in a window, you can drag one of its borders to change the size:

If you left on the Feedback With Sound option, you'll hear a clicking sound when you dock a toolbar along an edge of the screen.

Displaying Other Toolbars

Access usually displays the appropriate toolbar for the object on the screen. Other toolbars are optional, such as the Formatting (Datasheets) and Web toolbars. To see if Access recommends an optional toolbar, point to any toolbar and click the right mouse button. Any optional toolbar will be listed below the name of the default toolbar—click on it to display it.

You can also manually display additional toolbars. In most cases, however, another toolbar will only duplicate buttons in the toolbar already shown, or its buttons will be dimmed because they cannot be used with the current object. For example, if you display the Formatting (Datasheet) toolbar when a datasheet is not onscreen, the buttons will be dimmed and the text boxes will be empty. If you want to display another toolbar, however, right-click on a toolbar, choose Customize from the shortcut menu, and click on the Toolbars tab to see this dialog box:

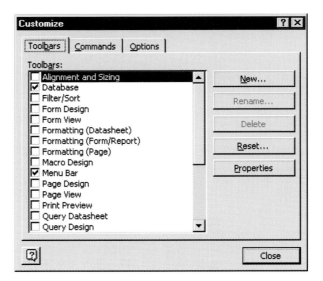

The check boxes of the toolbars already displayed will be checked. To display another toolbar, click on its check box. The toolbar appears as soon as you click; you do not have to exit the dialog box.

Deselect the box to remove the toolbar from the screen. If you turn off all of the toolbars by mistake, preventing you from right-clicking to display the shortcut menu, choose View | Toolbars to see the Toolbars dialog box, and then click to select the proper toolbar.

Removing and Adding Standard Buttons

Each toolbar includes a set of default buttons. You can quickly remove any of the default buttons that you do not use, or reinsert them. Click the arrow at the far right of a toolbar, and then click the Add or Remove Buttons option that appears to see a list of default buttons, as shown here:

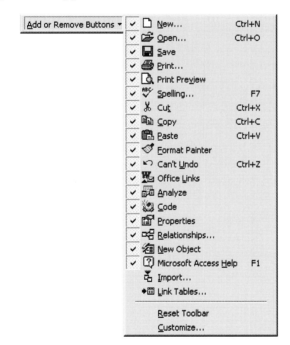

The check marks indicate which buttons are already displayed. Click an option in the list to remove the button from the toolbar, or to reinsert it if the check mark is not shown.

Click Reset Toolbar to restore all of the default buttons, or click Customize to create a custom toolbar, as you'll learn next.

Creating Your Own Custom Toolbars

Microsoft has done a good job of designing the toolbars, but even Microsoft isn't perfect. For example, you may find yourself changing the page layout frequently, sometimes adjusting margins, page orientation, or grid settings until you like what you see on the preview, or until you get a printout that you like. In this case, you may get tired of pulling down the File menu and selecting Page Setup. Another example is pulling down the File | New Object submenu to create a form or report when you're looking at a datasheet. Wouldn't it be better to just click on a single button to create a form for easier data entry? You can add the Page Setup and AutoForm buttons to your own toolbar so you can perform these functions with a single click.

Page Setup   AutoForm

Luckily, Access lets us modify the toolbars by adding other buttons to them. First, make sure that the toolbar you want to add a button to is displayed on the screen. Either use the Toolbars dialog box, or do whatever you have to do to display the toolbar. If you want to add a button to the Form View toolbar, for example, open a form, any form.

Next, right-click on any toolbar, choose Customize from the shortcut menu, and click on the Commands tab. (You can also select Customize from the Add or Remove Buttons list.) Then use the steps shown in Figure 5.6.

Before striking out on your own, here are a few extra words of caution. You can add a button for a command on a menu by dragging it from the menu to the toolbar. (You can even add an entire menu to a toolbar.) When you drag the command from the menu to the toolbar, however, hold down the CTRL key. This will display a plus sign next to the pointer indicating you are copying the item, not moving it:

CAUTION

If you do not hold down the CTRL key you will remove the item from the menu.
If you later delete the item from the toolbar, without restoring it to the menu, the item will no longer be available.

To access a menu item, click on the menu so the pull-down list appears. In fact, release the mouse button to make certain that the menu stays down. If you act too fast, you may end up dragging the

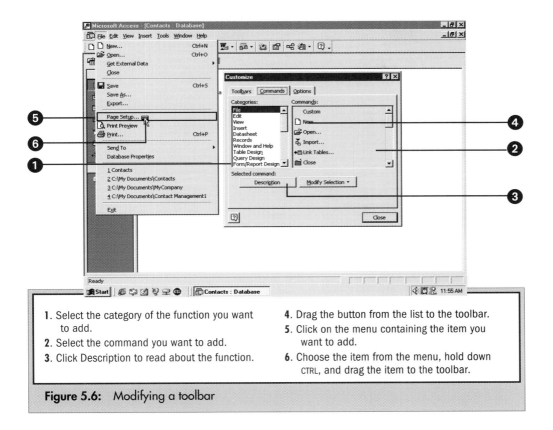

Figure 5.6: Modifying a toolbar

1. Select the category of the function you want to add.
2. Select the command you want to add.
3. Click Description to read about the function.
4. Drag the button from the list to the toolbar.
5. Click on the menu containing the item you want to add.
6. Choose the item from the menu, hold down CTRL, and drag the item to the toolbar.

entire menu itself, rather than an item from the menu. In this case, the pointer will look like this:

If you then accidentally drag the icon down into the window and release the mouse button without holding down CTRL, the entire menu will be deleted from Access.

As an example of customizing a toolbar, we'll add an AutoForm button to the Table Datasheet toolbar, the toolbar that appears when you open a table in Datasheet view. With this button, you can

To change a button's name, appearance, ToolTip, or other property, right-click the button in the toolbar, or click the button and then click the Modify Selection option in the Customize dialog box.

instantly create a form for entering and editing information. We will also add a button for the Page Setup command. Just follow along.

1. Open the Contacts database.

2. Open the Contacts table to see the Table Datasheet toolbar.

3. Right-click the toolbar and choose Customize.

4. Click on the Commands tab.

5. If necessary, drag the dialog box down out of the way so you can see the entire toolbar.

6. Click Insert in the Categories list. This is the category that contains the AutoForm command.

7. Scroll through the Commands list, click AutoForm, and then drag it so the large I-beam is just to the left of the New Object button.

8. Release the mouse button.

Now, let's add a Page Setup button to the toolbar.

1. Click the File menu. Release the mouse and make sure the menu remains displayed.

2. Click Page Setup.

3. Hold down the CTRL key and drag the Page Setup item to the toolbar.

4. Release the mouse button and the CTRL key.

5. Close the Customize dialog box.

That's all there is to it. The next time you're looking at a datasheet and decide to enter or edit information with a form, just click the AutoForm button.

EXPERT ADVICE

The toolbar in Datasheet view has the same default buttons as the toolbar in Form view, but they are not actually the same toolbar. If you display a form, your Find Next button will not appear. To add the button to the Form View toolbar, repeat the above procedure when a form is displayed.

To remove a button from a toolbar, or a command from a menu, display any tab of the Customize dialog box, and then drag the button down off of the toolbar, or drag the menu item down into the window. When you release the mouse, the button or menu command will be gone. You can also drag a toolbar button to a menu.

If you mess up one of the default toolbars by deleting or adding buttons by mistake, display the Toolbars dialog box, click the name of the toolbar, and then click Reset.

You use the New button in the Toolbars tab of the Customize dialog box to create your very own toolbar. Click New, and then enter a name for the toolbar in the dialog box that appears. A small blank toolbar will appear onscreen. Use the Customize box to add buttons to it. If you decide to later delete the entire toolbar, click on its name, not its check box, in the Toolbars dialog box and select Delete. Use the Rename option in the Toolbars dialog box to change the name of the selected toolbar.

EXPERT ADVICE

Use the same procedure you learned for customizing toolbars to customize menus. When the Customize box is displayed, drag a command or item from one menu to any other menu.

Now It's Your Turn

Use the Options dialog box to customize Access to the way you like to work. Experiment a little with the choices in the Keyboard page to find the most comfortable combination of settings.

Next, add new buttons to the Print Preview toolbar to make the toolbar more useful. Open any report in Preview, right-click the toolbar, and choose Customize to display the dialog box. Add the Page Setup command from the File menu, and copy the Eight Pages command from the View menu. Be very careful when selecting the Eight Pages command—be certain that you do not drag the entire View menu to the toolbar.

EXPERT ADVICE

Remember to hold down the CTRL key when you drag menu items to copy them to the toolbar, not move them from the menu.

The Eight Pages button will have text but not an icon on it:

Eight Pages

Add an icon to the button to make it more attractive. When the Customize box is open, right-click the button to display the shortcut menu:

Point to the Change Button Image command and choose an icon from those that appear:

The ampersand (&) before the letter E in the name text box means that the letter E will be underlined on the button. You now have some choices:

- Choose Text Only (Always) to display the words "Eight Pages" on the button.
- Choose Change Button Image to select an icon provided by Office 97.
- Choose Edit Button Image to design your own icon.
- Choose Image and Text to display both the words "Eight Pages" and your selected icon.

Summary

By setting options and customizing toolbars, you can really make Access your own. As you learned in this chapter, open a database and select Tools | Options. Don't be afraid to experiment with different settings; you can always go back and change the settings at any time. In this chapter, you also learned how to customize and create toolbars. When you have time, choose the various items in the Categories list, and then look at the commands that are available. From the Categories list, for example, you can select to display lists of your tables, forms, reports, and other database objects that you want to open with a click on a toolbar button.

It's time to move on, away from the security of Almost Instant databases. In the next chapter, I'll show you how to create your own databases and tables, and how to modify tables once you create them. Heavy stuff.

CHAPTER 6

Creating a Custom Database and Tables

INCLUDES

- Creating a new database
- Creating tables with Table Wizard
- Creating tables from scratch
- Modifying tables and field properties
- Working with fields and properties

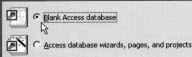

Create a Database ➡ p. 121

1. Select Blank Access Database from the Startup menu, or click the New Database button and double-click Database.
2. Type the database name.
3. Click OK.

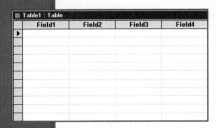

Create a Table in Datasheet View ➡ pp. 121–124

1. Display the Table page of the Database window.
2. Click New.
3. Select Datasheet View.
4. Click OK.
5. Double-click column labels and enter field names.
6. Enter information in rows of the datasheet.
7. Click the Save button.
8. Enter the table name and click OK.

Use the Table Wizard ➡ pp. 124–128

1. Display the Table page of the Database window.
2. Click New.
3. Select Table Wizard.
4. Click OK.
5. Complete the Wizard dialog boxes as they appear, clicking the Next button after choosing options from the dialog box.
6. Click Finish in the last dialog box.

Create a Table in Design View ➡ pp. 129–145

1. Display the Table page of the Database window.
2. Click New.
3. Select Design View.
4. Click OK.
5. Enter the field name.
6. Select the field type.
7. Set the field properties.
8. Repeat for each additional field.
9. Click the Save button.
10. Enter a table name and click OK.

Modify a Table ➡ pp. 145–146

1. Display the Table page of the Database window.
2. Click on the table.
3. Click Design.
4. Add, delete, or modify the fields.
5. Click the Save button.

Almost Instant databases are great, but they certainly don't do everything you'd need a database for. You may want special fields that Microsoft never even thought of giving you, or you might want a combination of properties for controlling what the user can input. Sure, you could probably live with the Almost Instant databases, but you can also get *mucho* frustrated trying to fit your information into someone else's database design. That's when you have to create your own database and tables, or at least change those created by the Database Wizard.

Get Ready to Rumble

First a little preamble to explain the rules of the game.

If you want to record some simple information about your stamp collection, all you might need is a single table. Of course you can't have a table without a database to store it in. Rather than create a separate database for your table, you could add the table to one of your existing databases. For example, you could store your stamp collection table in the Contacts database, or in any other. You could, but it's not recommended.

In theory, if there are several tables in a database, they should all relate to the same general theme—your business, your household accounts, your Edward D. Wood, Jr. fan club, or the like. They should never be mixed. The Guru will tell you never to put a table about something personal in your business database, or add a stamp collection table to your bowling league database. That's the theory, and it is a nice goal.

But in reality, you can have any number of unrelated tables in the same database. So you could have one database holding your household inventory, your membership records, your bowling scores, or whatever. If that's how you want to do it, go ahead. We don't always have to live by the rules, do we? All you have to remember is that everything in this chapter about creating tables can be applied to any database. Even if I show you how to add a table to a business database, you can use the same techniques to add any table to any database.

Just for the busy person, I'll show you how to create a database and tables with as little work as possible. Then I'll show you how to design a database when you need something special, and when you have the time. Now let's boogie.

Creating a Database

Creating a database is about the easiest thing you can do with Access. When you start Access, select Blank Access Database from the Startup menu. If you select Access Database Wizards, Pages, and Projects from the Startup menu by mistake, select the Database template in the General page of the New dialog box. When you click OK, the File New Database dialog box will appear. Access suggests the name db1 (or db2, and so on). Since that doesn't tell you much about what the database is used for (or say much for Microsoft's imagination), type your own database name and then click Create. Access will display the Database window for your new database. Couldn't be any quicker, so create your own database now, naming it My Company.

If you're already in Access, select New from the File menu or click on the New Database button in the toolbar. Any database you already have open will be closed when the new database is opened. You'll see the list of templates to select. Double-click the Database option.

Creating Tables

A database won't do you much good without a table. There are a lot of ways to create a table, and how you do it depends on how much work you want to do and how fancy you want the table to be. First, in the Database window, make sure the Table page is displayed. You can then use the New Object Shortcuts or a dialog box. The New Object Shortcuts offer these options:

- *Create a Table in Design View* lets you create a totally custom table, but requires the most work.
- *Create a Table by Using Wizard* lets you create a table by selecting fields and design elements from dialog boxes—quick, easy, and elegant.
- *Create a Table by Entering Data* lets you create a table by simply naming fields and entering data—not very elegant tables but quick.

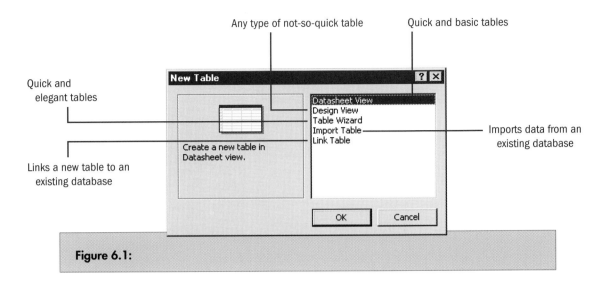

Quick and elegant tables

Links a new table to an existing database

Any type of not-so-quick table

Quick and basic tables

Imports data from an existing database

Figure 6.1:

As an alternative to using the shortcuts, click on the New button in the Database window to see the dialog box shown in Figure 6.1.

You can also create a table without returning to the Database window. Pull down the New Object button in the toolbar and select Table:

Creating a Quick and Basic Datasheet Table

Datasheet view is a great way to create a simple table when you need to enter information right away. You create a table by naming the fields and entering data. Nothing fancy or elegant, just fast and convenient. You won't be able to catalog the Library of Congress by creating tables in this view, but you can't beat it for speed and ease when all you need is a simple table. Anyway, you can always modify the table later in Design view to add all of the bells and whistles.

In fact, create an inventory table now.

1. Double-click on the Create A Table By Entering Data shortcut in the Table page of the Database window. (You can also click New and choose Datasheet View from the New Table dialog box.) A blank datasheet with 20 columns appears, with the columns labeled Field1, Field2, and so on.

2. Double-click on Field1 (or click anywhere in the column and then choose Rename Column from the Format menu) to select the field name.

3. The text of the field name will be selected, so type **Item** and then press ENTER.

4. Double-click on Field2 and type **Quantity**. You cannot use ENTER, TAB, or the arrow keys to move from one field name to another; you must double-click on the field name.

5. In the same way, rename Field3 as Cost, Field4 as Expires, and Field5 as VendorID.

Now enter some information into the datasheet. Access is going to know the type of field by the information that you enter, so be consistent. In the Quantity and Cost fields, for example, always enter numbers. In the Expires field, always enter a date. Complete the datasheet so it looks like this:

Table1 : Table

Item	Quantity	Cost	Expires	VendorID
Jelly, Cherry	76	4.5	3/6/99	105
Jelly, Grape	34	3.75	2/26/99	105
Cider, Apple	102	2.15	11/3/99	102
Coffee Beans	56	5.76	10/3/99	103
Jelly, Orange	46	4.26	1/4/99	101
Cider, Grape	97	2.79	10/1/99	102
Apricots, dried	56	7.76	5/3/99	104
Bananas, dried	87	6.57	6/5/99	104
Cider, Cherry	78	3.45	8/14/99	102
Figs, dried	56	8.90	4/16/99	104
Jelly, Lime	12	3.14	9/23/99	101
Peaches, dried	68	10.87	7/3/99	104

CAUTION

You can use the same technique to rename a field in any table. However, don't try that yet in your Almost Instant databases. Depending on how the Name AutoCorrect options are set, as you learned in Chapter 5, after renaming a field, Access may not be able to use the field in existing forms and reports.

CAUTION

Do not use the field name ID if you want Access to create a primary key for you. That field name will be used automatically by Access, as you will learn later in this chapter.

CAUTION

If you do not enter data into at least one record, Access will define each field as text. You'll learn all about field types later on.

Click the Save button to display the Save As dialog box. Access will imaginatively suggest the name Table1 (if it's the first table you created so far). We can do better, so type **Inventory** and then click OK.

A dialog appears warning you that you do not have a primary key. A primary key is not absolutely necessary for a quick and dirty table like this, so you *could* select No and go on your merry way. But primary keys make things a lot easier, so click on Yes now to see what Access does. The table appears on the screen with an AutoNumber field as the first column labeled simply ID—Access's default name for the primary key field. Let's name it something else. Double-click on the blank cell, type **ItemID**, and then press ENTER.

You're done. The table is created, so close it to return to the Database window. What Access has done is create the table for you. It has assigned field types based on the information you entered. Cost, Quantity, and VendorID will be number fields; Expires will be a date field; and Item will be a text field. When you next open the table, the data in the number fields will be aligned on the right, as they should be.

Creating a Quick and Elegant Table

So much for quick and basic. Now let's look at quick and elegant using the Table Wizard. The Table Wizard is to tables as the Database Wizard is to databases. It will create a complete table for you, letting you select from various purposes and fields. Instead of trying to decide what fields you'll need, you can let Access create them for you.

The Table page of the Database window should be displayed, so double-click on Create Table By Using Wizard. (You can also click on New, select Table Wizard, and then click on OK.) You'll see the first Wizard dialog box (Figure 6.2). The list on the left shows some sample tables. Above the list are the option buttons Business and Personal. The option selected determines the types of tables listed. Click on Personal to see suggested tables for personal pursuits; click on Business for typical business tables.

Now scroll the Tables list to see the types of tables available. When you select a table, suggested fields appear in the list box in the center.

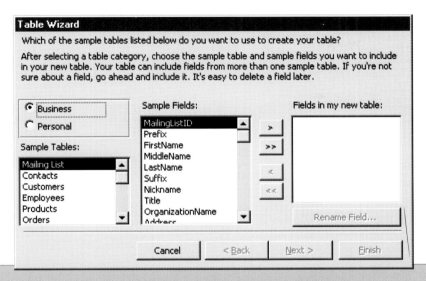

Figure 6.2: Select the type of table, the table itself, and then the fields

Click on Customers, because we're going to create a Clients table for our company database.

The trick now is to move the fields you want to use from the list box in the center into the list box on the right. To move an individual field, click on its name in the list and then the > button. If you want to use all, or almost all of the fields, just click >> (you can then remove the individual fields that you do not want included).

Continue to follow these steps:

1. We want all of the fields except one, and we want to change the position of another, so click the >> button.

2. Now remove the EmailAddress field by clicking on it in the right-hand list box and then clicking <.

3. In the same way, remove the Country field.

4. Now to replace the EmailAddress field, but in another position, scroll the list on the right and click on the Extension field.

5. Click on EmailAddress in the center list box and then click >. The field will now follow Extension.

> ## EXPERT ADVICE
>
> You can mix and match fields from any number of sample tables. Move the field from one table into the list box on the right, then choose another table, from either category, and select additional fields as you want.

6. Next, rename the field CustomerID to ClientID—client sounds more professional than customer (don't you think?). Click CustomerID and then the Rename Field button.

7. Delete the old field name in the dialog box, type **ClientID**, and then click OK.

When the list box on the right contains all of the fields that you want, click Next to see the dialog box shown in Figure 6.3. Here you give the table a name and choose if you want Access to set the primary key for you. Delete the suggested table name, type **Clients** as the table name, and click Next to let Access create the primary key for you. Access will select an appropriate field—in this case ClientID—as the primary key field and assign it an AutoNumber type.

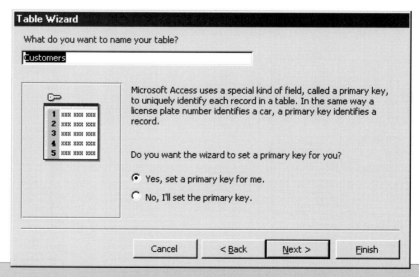

Figure 6.3: Name your table and have Access assign it a primary key

You'll now see the dialog box in Figure 6.4. This box only appears when there are already tables in the database. If a table has a field that matches the primary key of your new table, Access will suggest a relationship. You can accept Access's choice, remove the relationship, or create a new one on your own. We'll look at relationships in the next chapter, so just click Next.

The final Wizard appears with three options:

- The Modify the Table Design option opens the table in Design view. You use this option to change the table, add fields, change the field types, or change the way the field accepts data.

- Enter Data Directly Into the Table just opens the table in Datasheet view.

- Enter Data Directly Into the Table Using a Form the Wizard Creates for Me (probably the longest option name in history), will create a form and display it on the screen for entering information. This is a great option to select because it saves you the trouble of creating a form later on (although it only takes two or three clicks to do it any way).

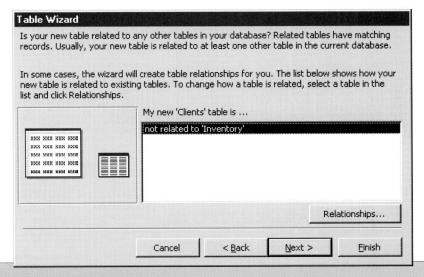

Figure 6.4: Access may suggest relationships with other tables

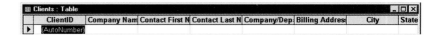

	ClientID	Company Nam	Contact First N	Contact Last N	City	State/Province	Postal Code	Contact Title
	1	Chesin Foods	Jane	Seymore	Alameda	CA	94701-	President
	2	Brandon Shops	Brandon	Lee	Margate	NJ	08402-	Owner
	3	Adam's Aunt	Barbara	Elayne	Longport	NJ	08404-	Owner
	4	Kaufman's	Sandra	Kaufman	Tampa	FL	87612-	President
	5	Zakuto's Barn	Alan	Zakuto	Berksville	CA	94198-	Owner
	6	Shell Shop	Bonnie	Moses	Tampa	FL	87612-	President
▶	7	Marvin Gifts	Marvin	Gins	Berkeley	CA	94817-	Owner
✱	(AutoNumber)							

Figure 6.5:   Enter this information into the table

For now, select Enter Data Directly Into the Table and click Finish. Your table will appear as shown here:

⊞ Clients : Table							_ □ ×
	ClientID	Company Nam	Contact First N	Contact Last N	Company/Dep:	Billing Addres:	City	State
▶	(AutoNumber)							

Enter the information shown in Figure 6.5 into the table and then close the table to return to the Database window. In Figure 6.5, we've only shown the fields where we want specific information, so the fields are not in the same order as those on your screen. Make up your own data for the columns that aren't shown in the figure, and then close the table to return to the Database window.

Modifying Tables in Datasheet View

Before we delve into the inner sanctum of tables in Design view, you should know that you can rename, add, and delete fields directly in a datasheet. You can modify any table in Datasheet view, no matter how it was created.

To rename a field, double-click on its field name and type a new name.

To delete a field, click anywhere in the column and choose Delete Column from the Edit menu. A box appears warning that deleting the column will permanently delete the field and the information in it. Select Yes only if you are sure.

To add a field to the datasheet, and thus to the table, click anywhere in the column that you want to follow your new field. Then

CAUTION

Before changing a field name, check the Name AutoCorrect settings in the General page of the Options dialog box. If the Track Name AutoCorrect Info and Perform Name AutoCorrect check boxes are not selected, forms and reports will still be looking for information in the original field, and will display an error message.

choose Column from the Insert menu. A new column will be added, labeled Field1, or the next highest field number. Change the name and enter data.

You can also rename, delete, and insert columns using the shortcut menu. Right-click on the field name to select the column and display the shortcut menu, then choose Insert Column, Delete Column, or Rename Column.

Designing a Table

Finally, we come to creating a table in Design view. Now I know you're busy, but if you want to have complete control over your table, for a really professional database, then you'll find this useful. Creating a table in Design view is not for the fainthearted, or for those who are really busy and find that Table Wizard fits all of their needs. It's good to learn about Design view, however, even if you do use the Wizard or Datasheet view, because you'll learn how to change a table in ways that cannot be done using the Datasheet view. All of the techniques that you'll learn here, in fact, can be applied to making a table as well as modifying one.

In Design view, you not only type the names of fields, but you must select their data types. Additionally, you have the opportunity to set their properties. The Data Type tells Access what kind of entries are allowed in the field. Properties determine how you can enter information into a field, how it appears onscreen, and how it is stored with the database.

To create a table in Design view, double-click on Create Table in Design View in the Database window, or choose Design View from the New Table dialog box. Create the table fields, using the steps shown in Figure 6.6.

As you work with Design view, look in the preview panel in the lower right for instructions or tips. It can be a valuable resource.

Access lets you use field names up to 64 characters, including spaces. Most other database programs do not let you use spaces. While

You'll learn how to insert a hyperlink column in Chapter 7 and a lookup column option in Chapter 8.

Look at the Tables/Queries page of the Options menu to see what default values you can set for new tables. Refer back to Chapter 5 if you need a refresher.

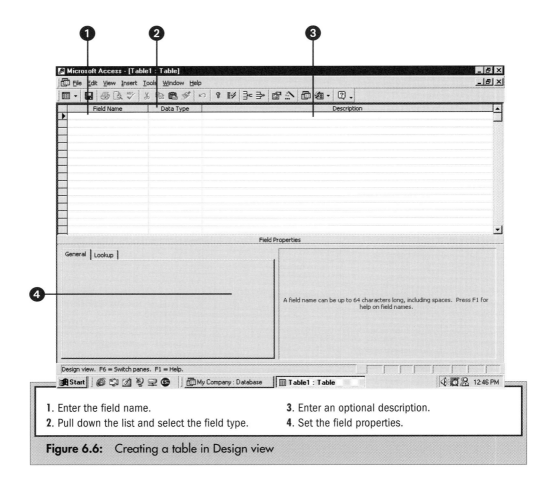

1. Enter the field name.
2. Pull down the list and select the field type.
3. Enter an optional description.
4. Set the field properties.

Figure 6.6: Creating a table in Design view

you might never imagine sharing your Access table with another program, you never know what's down the road, so use field names without spaces to give you more flexibility in the future.

Now there's a lot to explain about Design view, especially if you want to take advantage of field properties. This means that I'll have to interrupt this current flow of instructions with some explanations. But don't get too hung up on these details. If it's something you don't think you'll need, just scan the material and go on. You can always return to Design view to modify your table later on. Once you get the basics down pat, you can concentrate on the subtleties of field properties. OK? Let's continue.

Creating a Field to Number Records

The AutoNumber field is convenient because it will number your records for you. Use it for client numbers or any field that must be unique for each record. You're only allowed one AutoNumber field in a table, so pick it wisely.

1. In the first blank cell under Field Name, in the top row, type **OrderNumber**.
2. Click in the Data Type column. The down arrow button appears, indicating a pull-down list.
3. Click the arrow to see the field types, and select AutoNumber. You see, not every AutoNumber field must end with the letters ID.

Understanding Field Types

Before going on to the next field, here are the ten types of fields that you can create:

- **Text** Use for any field that won't be used for performing calculations or doesn't fit into any of the other field categories; entries can be up to 255 characters.

- **Memo** Use when you need to type more than 255 characters—sort of a mini-word processor for up to 64,000 characters in the field.

- **Number** Use only when you need to perform math and when you don't need it formatted as currency.

- **Date/Time** Obvious—use only when you need to enter dates and times; by specifying this type, you can perform math on dates, such as calculating the number of days between two dates.

- **Currency** Similar to the Number field type, but with a fixed number of decimal places, and a dollar sign (if you're using the American version of Access, that is).

- **AutoNumber** Use when you want Access to automatically number the record for you. In previous versions of Access, this was called the Counter type.

SHORTCUT
You can quickly create a field by clicking on the Build button in the toolbar. In the dialog box, select Business or Personal, choose the table containing a field you want to use, and then double-click the field to add it to your table.

You move around the Design view screen just as you do with a datasheet. Click where you want to enter information, or use the TAB, SHIFT-TAB, ENTER, and ARROW keys.

- **Yes/No**   Use only when a field can be either a yes or no value, such as Paid?, High School Graduate?, or Passed Inspection? The field will appear with a check box. Checked means Yes; unchecked means No.
- **OLE Object**   Use for pictures, sound files, or graphs.
- **Hyperlink**   Use for text that serves as a link to a site on the World Wide Web. The contents of the field are Internet addresses. You'll learn about hyperlink fields in Chapter 7.
- **Lookup Wizard**   Use to create a field that lets you select a value from a field in another table or to enter a list of specific items to choose from.

Investing in Property

We accepted all of the default properties for the first field. In general, if you don't have to change something, just leave it. There are times, however, when you'll want to set special properties. For example, suppose you want to control how you enter the date into a table or form, and how it should appear on the screen. Or, perhaps you want Access to enter the date automatically to make it easier to complete a record. That's when you need to set the field's properties:

1. In the second row under Field Name, type **Date**.
2. Click in the Data Type column.
3. Pull down the list and click Date/Time.
4. Click in the Format text box in the Field Properties pane at the bottom of the window.
5. Pull down the list to see the date and time formats allowed.
6. Click on Short Date. This determines how the date appears *after* you've entered it.
7. Click the Input Mask text box, and type **99/99/00**. This determines the way you must enter the date. The number 9 means that you can enter either a digit or space in that position, but that it is not required. The zeros represent required characters.

8. Click on the Caption text box and type **Order Date**. Order
   Date will appear in the datasheet and when you create forms
   and reports, rather than the name of the field. You can still use
   the shorter field name in expressions and calculations.

9. Click in the Default Value box and enter =**Date**(). This
   function automatically inserts the current date set on your
   computer for you, for all new records. The field should now
   appear like this:

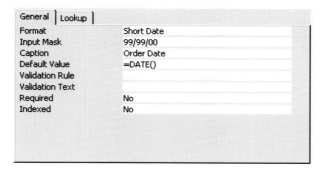

General	Lookup	
Format	Short Date
Input Mask	99/99/00
Caption	Order Date
Default Value	=DATE()
Validation Rule	
Validation Text	
Required	No
Indexed	No

Now let's see what you just did and look at some field properties in
detail. (Even If you don't care, please scan through the section anyway.)

Customizing a Field with Properties

Properties determine how a field is entered, displayed, and stored. The
properties shown in the Field Properties pane depend on the data type
assigned to the field. Some properties will have default values; others
will be blank. If you don't want to bother about the properties, you
can just go on. However, properties do give you greater control over
your database, and they ensure that your information is valid. Here's a
summary of the properties used by Access. Just remember that not all
of these properties will appear for each field type.

- **Field Size**   For text and number fields. With text fields, set
  the number of characters from 1 to 255; the default is 50. For
  number fields, select Byte, Integer, Long Integer, Single,
  Double, or Replication ID. A Byte can accept numbers from 0
  to 255 only. Integers and Long Integers are numbers without

decimal places. Integers can be between negative and positive 32,768; Long Integers between negative and positive 2 billion. Single and Double numbers can include decimals; Single to 38 places and Double to 308. The Replication ID type is used for primary key fields with tables in briefcases. A briefcase lets you synchronize files to maintain up-to-date copies (replicas) between computers, such as your desktop and laptop.

- **Format**   Determines how the information appears onscreen and when printed. With text fields, for example, the most common entry is >, which converts all lowercase characters to uppercase, such as for state abbreviations.

- **Decimal Places**   Sets the number of decimal places for number and currency fields.

- **New Values**   For AutoNumber fields, select either increment (1, 2, 3...) or random (who knows?).

- **Input Mask**   Specifies the format used when information is entered.

- **Caption**   A more descriptive name for the field to be used in forms and reports. Use a caption to help explain what your field means when you enter a short, nonintuitive field name to fit in a datasheet column, or when you're conforming to other database naming conventions.

- **Default Value**   Information that will appear in the field automatically, but that you can change in the datasheet or form. The entry =Date() is a special function that tells Access to insert the current date. If all of your clients are in California, you'd enter CA as the default value in the property for the State field.

- **Validation Rule**   A logical expression that determines whether Access accepts your field entry. Once you assign a validation rule, you cannot leave the field blank.

- **Validation Text**   A message that appears if information violates the validation rule.

- **Required**   Determines if an entry must be made in the field.

- **Allow Zero Length** Too complicated to explain here; see the explanation in the section of this title later in the chapter.
- **Indexed** Determines if an index will be created to provide faster searches. You'll learn more about indexes later in the "Keys and Indexes" section of this chapter, and in Chapter 8.

Input Mask

Short and simple, input masks do two important things. They save you the trouble of entering certain characters—like the parentheses and hyphen in the phone number—and they ensure that even the most careless person can't screw up your database. Sure, you can set up rules, write procedures, and train staff. But it doesn't mean that everyone follows the rules or pays attention during the training session.

Here's an example. For some reason, companies come up with the weirdest conventions for inventory stock numbers. So suppose your company decides to assign an inventory code that starts with the letters XY (the initials of the owner's wife), followed by five numbers. I can just bet that sometime, somehow, someone will forget the rule (or to give the benefit of doubt, will make a typographic error).

When you want to ensure that data gets entered in the correct format, use an input mask. The mask characters are shown in Table 6.1. Any other character is a literal. For example, use (999) 000-0000 in a telephone field to display the parentheses and hyphen in the mask. For your inventory numbers, use the mask XY00000. The letters XY will appear on the screen, and the user must enter five numbers. Want a five- or nine-digit ZIP code? Use the mask 00000-9999.

In addition to the definition characters, the mask can have two optional parts, separated by semicolons:

- **Part 1** By default, only characters that you type in the field are saved on the disk. All literal placeholders (such as the parentheses and hyphen in the phone number mask) appear onscreen and when printed, but are not actually saved with the table. This is good because it saves disk space. If you follow the mask with the number 0, however, as in (999) 000-0000;0, the

DEFINITION

Input mask: A series of special characters that establish the pattern for your entries. It lets you control what gets entered and what appears on the screen.

A Format property takes precedence over an input mask. For example, if the Format is < (for lowercase) and the input mask is >LL (for uppercase), the text will appear as lowercase.

literals will actually be saved. Use the number 1 if you want to indicate the default setting.

- **Part 2**   The second option determines which character fills in the spaces in the mask. By default, spaces are shown with an underline character (_), but you can designate any other. For example, the mask 00000-9999;1;* will display *****-**** in the field. To display a blank space, use two quotation marks around a space, as in " " .

0	Only digits 0 to 9, required
9	Optional digit or space
#	Digit or space, as well as plus and minus signs
L	Letter A to Z, required
?	Optional letter A to Z
A	Any letter or digit, required
a	Any optional letter or digit
&	Any character or a space, required
C	Any optional character or a space
.	Decimal point
,	Thousands separator
: ; - /	Date and time separators
<	All characters following will be converted to lowercase.
>	All characters following will be converted to uppercase (use >LL in a state field, for example).
!	Characters will appear from right to left, rather than from left to right. Only works when characters on the left are optional.
\	Displays the next character, even if it is an input mask character (using \& will actually display the & character)
"Password"	Displays an asterisk for each character typed

Table 6.1:   Input Mask Characters

Input Mask Wizard

For phone numbers, dates, ZIP codes, and other common types of text and date field entries, use the Input Mask Wizard. After entering the Input Mask property text box, click the Build button to the right to see the dialog box shown in Figure 6.7. The list box shows some general types of entries and how the corresponding information appears onscreen. Select the type of entry, and then test how it will work by clicking in the Try It box and typing a sample entry.

Click on the Edit List button if you want to modify the default Wizard options or to add your own input masks to the Wizard list.

Build button

When you select the entry type, click Next. For all but password entries, Access will display a dialog box where you can edit the mask and select the placeholder for spaces, as shown in Figure 6.8. (For passwords, the final Wizard box appears, so just click Finish.) Make any changes you want to the mask or placeholder and then try it out. When you're satisfied, click Next. For all but date fields, the final box

To use the Input Mask Wizard, you must install the Developer Tools as part of the Office setup.

Figure 6.7: Input Mask Wizard

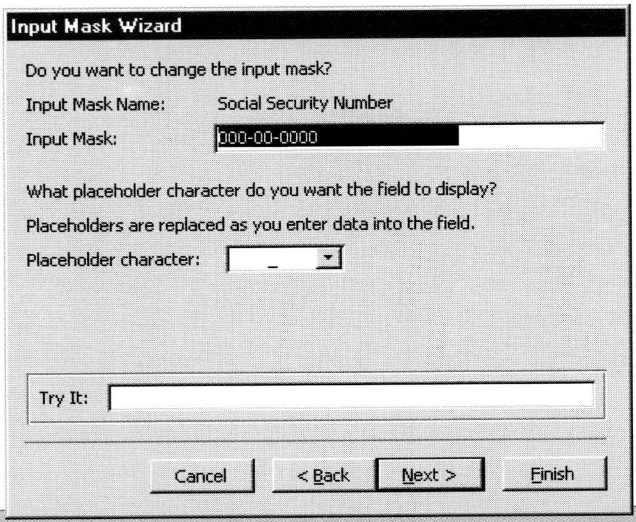

Figure 6.8:   Edit the input mask and select a placeholder

asks if you want to store the literals with the field or not. Make your choice and then click Finish.

Validating Field Data

Input masks help, but your table can still fall victim to that loose cannon in the office. Your next line of defense is the validation rule. Create a text field called ShipBy and set its properties like this:

1. Set the Field Size at **5**.

2. Enter > in the Format property to convert your entries to uppercase characters.

3. Set the Default Value at **UPS**. When you move to another property box, Access will surround the text with quotation marks.

4. Enter a Validation Rule of **In (UPS, FEDEX, DHL, AIR, BOAT)**. When you move to another property box, Access will surround each item in the list with quotation marks.

5. Enter the Validation Text **Must be UPS, FEDEX, DHL, AIR, or BOAT**.

6. Set the Required property to **Yes**. The field looks like this:

General	Lookup	
Field Size	5	
Format	>	
Input Mask		
Caption		
Default Value	"UPS"	
Validation Rule	In ("UPS","FEDEX","DHL","AIR","BOAT")	
Validation Text	Must be UPS, FEDEX, DHL, AIR, or BOAT	
Required	Yes	▼
Allow Zero Length	No	
Indexed	No	
Unicode Compression	Yes	

The validation rule property determines the valid entries that Access will accept. The rule is actually a logical expression. If your entry meets the expression criteria, then it is allowed. If the entry does not meet the rule, then when you try to move to another field, a box will appear containing the validation text. In this case, the rule uses the In operator, which tests if your entry is one in a series of values. So in our example, you must enter **UPS**, **FEDEX**, **DHL**, **AIR**, or **BOAT**. You can enter it in lowercase as well because the format property converts it to uppercase for you.

To test for numeric values, use any of these operators:

>	Greater than
>=	Greater than or equal to
<	Less than
<=	Less than or equal to
=	Equal to
<>	Not equal to

For example, if you were entering information in the Hourly Wage Rate field, you'd want to be sure you wouldn't enter $75.00 instead of $7.50. To avoid this problem, use a validation rule such as <10 to

SHORTCUT

If you have just two or three options, you could also use the OR command, as in UPS or FEDEX. With more entries it pays to use the IN command.

Once you create a validation rule, you cannot leave the field blank, unless the rule specifically indicates that it can be a null.

ensure that only rates less than $10 can be entered. To test to see if a value is within a certain range, use the Between...And operator. It works like this: Between 5 and 8.25. If the field is a date/time field, the validation rule can test for dates. After you type something like >10/22/99, Access displays it as >#10/22/99# to ensure that the date entered is after October 22, 1999. You do not have to type the # symbols yourself.

Text and memo fields offer even more opportunity for controlling input. You can test the entry to determine if certain characters are in specific positions, and you can limit the input to specific characters. All this is done with the LIKE operator and the wildcards: ? (any single character), * (any number of characters), and # (any single number). The LIKE expression means that the input must look "like" a certain pattern.

This is similar to the action of an input mask but with the added advantage of a personal error message. For example, if you use an input mask to check for a valid ZIP code, Access will display a rather cryptic message if the user gets it wrong. Instead, use a validation rule such as LIKE "#####" OR LIKE "#####-####". This rule means that the input has to look like five numbers in a row, or five numbers followed by a hyphen and four other numbers. You can then use validation text such as, "Enter either a correct 5 or 9 digit ZIP code."

To control which specific characters are allowed—something you cannot do with an input mask—enclose the valid characters in brackets. For example, suppose you use an inventory product code to identify the item's location in the warehouse. The code must start with the letters A, B, C, or D, representing the section number, followed by the numbers 1, 2, 3, or 4, representing the bin number. These are followed by a hyphen and then up to four numbers to identify the item, such as A1-1234 to represent item 1234 in bin 1 of section A. Sounds complicated, but it's not.

Start with this input mask: L0-####. This requires a letter and a number, and displays the hyphen so you don't have to type it. Then, enter the validation rule of LIKE [ABCD][1234]####. Now only valid ID numbers can be entered—only the letters A, B, C, or D in the first position, and the numbers 1, 2, 3, or 4 in the second position.

Since this will be a text field, Access will format the mask as L0\-#### to designate the hyphen as a literal, not a date or time separator.

Finally, you can add specific validation text, such as "You must enter a product code in the format A1, followed by the item number."

To specify values that cannot be entered, by the way, precede them with an exclamation point. For example, LIKE "[!XYZ]" would allow any character except X, Y, or Z.

Allow Zero Length

This is one of those strange properties that takes some extra explanation. If you do not enter anything into a record for a text or memo field, then what's there? And no, it's not like, "If a tree falls in the forest, and no one is there, does it make a sound?".

Null is a special computer word meaning that a field is blank, empty, there's nothing there. A Zero Length string is actually this: "", a string with nothing in it. The two are not the same. For example, suppose you have a field called Fax Number. Entering a zero length string by typing "" means, "I know the client does not have a fax number." Leaving the field empty—a Null field—means, "I don't know if the client has a fax number."

Is it that important a distinction? Yes. Do you have to worry about it now? No.

Keys and Indexes

You can create a primary key, as well as establish one or more indexes. The primary key maintains the order of the records and uniquely identifies each record in the table. Indexes help speed up searches and other operations.

To set the primary key, click on the field that you want to use for the key, and then click the Primary Key button in the toolbar. Do that now. Click anywhere in the row for OrderNumber and then on the Primary Key button. Access places a key symbol on the field's selector bar. Notice that it also sets the Indexed property to Yes (No Duplicates). This means that the field will be indexed and that you cannot have the same value in more than one record. All primary key field entries must be unique.

CAUTION
The key field can be any type except Memo, OLE Object, and Hyperlink. It can be a Yes/No field, but then you'd only be able to have two records.

Let's talk about the primary key for a moment. You know that Access maintains your records in primary key order. If you sort the table using some other field, you can quickly return to the primary key order using the Remove Filer/Sort command in the Records menu.

When you use an AutoNumber field as the primary key, Access inserts the value for you and ensures that it is unique. That's why an AutoNumber field is a perfect candidate. If you use some other type of field for the primary key, then you can enter the value yourself, or edit it. Not to worry. Access will ensure they are unique by not letting you enter a duplicate value. If you enter a value that is already used as a primary key in another record, a warning box will appear, and you'll have to try again to enter a unique primary key.

In addition, you do not have to enter the records in primary key order. Suppose you use the OrderNumber field as the primary key, but make it a regular number field, or even a text field. You can enter the records in any order of the key value you want—OrderNumber 4, then 1, then 100, or anything. When you change views—such as from Datasheet to Form—or close and then open the table, Access will automatically arrange the records in order of their primary keys.

Creating an Index

You can also set the Indexed property for other fields. By indexing a field, it speeds up searches and other database operations, but it may slow down data entry somewhat.

Click on the Date field, click on the Indexed property, and then pull down the list. In addition to No, for no index, you can select Yes (Duplicates OK), and Yes (No Duplicates). Select Yes (Duplicates OK). This means that you can have the same value in more then one record. In this case, we might have any number of orders placed on the same day, so select Yes (Duplicates OK). We're just indexing them to make it easier to find records by their date and produce statistical information for things such as aging reports.

SHORTCUT

If you want to change the primary key field, just click in another field while in Design view, and then on the Primary Key button.

When you end a field name with ID, Access sets the Indexed property automatically to Yes (Duplicates OK).

You'll learn more about primary keys and indexes in Chapter 8.

Yes/No Fields

Finally, create a Yes/No type of field. In the fourth row under Field Name, type **Rush** and choose Yes/No as the data type. The Format

Property will appear as Yes/No. You can also select a format of True/False or On/Off. How the value actually appears in the datasheet, however, depends on a setting in the Lookup page of the properties. Click on the Lookup tab to see the option Display Control. This property will be set at Check Box. This means that a check box will appear in the field. When entering data, click in the box to indicate either an on or an off condition, just like a check box in any Windows dialog box.

You can also set the Display Control at Text Box or Combo Box. A text box will display the value as either True or False, Yes or No, or On or Off, depending on the Format property. You can enter any positive value (True, Yes, On, 1, or –1) or any negative value (False, No, Off, or 0). Access will convert your entries to the appropriate format. For example, if you choose the True/False format, Access will convert all other positive entries to True, and all negative entries to False.

Leave the option set at Check Box and click on the General tab. The field looks like this:

If you enter negative and positive values into a field when either creating a table or adding a field while in Datasheet view, Access applies no default format. Positive entries appear as **–1**, negative entries as **0**. Use Design view to set the format as desired.

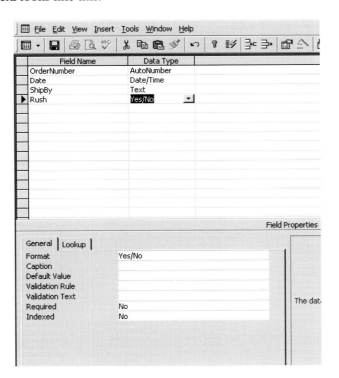

Setting the Table Property

A field's Validation Rule sets criteria that the entry must meet before you can leave a field. You can also create a record validation rule. This is a criteria that must be valid before you can save the record, or add a new one. Record validation rules generally compare the values in more than one field.

For example, suppose we don't want to ship rush orders by BOAT. We don't want to leave a record if BOAT is in the ShipBy field and the Rush field is checked. Here's how. Click the Properties button in the toolbar or choose Properties from the View menu; then set the properties like this:

1. Enter this rule that must be obeyed.

2. Enter this text to appear when the rule is broken.

3. Close the box.

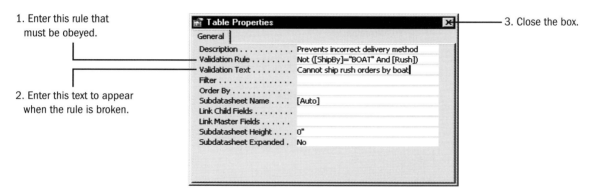

CAUTION

Type the validation rule exactly as shown, being careful to distinguish between the square brackets and the parentheses.

The validation rule we used contains two parts combined into an AND operation. It begins with the word NOT, showing Access what is not allowed. In this case, what's not allowed is the combination of [ShipBy]="BOAT" and [Rush]. Since Rush is a Yes/No field, [Rush] by itself means that it equals Yes. So, the validation rule means what is NOT allowed is the combination of shipping by boat ([ShipBy]="BOAT") and a rush order ([Rush]).

The Filter and Order By properties determine what filter and sort order will be used if you click on the Apply Filter button. Specifying a filter or order property applies whenever you open the table in either Datasheet or Form view. If you applied a filter/sort in Datasheet view and did not clear the filter grid, you would see those specifications in the Table properties dialog box. Changing these two properties will also change the specifications in the filter grid.

EXPERT ADVICE

The best way to learn the syntax for these properties is to create an Advanced Filter/Sort and then look at the table properties.

The format of the Filter property can be quite complex, as in (((City)="Orlando") AND ((StateOrProvince)="FL")). Each field name and the entire expression must be enclosed in parentheses. To specify a sort, just enter the field name in the Order By property, starting it with a minus sign to indicate a descending sort.

Use the Subdatasheet Name property to control where subdatasheets appear. Remember, subdatasheet means that you can view the contents of related records by clicking on a plus sign next to a record in a datasheet. When set at [Auto]—the default setting—you can access subdatasheets at every level. If you removed them using the Format menu, this property will be set at [None]. Change the property to [Auto] to reinstate the subdatasheets. Other options let you choose specific tables for subdatasheets; do this when you do not want every related table available.

Saving the Table

When you have finished creating your table, you must save it. Click on the Save button to save your table, and name it Orders. If you try to change to Datasheet view before saving the table, a dialog box appears telling you that you must save it first. Click Yes to save the table and change views.

Don't panic if this table doesn't seem complete. We'll be adding another field to it in the next chapter.

Then click the Datasheet View button to see the completed table. You can close the table for now; we'll be adding records to this table in the next chapter. Sit back and relax, and read the rest of the chapter.

Modifying a Table

All of the techniques that you've just learned can be applied to changing an existing table, as well as creating a new one. Just open the table in Design view. Click on its name in the Datasheet window and then select Design, or open the table and click the first button on the left of the toolbar. You can modify a field's name, type, or properties by editing the name, selecting a new type, and choosing new properties.

To add a new field at the end of the table, just enter the field information in the first blank row. To insert a field within the table, click anywhere in the field that you want to follow the new one, and then click the Insert Rows button in the toolbar. You can also select the field by clicking in its row selector and then pressing the INS key on the keyboard to insert a row.

To Delete a field, click anywhere in the field and then click the Delete Rows button. You can also select the field and then press the DEL key on the keyboard.

To reposition a field, select it and then point to its row selector so the pointer appears like a large white arrow. Then drag the field up or down to its new position.

You can also change the field type and its properties. However, once the table has information in it, changing its type or properties could produce some unwanted results. Some information may be lost, such as characters in a text field when you change it to a number field. If you are creating or changing a validation rule, Access will ask if you want to check the existing information against the rule. If you select Yes, Access will report if it finds information that violates the rule, but it will not delete it. This lets you know that you should review your information and decide if you want to change it to conform to the new rule.

If you set a new primary key, Access will not be able to save the changes if any duplicates exist in the new primary key field. You'll have to remove the primary key, return to the table, and correct the duplicated information before changing the primary key.

Summary

So now you know three ways to create a table. Datasheet view is easy, and you can create the table and add records at the same time. Using Table Wizard lets you take advantage of Access's suggested tables and fields. Design view gives you complete control over everything—field names, data types, and properties. Just remember that you can use any method to create the table, and then modify or customize it in Design view at any time.

Once you create your database, why keep it all to yourself when you can share it with the world? Ever hear of the Internet and the World Wide Web? Been living in a cave somewhere for the past five years? You can easily publish your database to the Web so others can view the information. In the next chapter, you will learn how to publish your database tables onto the Internet and how to create *Data Access Pages* that you can use from within Access, as well as your Web browser. Read on, Web surfer dude!

CHAPTER 7

Access on the Internet

INCLUDES

- Using the Web toolbar
- Creating hyperlink fields
- Publishing to the Web
- Saving HTML files

Display the Web Toolbar ➡ pp.153–154

1. Right-click on any toolbar.
2. Select the Web Toolbar from the menu.

Connect to the Web ➡ pp. 154–155

- Click on the Start Page button.
- Click on the Search the Web button.

Use Favorites ➡ p. 155

To add a Web site to the Favorites list:

1. Display the Web toolbar.
2. Launch Internet Explorer and navigate to the site.
3. Pull down the Favorites list and click Add To Favorites.
4. Click OK.

To move to a favorite site from Access:

1. Display the Web toolbar.
2. Pull down the Favorites list and select the Web site from the bottom of the list.
3. If the site is not on the menu, click Open Favorites, then double-click the shortcut for the site.
4. Click Connect if the Connect To box appears.

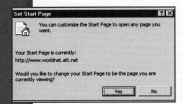

Change the Start Page to an Access Document ➡ p. 156

1. Open the database to use for the Start Page.
2. Display the Web toolbar.
3. Pull down the Go list.
4. Click Set Start Page.
5. Click Yes.

To set a Web Start Page:
1. Launch Internet Explorer.
2. Choose Tools | Internet Options.
3. Click on the General tab.
4. Enter the site in the Address text box.
5. Click OK.

Create a Hyperlink Field ➼ pp. 156–159
1. Create or edit the table in Design view.
2. Enter the name of the field.
3. Pull down the Data Type list and select Hyperlink.
4. Specify properties as desired.

Jump to a Hyperlink ➼ p. 157
1. Open the table, form, or report containing the hyperlink.
2. Click the hyperlink.
3. Click Connect if the Connect To box appears.

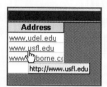

Edit a Hyperlink ➼ pp. 159–160
1. Open the table, form, or report containing the hyperlink.
2. Move to the hyperlink with the TAB key.
3. Press F2.
4. Edit the hyperlink.

Create a Web Page ➡ pp. 160–161

1. Select the object in the Database window.
2. Choose File | Export.
3. Pull down the menu for the Save As Type box and choose the type of page you want to create:
   - HTML Documents for a static page
   - Microsoft IIS 1-2 for a dynamic page
   - Microsoft ActiveX Server for an ActiveX dynamic page
4. Enter the filename and designate the folder, as you would when saving any document.
5. Click Save.
6. For a dynamic type, specify the Data Source Name, User Name, Password, Server URL, and the Session Timeout.

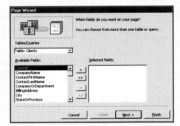

Create a Data Access Page ➡ pp. 162–165

1. Click Pages in the Database window.
2. Double-click Create Data Access Page By Using Wizard.
3. Select the fields that you want to add to the Web page, then click Next.
4. Choose a grouping level, if desired, and then click Next.
5. Choose up to four sort fields, then click Next.
6. Enter a page name and select to use a theme, and then click Finish.
7. Choose and theme and click OK.
8. Choose File | Save, and then click Yes.

There's no reason to panic, but the world seems to be getting smaller—at least figuratively. Ever try to rush anywhere during rush hour? So many people in such small a space. And furthermore, it's as easy to talk to someone on the other side of the globe as it is to call around the corner. Now with the Internet and the World Wide Web, you can share information, graphics, and even your Access databases with a few keystrokes or clicks of the mouse. Because Internet connectivity is built into Office 2000, you've got the power of this valuable resource right at your fingertips. (Of course, you need to have access to the Internet, or a company intranet, to take advantage of this power). And the only traffic you'll have to fight will be with others trying to dial in or connect at the same time.

Using the Web Toolbar

Office 2000 gives you several ways to access the Internet, but one of the most versatile is Access' Web toolbar. Displaying the toolbar is like having Internet Explorer open right in the Access window. In fact, the toolbar (see Figure 7.1) looks amazingly similar to the buttons in Internet Explorer itself—which should be no surprise because both were created by the same company that we've grown to know and love. Not only are the toolbars similar, but they share common elements. Recently used sites, favorite sites, and the home page you set in Internet Explorer will all be available from within Access as well.

If you're on a network intranet, or already connected to the Net, use the toolbar just as you would your browser. If you are not connected, selecting a site with the toolbar will launch your browser and make the connection for you.

The Web toolbar will appear automatically when you open a table or form containing a hyperlink field. To display the toolbar when you're viewing a table or form or designing a report that does not contain a

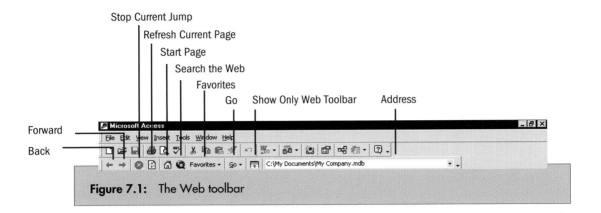

Figure 7.1: The Web toolbar

hyperlink, right-click on any toolbar and choose Web Toolbar from the shortcut menu, or use the Toolbars tab of the Customize dialog box explained in Chapter 5. The functions of the toolbar buttons are explained in Table 7.1.

If you are at all familiar with Internet Explorer, or any other Web browser, then you'll feel right at home with the Web toolbar. Clicking

Button	Functions
Back	Moves back through the previously opened Web pages.
Forward	Moves forward through the previously opened Web pages.
Stop Current Jump	Stops loading the Web page being transferred to your computer.
Refresh Current Page	Reloads the currently displayed page.
Start Page	Jumps to the configured designated home page on that system.
Search the Web	Lets you search the Internet.
Favorites	Lets you create bookmarks or jump to a hyperlink for frequently used sites, to specific sites, or to open documents.
Go	Lets you jump to a site, navigate through recently used sites, or set the Start Page and Search Page.
Show Only Web Toolbar	Toggles off and on the display of other toolbars.
Address	Lists recently visited sites and lets you move to a specific site.

Table 7.1: Web Toolbar Buttons

on Start Page, for example, will cause you to jump to the home page set in Internet Explorer, or to the Microsoft Corporation home page if you are using another browser. Access will launch your Web browser if you're not already connected. Once you're connected, of course, you can jump to any other site by using the toolbar or your browser.

If you click on Search the Web, you'll jump to a page that lets you search for information, e-mail addresses, maps, and telephone numbers.

Playing Favorites

As you surf the Web, you'll find sites that you'll want to return to time and again. If you are using Internet Explorer, you can designate these sites as your favorites, so you can quickly jump to them without entering their Web addresses or navigating through a series of other sites. You can also add a database to the Favorites list, whether it is on your computer or the network.

To add a site to the Favorites list, follow these steps:

1. Use Internet Explorer to navigate to the site you want to add as a favorite.

2. Pull down the Favorites list in Internet Explorer, and then click Add To Favorites.

3. Click OK in the Add to Favorites dialog box.

To add a database to the Favorites list, open the database in Access, and display the Web toolbar. Pull down the Favorites list in Access, click Add To Favorites, and then click Add.

To move to a favorite site, pull down the Favorites list in either Access or Internet Explorer. A list of your recently added favorites will be listed at the bottom of the menu, so just click on the location you want to jump to.

If you have Netscape or another Web browser installed on your system, the Favorites folder may also contain the item Imported Bookmarks. This will list the bookmarks that were found in your other Web browser.

Using Go

The Go list on the Web toolbar gives you another way to navigate the Internet. It offers many of the same features as the toolbar itself, and also lets you change the Start Page and Search Page, as shown in Figure 7.2.

Creating and Using Hyperlinks

Hyperlinks are the engine that makes the Web work, and you can use hyperlinks within your database just as effectively. You can add a hyperlink button to a form, for example, to jump to your corporate home page, or to look up product information at a vendor's site. Hyperlinks give you the ability to quickly move to locations like the following:

- A location on the Internet or an intranet
- An object in your database or in another database
- A document on your computer
- Another computer on your network

The easiest way to use a hyperlink in Access is to create a hyperlink field that will move you to a Web location with a click of the mouse.

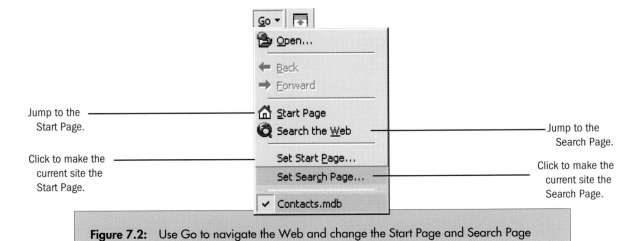

Figure 7.2: Use Go to navigate the Web and change the Start Page and Search Page

So, for example, you can include a hyperlink field listing the Web sites of your suppliers, as shown here:

⊞ Supplier Web Sites : Table	
SupplierID	**Web Site**
1	www.cajun.com
2	www.tokyotrade
3	www.coop.com
4	www.exo.com
*	(AutoNumber)

When you want to jump to a site—to look up product information or send e-mail, for example—just click on the hyperlink field in the supplier's record.

Creating a hyperlink field is easy. When you create a table in Design view, define a hyperlink field by entering the field name, then by pulling down the Data Type list and selecting Hyperlink. If you are already in datasheet view, add a hyperlink field by choosing Insert | Hyperlink Column.

Entering the address in the field, in either Datasheet or Form view, is just as easy. Just move to the blank field and type the address. Because the field is defined as a hyperlink, the text will appear in blue (the Not Yet Followed color) and be underlined by default. You can leave off the http:// notation—Access will figure that out for you. So you can enter, for example, **www.ufl.edu**, if you want to jump to the University of Florida, or **www.udel.edu** for the University of Delaware. Access will automatically add the prefix when it makes the jump. If the hyperlink is a path to a file, Office 2000 will open that document when you click on the link.

You can also use the dialog box shown in Figure 7.3 to create a link when you are in a Hyperlink field. If you want the reader to see something other than the actual address of the link, type some text that you want the reader to click on. For example, you could select the phrase "Click here for more information" to use as the link. Then, click the Insert Hyperlink button in the datasheet or form toolbar, or select Insert | Hyperlink. (The button and menu command are dimmed when you are not in a hyperlink field.)

Enter or edit the
text to appear
in the document.

Enter the
address of the
link to jump to.

Click to create
a custom
ScreenTip.

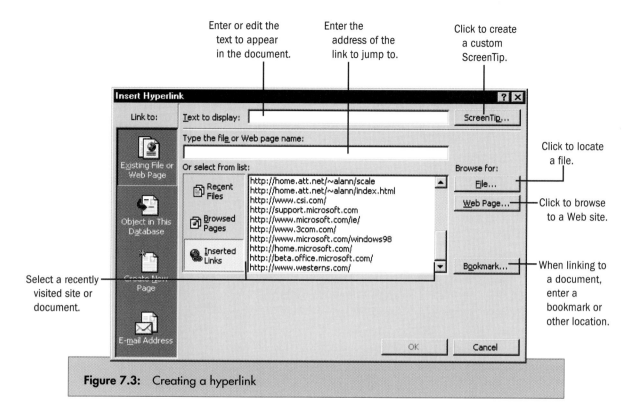

Click to locate
a file.

Click to browse
to a Web site.

When linking to
a document,
enter a
bookmark or
other location.

Select a recently
visited site or
document.

Figure 7.3:   Creating a hyperlink

If you are not sure of the address, click the Web Page button to launch your browser. Navigate to the site, then switch back to the dialog box. Click OK to accept the address, and then close your browser.

Here are two other ways to create a hyperlink:

- Use copy and paste. Copy the address from another location in the database and paste it into the field. To create a link to another Office 2000 document—such as a Word document or Excel worksheet—copy text from the document and then select Insert | Paste as Hyperlink to place it into the field. Clicking the hyperlink opens the document.

- From another Office 2000 application, drag and drop a defined hyperlink field, a Web address, or the text that you want to jump to into the defined hyperlink field.

Editing Hyperlinks

When you first enter the link in the hyperlink field, you can edit it just as you would any other text in a table or form. Once you move to another field, however, things change.

When you use the mouse to point to a hyperlink, the cursor appears as a hand, and clicking makes you jump (or try to jump) to the site, so you cannot click on a hyperlink field to edit it. To edit a hyperlink, move to it (in either table or form) with the TAB or arrow keys, and then press SHIFT-F2 to display the address in the Zoom box. Edit the text of the link and then click OK.

You can also edit a hyperlink by moving into the field and pressing F2. However, you have to be careful here. Once you move out of the record and then return to it, pressing F2 in a hyperlink field will display the link address following the text you entered, surrounded by # symbols and with the http:// prefix, like this:

www.ufl.edu#http://www.ufl.edu#

You entered www.ufl.edu as the address, and Access created a link to http://www.ufl.edu. The information between the # symbols is the actual link address, not what you originally typed. So to edit the link, edit the address within the # symbols. When you move to another field, the address in between the # symbols will no longer appear, although it is saved with the field. The displayed link—the text that you entered or pasted into the text box—will not change to reflect the changes you made to the link. If you want the display text updated as well, you have to edit it also. So editing just the address to #www.udel.edu# will still display www.ufl.edu in the field (the link will be to www.udel.edu). You don't have to worry about this if you use the Zoom box, where editing the text changes what's displayed in the field and the link itself.

You can also edit the hypertext field by right-clicking on it and choosing Hyperlink from the shortcut menu to see these options:

Choose Edit Hyperlink to edit the link in the dialog box shown in Figure 7.3. To change just the displayed text, not the link itself, edit or enter the text in the Display Text box in the shortcut menu.

Publishing Your Database to the Web

TIP

Beware of geek-speak. When it comes to dynamic Web pages there's a lot of complex terms that will mean nothing to you if you're not a Web page designer. Don't worry—be happy!

So far, we've discussed using Access to browse the Web or to move to specific sites. That's just the tip of the iceberg. You can also publish your databases on the Web itself. This means that other Internet road-warriors can view your tables, forms, and reports. You perform all of this magic using the Export option in the File menu.

Access lets you save Web pages in three formats:

- HTML Document
- Microsoft IIS 1-2
- Microsoft Active Server Pages

With the HTML document format there is no link between the HTML page and the data itself. Once you create the page and upload it to the Net, any changes to the information in the database will not be reflected in the Web page.

The other two options, Microsoft IIS 1-2 and Microsoft Active Server Pages, create dynamic pages so Net users will always see the most current information in the database. The information on the page will be updated each time it is accessed. The dynamic options are designed for users of the Microsoft Internet Information Server.

The Microsoft IIS 1-2 option creates two files that tell the Internet Server how to use ODBC (Open Database Connectivity) to access the data and how to format it as an HTML document. A file with the IDC extension tells the server the names of both the data source and a file with the HTX extension, and includes a SQL statement to access the information from the file. The file with the HTX extension serves as a template to specify how to format the data as an HTML document. When a user accesses the Web page, the files retrieve the information from the database and display it on the screen.

The Microsoft Active Server Page option is for use with the ActiveX component of the Microsoft Internet Information Server 3.0 or later. The ASP (Active Server Pages) file contains HTML formatting commands as well as SQL statements needed to access the information, along with Visual Basic code that references ActiveX Server Controls.

To publish your database to the Web, follow these steps:

1. In the Database window, select the table, form, query, or report that you want to publish to the Web.
2. Choose File | Export.
3. Pull down the Save As Type box and choose the type of page you want to create:
   - HTML Documents for a static page
   - Microsoft IIS 1-2 for a dynamic page
   - Microsoft Active Server Pages for a dynamic page

   Reports can only be saved in the HTML document format.
4. Enter the filename and designate the folder, as you would when saving any document.
5. Click Save.
6. If you selected a dynamic type, the next dialog box asks you to specify information the server needs to access and update the information. You'll need to enter the Data Source Name, User Name, and Password. If you chose the ASP type, you'll also have to specify the Server URL and the Session Timeout options.

DEFINITION

ODBC (Open Database Connectivity): A set of standards for working with information in SQL database servers, allowing various programs to access the same information.

Creating Data Access Pages

When you use the Export command, Access creates a page that can be opened and accessed by your Web browser. As an alternative, you can create a data access page that can be used from both within Access and on the Internet.

A typical data access page is shown in Figure 7.4. Like a form, it displays fields in text boxes in which you can view, edit, and add information. At the bottom of the page is a special toolbar containing the familiar buttons to navigate, add, and delete records as well as buttons to save and undo record changes, sort the table, and create and apply filters.

When you open a data access page you are actually looking at a Web page. Right-clicking on the page displays your browser's shortcut menu rather than Access' shortcut menu.

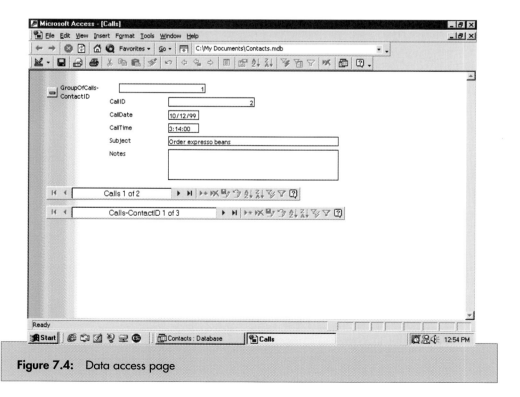

Figure 7.4: Data access page

To create a data page in as few steps as possible, click Pages in the Database window, then double-click Create Data Access Page By Using Wizard.

In the first wizard dialog box, shown in Figure 7.5, select the fields that you want to add to the Web page, including fields from related tables. To create a data access page using multiple tables, pull down the table list and select the "one" table in a one-to-many relationship, then add the fields that you want from the table to the form. Next, pull down the table list and select the next table, the "many" side of the relationship, and add fields from it. You can then repeat the process for any other tables that have one-to-many relationships.

The next wizard dialog box, shown in Figure 7.6, lets you choose the grouped arrangement. A grouping level will organize the information according to the field that you designate. However, it will also make the page read-only so the information cannot be changed using the data access page.

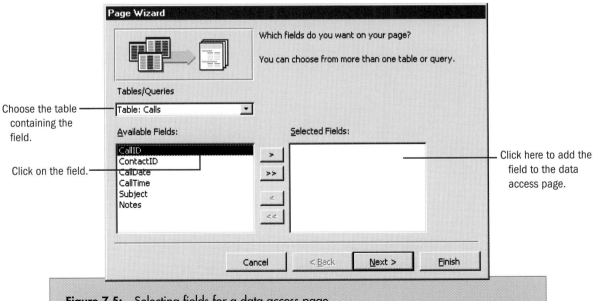

Figure 7.5: Selecting fields for a data access page

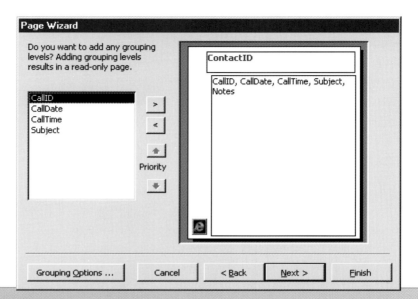

Figure 7.6: Selecting a grouping level

The next dialog box lets you choose if you want to organize the detail information by any other field. You can choose up to four fields, each in either ascending or descending order.

In the last wizard dialog box, type a name for the page and select a theme if you wish. Then click Finish.

Choosing a theme lets you format the data access page with a background and other graphic elements. If you chose to apply a theme, you'll see the dialog box shown next.

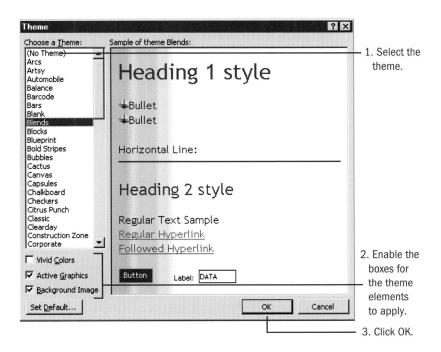

1. Select the theme.

2. Enable the boxes for the theme elements to apply.

3. Click OK.

You will then see the data access page in Design view. You'll learn more about designing custom forms and data access pages in Chapter 13. To save the data access page at this time, however, select File | Close, then click Yes to the message that appears asking if you want to save the page.

To view a data access page on your Web browser, right-click on it in the Database window and choose Web Page Preview from the shortcut menu.

Summary

As you learned in this chapter, you can use your database to access the Web. Create and use a hyperlink field to link your table or form with Web sites or files on your network or computer. You can also easily create a Web page to share your information with the world. If you do publish your database to the Internet, however, make sure it is information that you really want to share and make public. Using a static page type lets you control what appears on the page, giving you the option to keep changes from prying eyes.

Seems too easy? There's just gotta be a catch. Well, yes and no. There are some more sophisticated things you'll have to know—such as creating lookup fields and relationships—to make something more than a very simple database. In Chapter 8 you'll tackle some of the more sophisticated tasks in creating a database.

Stuff to Make the Guru Happy

INCLUDES

- Designing databases
- Using lookup tables
- Creating indexes
- Defining table relationships
- Printing database specifications

Create a Lookup Field ➡ pp. 172–178

1. Open the table in Design view.
2. Name the field and click in the Data Type column.
3. Pull down the Data Type list and select Lookup Wizard.
4. Complete the wizard dialog boxes as desired.

Create a Multiple-Field Index ➡ pp. 178–180

1. Open the table in Design view.
2. Click the Indexes button.
3. Enter the index name.
4. Select the index field.
5. Choose a sort order.
6. Set the index properties.
7. In the next blank index row, select another field and sort order.
8. Repeat step 6 for each field to be added to the index.

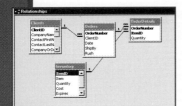

Define Relationships ➡ pp. 181–185

1. Open the database.
2. Click the Relationships button.
3. Click the Add Table button.
4. Double-click the tables to be added to the Relationships window, and then click Close.
5. Drag between related fields.
6. Confirm fields in the Relationships dialog box.
7. If desired, select Enforce Referential Integrity and other options.
8. Click Create.
9. Close the Relationships window. When prompted to save the layout changes, click Yes.

Print Table Information ➡ pp. 188–190

1. Open the database.
2. Choose Tools | Analyze | Documenter.
3. Select the object type, or click on the All Object Types tab.
4. Select each object you want documented, or click Select All.
5. Click Options, select the options to be included, and click OK.
6. Click OK to create the report.
7. Read or print the report.
8. Close the Report window.

You now know the basics for creating tables and databases. If the basics seem easy it's because they are. If you want to move on and create a professional database—one that a guru would be proud of—you can do it slowly, in stages, and with a lot of intestinal fortitude. This chapter will get you jump-started.

Database Design Rules

Granted, the Database Wizard can create a complete database for you, and a pretty fancy database. Not only are there tables, forms, and reports, but some complicated ones at that—switchboards, forms with fields from multiple tables, and the like. However, if you take the trouble to learn how to design your own database, you can create even more sophisticated and useful databases. You can add to your own databases all of the powerful elements that the Database Wizard provides. Creating this type of database by yourself, *sans* wizard, isn't that difficult—it just takes quite a few steps and a little more experience.

Before you dive head-first into developing all of your own databases and tables, you should learn a little about good database design. I know you're too busy to worry about all of the design principles that would satisfy the database guru in the office. However, it's always been my belief that if you start off with just a few basic good habits, the rest will somehow find its way into your brain.

So here's my basic set of rules:

- **Rule 1**   Never create a field that can be calculated from other fields.

  If you have an inventory table with fields called StockOnHand and Cost, don't bother creating a field containing the item's net value—the product of the two fields. For one reason, every time the amount on hand and cost change, you'd have to recalculate and edit the value in the net field. When you want to see the net value—or perform any other calculation on fields—you do so with a form, report, or query. This way you can see and print the results without wasting screen and disk space storing them in the table. In addition, you should never have a situation in which making a change on one field means that you have to make a change in another field. It's too easy to forget.

- **Rule 2**   Never create repeating fields.

  Repeating fields are those that basically contain the same type of information. For example, suppose your club wants to keep information about members' children. How many fields do you have and what do you name them? Child1, Child2, Child3, and so on? Are we interested in family planning here, or creating a good database? You have fields that repeat the same type of information—the name of a member's child. Actually, what you need to create are two related tables. You'll learn about that later in this chapter.

- **Rule 3**   Never create a field that has the same value in every record, and which you know will be the same value.

  Say you are licensed to trade only with customers in Kentucky. Do you need a field called State? No way. All of your customers must be in Kentucky. And don't worry about printing the state name on addresses. You can add the state's name once in a form, report, or mailing labels.

- **Rule 4**   Each record must be unique.

  No two records should be entirely the same. If you have two records that are exactly the same—in every field—then you did something wrong. OK, so suppose your baseball card collection has duplicates. Are they in exactly the same condition? If not, then you need a Condition field where you can record the condition of each card. If you do have exact duplicates then you need a Duplicates or Quantity field. Don't record the same information twice—just have a field that can indicate you have two of the same object.

- **Rule 5**   You should have a primary key, and it must be unique.

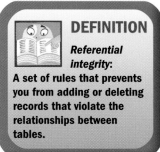

DEFINITION

Referential integrity:
A set of rules that prevents you from adding or deleting records that violate the relationships between tables.

A primary key helps keep your records in some type of order, and it enables you to form relationships. Enforcing a relationship's referential integrity is the best way to avoid serious errors in your database. If you do have a primary key, however, make sure that it will be unique for every record.

Streamlining Data Entry with Lookup Fields

There are a lot of times when you can only enter specific values in a field. Remember the ShipBy field in the Orders table in Chapter 6? The validation rule said you could only enter FEDEX, UPS, AIR, DHL, or BOAT. Rather than trust your user to remember what to enter, create a lookup field. A lookup field displays the possible choices, so all the user has to do is click the correct one.

This is a perfect way to make a database foolproof so just about anyone can use it. For example, while taking orders over the phone, you need to record the name or ID number of the client placing the order. What would happen if, by mistake, you write down an incorrect ID number, one for a client that does not exist? When you are ready to ship the order, you won't know where to ship to and whom to bill. To make sure this problem doesn't occur, use a lookup field. When taking the order, you can just pull down a list of client ID numbers and names. No mistakes and no problem.

The database that we've created needs a lookup field for this exact purpose, so you should add it now. Add a lookup field to the Orders table to let you pick the ClientID number from the Clients table:

EXPERT ADVICE

Use a lookup field whenever possible when information in a field must match a value in another table or in a list of valid entries. Lookup fields are a great time-saver.

You first have to add a field to the table in Design view.

1. Open the My Company database and, if necessary, click Tables in the Database window.

2. Click on the Orders table and select Design so you can add the field.

3. Click anywhere in the row for the Date field, then click the Insert Row button to insert a blank row. Now create the field.

4. Type **ClientID** as the field name.

5. Pull down the Data Type list and select Number. The field type must match the corresponding field to be looked up, but while the ClientID field in the Clients table is actually an AutoNumber field, it contains numbers.

6. Pull down the Data Type list again and click Lookup Wizard to see the first dialog box with the two options, as shown in Figure 8.1.

7. We want to look up information from another table, so leave the options at the default settings and click Next to see a list of the other tables in the database. This box is really asking, Where do you want me to get the information from?

8. Click on the Clients table and then click Next. The third wizard box is shown in Figure 8.2. Here you select the information that you want to be listed in the lookup table.

9. Click each field you want listed (in this case, the ClientID field), and then click the > button.

10. Now in the same way, add the CompanyName field to the list and then click Next. This next dialog box shows how the columns in the lookup list will appear. But only the CompanyName field

SHORTCUT

You can insert a lookup column directly in Datasheet view. Click in the column that you want to appear to the right of the lookup column, and then choose Insert | Lookup Column. Then complete the wizard dialog boxes as explained here.

Gets information from another table

Lets you enter items such as shipping options for the ShipBy field into the list while the wizard is running so the user can pick from valid choices

Choose an option and click Next to continue.

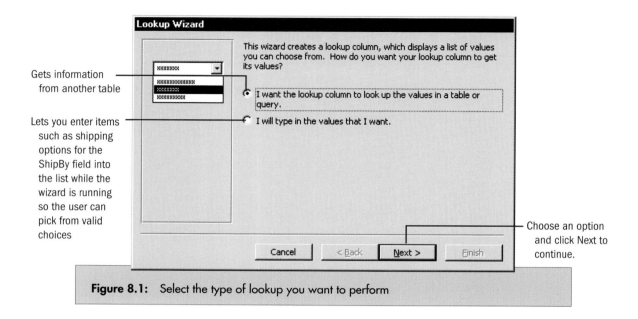

Figure 8.1: Select the type of lookup you want to perform

appears! That's because the Hide Key Column option is selected, and the ClientID field is the key to the table.

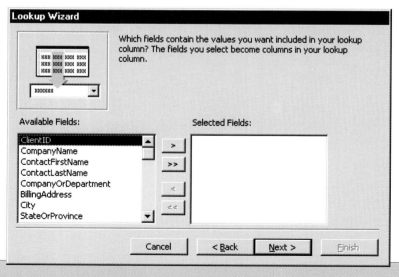

Figure 8.2: Select the fields that you want included in the lookup table

11. We want the key to appear so that we can double-check the ClientID as we record orders, so deselect the Hide Key Column check box to display the ClientID column.

12. Now, as the instructions say, you drag the column header buttons to adjust their width, or double-click on the right edge of a column header button to fit it to the heading. Because the first column will only contain a number, double-click the line on the right side of the column header button. The columns will appear like this:

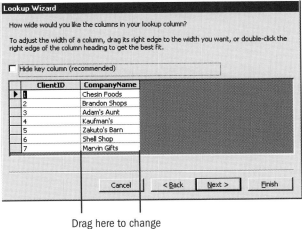

Drag here to change
column width.

13. Click Next to see the wizard dialog box shown in Figure 8.3. This is an important one. In this box, you select the field that you want inserted into the record. For example, when you select an item from the list, do you want the ClientID or Company Name inserted into the order record? We want the ClientID inserted, so make sure that field is selected and then click Next. We're almost there.

14. The final box asks for the label you want for the field. The default will be the field name, so let's leave it that way. You can also select to display Help information about formatting fields. But for now just click Finish.

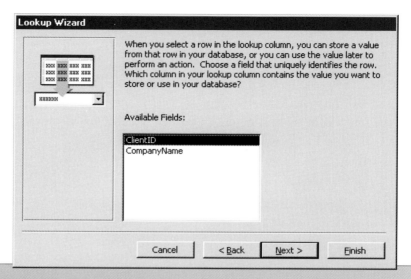

Figure 8.3: Pick the field that you want inserted into the record

On your own, try to create a lookup field for the ShipBy field, so the valid shipper choices are displayed. Select the wizard option that lets you enter the list values.

That's it, except for a box that appears, telling you that you must save the table before any relationships can be defined. Who said anything about relationships? Well, when you created the lookup field, Access realized that there is some connection between the ClientID field in the Clients table and the ClientID field in the Orders table, so it wants to create a relationship for you. To make Access happy, select Yes to save the table and to create the relationship—we'll look at it in more detail a little later.

Before seeing how the lookup field works, let's adjust one of its properties. First, notice that Access has set the Index property of the

EXPERT ADVICE

Avoid selecting more than two fields. Too many fields make the lookup list bulky on the screen. Use just enough fields to identify the records to choose from.

field to Yes (Duplicates OK). Now Click on the Lookup tab to see these options:

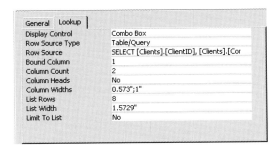

The Lookup Wizard has set these for you. They're not important unless you need to change them—a rather advanced operation. Here is a summary of some of these properties:

- The Display Control property determines the type of box. The default is Combo Box—that's a text box where you can enter information or choose from a drop-down list. You can also select a Text Box or a List Box for the property.

- The Row Source Type and Row Source properties define from where the information for the list is coming.

- The Bound Column property specifies which column from the combo box contains the information to be inserted into the record.

- The Column Count, Column Heads, and Column Widths properties specify how many columns there are, whether they have headings, and their width.

- The List Rows property is the number of values displayed in the list before scroll bars appear.

Now let's change one of these properties.

1. Click in the Limit To List property. When this is set to No, you can type an entry into the text box that does not exist in the list.

You can still type an entry for the field, rather than select it from the list, but it must be a ClientID number actually in the Clients table.

Since we're using the box to ensure that only valid ClientID numbers are entered, we want to change this property.

2. Pull down the list at the end of the box, and select Yes.

3. Click the View button. Access displays a box reporting that you must save the table—select Yes. If a box appears asking if you want to check data integrity, select Yes. Now on your own, add the following records to the table. As you do, however, try to place a rush order shipped by BOAT, and try to use a client number that does not exist. In both cases, Access will display a message telling you the input is improper. Click OK to clear the message box and enter valid information. When you're done, close the table to return to the Database window.

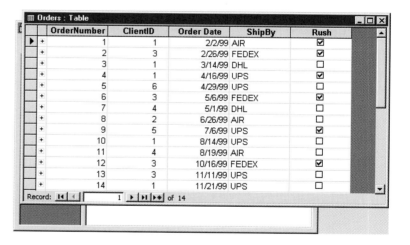

Speeding Searches with Multiple-Field Indexes

Each of our tables has a primary key. As you know, you can create the primary key in Design view by selecting the field and then clicking the Primary Key button. You can also create indexes for other fields by setting the Index property. Unlike the primary key, however, the indexed field gives you the option of using duplicate values. What I haven't mentioned so far is that the primary key or an index can be based on more than one field. I've been saving this little beauty for now.

EXPERT ADVICE

Use multiple fields in an index to minimize the number of duplicates. Multiple fields let you distinguish between records even when the first part of their keys are the same.

Here's an example: Suppose you have a database of students in your computer-training school. Because of some strange quirk of demographics, you have 50 students named Smith and 100 named Jones. You couldn't use the Last Name field as the primary key because there are plenty of duplicates (chances are you'd be using an assigned student ID or the social security number as the primary key anyway).

To speed searches using the student name, however, you could set the Last Name field to be indexed, with duplicates allowed. But because there are so many Smiths and Joneses, this wouldn't save Access a great deal of time, anyway. A more efficient method is to index combined fields to make duplicates less frequent, even if you cannot avoid them altogether. In this case, create an index using both the last and the first names. You can even add a third field, such as phone number, to further prevent duplications.

To see how this is done, create a multiple-field index for the Clients table that you created earlier. The index will combine the state and city of the contact's address to help you locate contacts based on their location. Open the Clients table in Design view. Now click the Indexes button in the toolbar (or choose View | Indexes) to see the dialog box shown here:

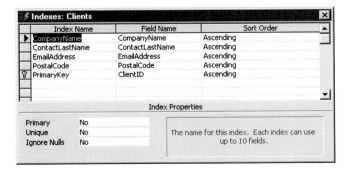

EXPERT ADVICE

The database has both a primary key and index on the same field. This is because it has used the field for some advanced purposes that we'll get to later.

Every index is assigned a name, a field that it is based on, and a sort order (either ascending or descending). The box shows several indexes and a primary key that were already defined for you by Database Wizard.

To create a new index, we have to first give it a name. Click on the first blank row under the Index Name column and type **Location**. The name you choose really doesn't matter as long as it is not used by any other key or index. Just make it somehow identify the purpose of the index.

When you create a multiple-field index, always start with the broadest field—the one that may provide the most duplicates—and work your way to the most narrow field. Click on the Field Name column in that row, pull down the list that appears to see the fields in the table, and select StateOrProvince.

Now before adding the next field to the index, look at the Index Properties. "No, No, No" means that the index is not the primary key, it is not unique (duplicates are allowed), and that null values are not allowed. You do not want to make the index unique because you may have more than one client in the same city.

Okay, so much for the first part of the index. To add another field, move to the blank row under StateOrProvince and select another field and sort order. Do not enter an index name because this second field is part of the same index, Location. So in the next blank row under Field Name, pull down the list and select the City field.

Close the Indexes box, either by clicking its Close box or the Indexes button in the toolbar. When you're done, close the table, saving the changes.

Notice that the Index Properties do not appear when you are in a row that does not have an index name. The properties are associated with the index itself, not any individual field. (I'll discuss multiple-field primary keys later.)

Building Good Relationships

We've skirted the issue of relationships several times, but unless your database is a very simple one, relationships are important to understand.

We have a perfect candidate for a one-to-many relationship in the My Company database that we've been developing: the relationship between the Clients and the Orders tables. Every client can have more than one order, that's why it's one-to-many. We should make the relationship official, sort of marrying the tables to prevent problems down the road. For example, we wouldn't want to create an order for a company not found in our client's table if we haven't checked out their credit rating, and if we don't have their address and other information on file.

We've taken care of that problem somewhat by making the ClientID field in the Orders table to be a lookup field from the Clients table. If you remember, we adjusted the property so if you did not select the ClientID from the list, you could only enter one that existed. Defining the relationship would do the same thing even without using a lookup field, but a relationship goes much further.

A relationship solves some other types of problems, too. Suppose the primary key for the Clients table is a type of field other than AutoNumber. This means you can change the value in a record's key field as long as it is unique. Without a relationship, you could assign a client a new ID number in the Clients table, but the ID number in their orders will not change. When you ask for a copy of their orders, none will print. With a relationship, changing the key value—the ID number—in the Clients table will automatically change it in all of the client's orders.

The relationship also helps cure the repeating field blues and avoids problems when deleting records. For example, remember that hypothetical table where we wondered what to do to record the names of member's children? The solution is to have two tables. One table has all of the member's general information. The other table contains their children's names. The two tables are related because they both refer to the member's ID number.

Without a relationship, you could delete a member from one table but forget to delete their children from the other table, creating database orphans. With a relationship, deleting the member automatically deletes their children as well.

Okay, get the idea? To see how to get all of this magic together, let's define the relationship between the Clients and Orders tables.

Open the My Company database and then click on the Relationships button in the toolbar. If you already have the database open, you'll have to return to the Database window to access the Relationships button. Access will open the Relationships window and display the Clients and Orders tables with a line between them. The default line shows that there is some relationship between the tables, but it doesn't show the exact type. Let's change that now.

Double-click on the line between the tables to see the Edit Relationships dialog box shown in Figure 8.4.

When you create a table with Table Wizard, Access will suggest relationships if another table contains the same field name as the primary key.

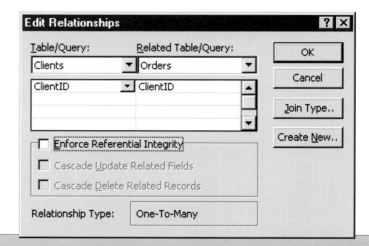

Figure 8.4:   Use the Edit Relationships dialog box to confirm the related fields and the type of relationship

The Table/Query list shows the name of the field in the "one" table. The Related Table/Query list shows the name of the field in the "many" table. If either is incorrect, click on the field name, pull down the list box, and select the correct field. The two fields can have different names as long as they are the same types and sizes. The field in the one table should be a primary key or a field that is indexed with no duplicates.

Next, click to select the Enforce Referential Integrity option. Referential integrity is what really gives the relationship its power, making sure you cannot have a "many" record that does not match a "one" record. This also lets you select the other check boxes:

- Cascade Update Related Fields will update the ClientID in the Orders table to match changes to a client's ID in the Clients table.
- Cascade Delete Related Records will delete orders for clients deleted from the Clients table.

Both of these are certainly noble options, but we actually don't want either. The ClientID field is an AutoNumber type. We can't change it anyway, so we do not need the Cascade Update option. If we delete a client—because they no longer want to do business with us, for example—we do not want to delete their orders. Doing so may delete any record of outstanding orders that have not yet been paid for. Instant bankruptcy.

Finally, notice the setting in the Relationship Type box. It is set at One-To-Many. You can't change this option. Access defines the relationship based on the fields. If the field in the related ("many") table is defined as an index with no duplicates, then Access knows the relationship is one-to-one. Do you see why it has to be? Because duplicates are not allowed, there can only be one of each in the table. When the field in the related table can have duplicates, then Access knows the relationship is one-to-many.

Now click OK. The Relationships window appears with the one-to-many relationship shown as a line from one field to the other as shown next.

In database-speak, the "one" table is called the *parent*, and the "many" table is called the *child*.

The Join Type command determines how records from the two tables are combined when creating certain types of queries.

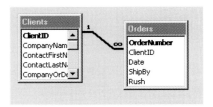

The numeral 1 next to the Clients table indicates the "one" side of the relationship; the infinity symbol shows the "many" side. You can no longer enter a ClientID in the Orders table that does not exist in the Clients table. Close the Relationships window, saving the changes.

Working with Relationships

That's how relationships are formed (and you didn't have to place an ad in the personal section of the local paper). In this case, Access displayed the two tables in the window for you when you created the lookup column. If the tables you want to relate don't appear in the Relationships window, click the Show Table button, then add other tables as shown here:

4. Define the relationships.   1. Select to list tables, queries, or both.

2. Double-click the object you want to add.   3. Close the Show Table window.

The tables will appear in the Relationships window as boxes containing lists of fields. To define the relationship, point to the field in the table that will be the "one" side of the relationship, hold down the mouse, and drag to the field in the table that will be the "many" side. When you release the mouse button, the dialog box for defining the relationship will appear.

Now, here are some other ways to work with the Relationships window.

- To delete a relationship, click the middle of the relationship line between tables and press DEL.
- To edit a relationship, double-click the middle of the relationship line to display the Relationships dialog box.
- To hide a table from the Relationships display, click on it and press DEL. The table will no longer appear in the window but its relationships are unaffected.
- To redisplay all relationships in the database, click the Show All Relationships button.
- To see if a table has any hidden relationships, click it and click the Show Direct Relationships button.

Now on Your Own

Our database is lacking one very important table. The Orders table contains general information about each order but not the individual details, such as the item ordered and in what quantity. Since an order can be for more than one item, these would be repeating fields—a definite no-no. We need this information, however, to complete the order, so we need a table to store it.

On your own, create a table called Order Details with these fields:

Field	Type
OrderNumber	Number, indexed with duplicates allowed
ItemID	Number, indexed with duplicates allowed
Quantity	Number

When you end a field with the letters "ID," Access automatically sets the properties to make it an index.

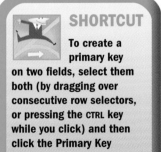

SHORTCUT

To create a primary key on two fields, select them both (by dragging over consecutive row selectors, or pressing the CTRL key while you click) and then click the Primary Key button.

Now, create two lookup fields. For the OrderNumber field, select the OrderNumber and ClientID fields from the Orders table, using the OrderNumber field as the bound column, and deselecting the option to hide the key column. This way, you can either enter or look up the order number. Follow the Lookup Wizard just as you did when you created the lookup field in the Orders table. If you are told that you must save the table, select to save it but opt against having Access create the key for you—we'll do that later. If a warning appears that Access cannot create a relationship, just close the warning box.

The other lookup field is for the ItemID field, and it will look up information in the Inventory table. When the Lookup Wizard asks you to select the fields, choose the ItemID and Item fields, then accept the default setting to hide the key column. Access displays in the datasheet the name of the item, but it will maintain a link using the item ID number. If you use the Find command to search through the column, for example, you search for ID numbers. Because the column is hidden, the ID numbers will not appear when you pull down the list.

Each record in the table will contain information about one item in one order. So if order number two is for five items, there will be five records, with the OrderNumber repeated in each. This creates a problem with the primary key. You cannot make the OrderNumber field the key because it has duplicates. You also can't make the Item field the key, because several clients may order the same item. The trick is to find some combination of items that is unique. In this case, an item will only appear once in each order, so combine the OrderNumber and Item fields into the primary key.

When you combine fields into a primary key, or into an index with no duplicates, only the combination must be unique. Each individual field can be duplicated, as long as they are not individually indexed without allowing duplicates.

Next, close and save the table and create relationships. Once you click the Relationships button, pull down the Relationships menu and click Show All. Access will display the Inventory and Order Details tables with lines between them. Create a relationship between the OrderNumber field of the Orders table and the OrderNumber field of the Order Details table, enforcing referential integrity. Then create a relationship between the ItemID field in the Inventory table and the same field in the Order Details table, again enforcing referential integrity. The relationships should look as shown in Figure 8.5.

Close the Relationships window, saving the changes. Finally, enter the records shown into the Order Details table, as shown in Figure 8.6. When you're finished, close the table.

U se the Show Table button to add the Order Details and Inventory tables to the Relationships window.

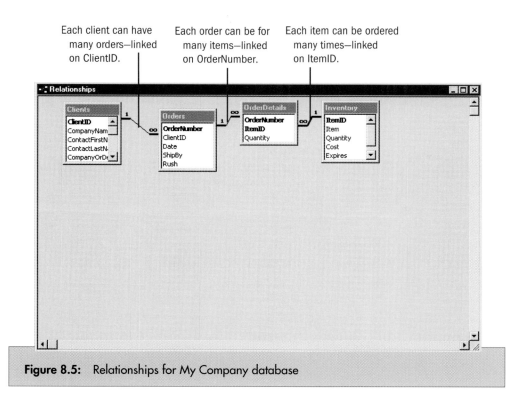

Figure 8.5: Relationships for My Company database

OrderDetails : Table

OrderNumber	ItemID	Quantity
1	Cider, Apple	4
1	Jelly, Orange	3
2	Cider, Grape	12
3	Coffee Beans	6
3	Cider, Grape	4
3	Bananas,drie	3
4	Jelly, Cherry	12
4	Jelly, Orange	4
5	Jelly, Cherry	13
5	Jelly, Grape	54
5	Jelly, Orange	4
6	Jelly, Cherry	10
6	Coffee Beans	12
0		0

Figure 8.6: Enter these records into your table

Documenting Your Work

Now that you've created your database and defined your tables, you might want a hard copy detailing your exhausting work. Keep it for your records in case your hard disk crashes and your backups are eaten by your pet iguana. The database Documenter can print a detailed report—sometimes in nauseating detail—showing the specifications of your database, tables, forms, reports, and other objects.

When you want to create a report, open the database and select Tools | Analyze | Documenter, or pull down the Analyze button menu in the Database toolbar and click Documenter. Select the items you want to document, as shown next.

1. Select the type of object. 4. Click OK.

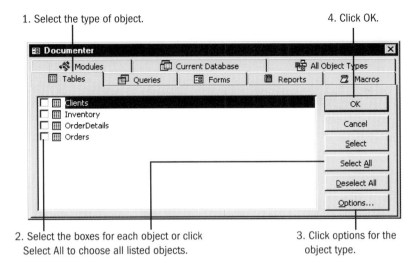

2. Select the boxes for each object or click
Select All to choose all listed objects.

3. Click options for the
object type.

To customize what gets printed about each object, select it and click the Options button. Your choices depend on the object. Figure 8.7 shows your choices for the table.

Click OK to create the report and to display it in a Report window. In the Report window, click the Print button for a hard copy reference.

EXPERT ADVICE

To print a complete report, click the All Object Types tab and click Select All. You can then deselect any individual objects that you do not want reported.

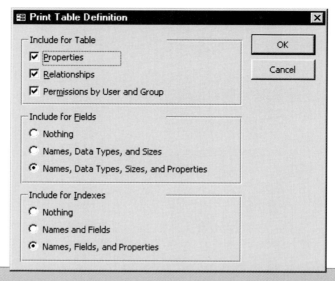

Figure 8.7: Choose the items to report for your tables

Summary

The company guru will now be proud of you. In this chapter, whether you realized it or not, you moved your database skills to a new level. You learned ways to create more sophisticated and accurate databases. Remember, good database design is critical if you want to use Access for any important or serious work. Lookup tables and indexes help speed your work and ensure that your information will be accurate, and building relationships between tables is the hallmark of a real database maven.

You know how to use them, now learn how to make them. Forms, that is. In the next chapter, you'll learn how to create forms for your tables, even forms that use information from up to three related tables at the same time.

CHAPTER 9

Creating Forms and Graphs with Form Wizard

INCLUDES

- **Creating instant AutoForms**
- **Using Form Wizard**
- **Creating forms with multiple tables**
- **Creating charts and graphs**

Create an Instant Form ➡ pp. 194–195

1. Select the table in the Database window.
2. Pull down the New Object button menu in the toolbar and click AutoForm.

Select an AutoForm Style ➡ pp. 195–197

1. Click on the table in the Database window.
2. Pull down the New Object button menu in the toolbar and click Form.
3. Select AutoForm: Columnar, AutoForm: Tabular, or AutoForm: Datasheet, and then click OK.
4. Save and close the form.

Use Form Wizard ➡ pp. 198–204

1. Display the Forms page of the Database window and select New.
2. Click Form Wizard, and then click OK.
3. Select the table and fields, then click Next.
4. Select Columnar, Tabular, Datasheet, or Justified, and then click on Next.
5. Choose the style, and then click Next.
6. Enter a form title, and select if you want to open the form or show it in Design view.
7. Click Finish to see the form.

Create a Form with Subforms ➡ pp. 204–205

1. Display the Forms page of the Database window and select New.
2. Click Form Wizard, and then click OK.
3. Select the parent table and fields, and then select the child table and fields.
4. Select how you want to look at the form, and if you want subforms or linked forms, and then click Next.
5. Select the look for each subform, and then click Next.
6. Select a style for the form, and then click Next.
7. Enter the form and subform titles, and click Finish.

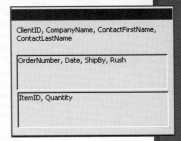

Create a Chart ➡ pp. 205–214

1. Display the Forms page of the Database window and select New.
2. Select the table, click Chart Wizard, and then click OK.
3. Select the fields to chart, and then click Next.
4. Select the chart type, and then click Next.
5. Choose the x-axis and y-axis fields, and then click OK.
6. Enter a chart title and choose whether to include a legend, and then click Finish.

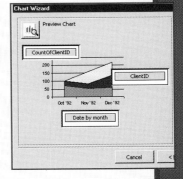

Forms are a great way to enter and edit information in your database. They're orderly and consistent, they're not intimidating, and they're easy to work with. So when you create your own table, probably one of the first things you'll want to do is to create a form. Remember all of the ways that Access gave you to make tables? You have even more ways to create forms. There's even one way that takes just two clicks. In fact, I recommend getting into the habit of making one of these two-click forms for every table you create. Then you have the immediate choice of using a datasheet or a form to work with information. In this chapter, I'll show you how to create forms in several ways, and how to create eye-catching charts and graphs.

Creating Instant Forms

The quickest way to create a form is with AutoForm. You just tell Access what table you want to use, and Access does all of the rest. Here's all you have to do:

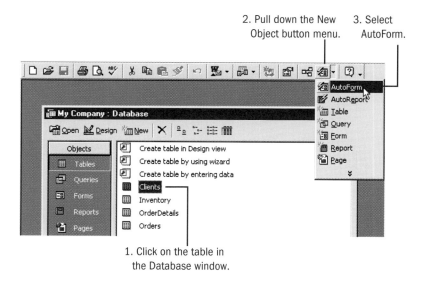

2. Pull down the New Object button menu.

3. Select AutoForm.

1. Click on the table in the Database window.

That's it. Try it now using the Clients table of the My Company database. Click on Clients in the Database window, pull down the New Object button menu, and select AutoForm. Access creates what's called a columnar form and opens it so you can start using it. A columnar form for the Clients table looks like the one shown in Figure 9.1. The form contains all of the table's fields, and you see one record at a time onscreen. Click the Save button in the toolbar, type the form name—let's call it **Clients**—and then click OK. Now close the form to return to the Database window.

CAUTION
You must have a table selected in the Database window to create an AutoForm, otherwise the AutoForm option will be dimmed.

Choosing an AutoForm Style

Just as in the fast food business, "instant" doesn't have to mean "lack of choice." You don't have to settle for one type of form just because you're too busy to design the form yourself from scratch. Have it your way. When you use the New Form command, you can select one of three styles of AutoForms, as well as other ways to create even more

In many dialog boxes, you can select either a table or a query. This is because every time you can use a table, you can also use a query. You'll learn about queries starting in Chapter 10.

Clients	
ClientID	1
Company Name	Chesin Foods
Contact First Name	Jane
Contact Last Name	Seymore
Company/Department	
Billing Address	
City	Alameda
State/Province	CA
Postal Code	94701-
Contact Title	President
Phone Number	
Extension	
Email Address	
Fax Number	
Notes	

Record: 1 of 7

Figure 9.1: A columnar form lists all of the fields down the screen

sophisticated forms. Select Form from the New Object button menu in the toolbar, or click New in the Forms page of the Database window. Access will display this dialog box:

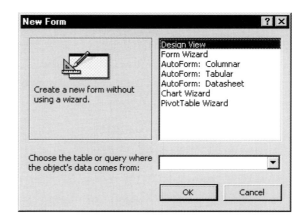

Select the table to serve as the basis of the form. If you select to start a new form when a table is open in the foreground window, or select a table in the Database window, then that table's name will automatically appear in the dialog box. If no name appears, or the name of the wrong table appears, pull down the list and select the table that you want to use.

Next, decide which of the three AutoForm styles you want. You can select columnar, tabular, or datasheet. In a tabular form, the fields appear across the screen like columns, so you can see more than one record at a time—although you may have to scroll left and right to see all of the fields. A datasheet form looks just like a datasheet.

Go figure. The AutoForm: Datasheet option displays a datasheet, just as if you had opened the table. However, it actually creates a tabular form containing just one record at a time. If you pull down the Form View button and select Form View, you'll see the form as a form. Use this option if you want a tabular layout for single records.

To create a tabular form for the Orders table, follow the steps shown in Figure 9.2.

Review the form when it appears (Figure 9.3). Click Save, type a form name, call it **List of Orders**, and then click OK. Now close the form to return to the Database window.

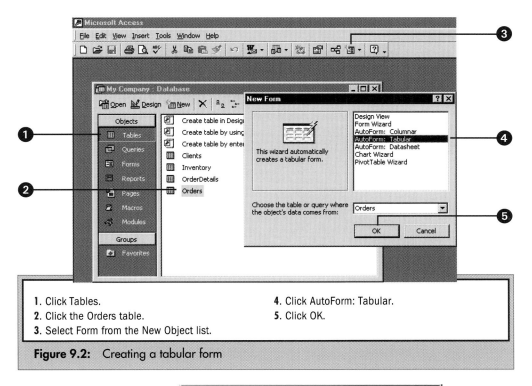

1. Click Tables.
2. Click the Orders table.
3. Select Form from the New Object list.
4. Click AutoForm: Tabular.
5. Click OK.

Figure 9.2: Creating a tabular form

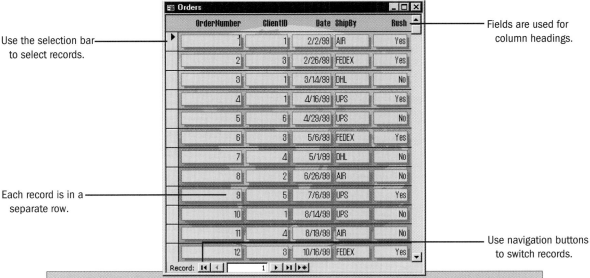

Use the selection bar to select records.

Each record is in a separate row.

Fields are used for column headings.

Use navigation buttons to switch records.

Figure 9.3: A tabular form looks like a very fancy datasheet

Using Form Wizard

Columnar, tabular, and datasheet are the Moe, Larry, and Curly of the form world. They're great fun to have around, but would you trust your business to them? When you want an award-winning performance, try Form Wizard. Like other wizards, Form Wizard lets you select options so you can customize the form's appearance. It only takes a few steps, so it's not really any more difficult or time-consuming than using AutoForm.

We'll make two forms using Form Wizard. The first is a simple columnar form for the Clients table. Instead of using all of the fields, however, we'll just use selected ones. This time, we'll use the New option from the Forms page of the Database window, just for a little variety. Start by following the steps shown in Figure 9.4.

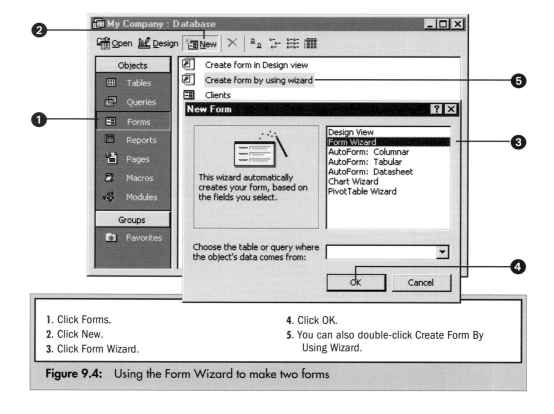

1. Click Forms.
2. Click New.
3. Click Form Wizard.

4. Click OK.
5. You can also double-click Create Form By Using Wizard.

Figure 9.4:   Using the Form Wizard to make two forms

The first wizard dialog box (Figure 9.5) asks you to choose the fields that you want in the form. The box includes a message that says you can select fields from more than one source; we'll use fields from several tables later on. You add fields just as you learned when using Table Wizard.

SHORTCUT
You do not have to select a table first, since you'll have the opportunity in the Form Wizard dialog box. However, if you do pick a table now, its fields will be shown in the first Form Wizard dialog box automatically.

1. If Table: Clients is not listed in the Tables/Queries box, pull down the list and select it now.

2. Click the ClientID field and then click the > button.

3. In the same way, add the following fields: CompanyName, ContactFirstName, ContactLastName, PhoneNumber, Extension, and EmailAddress.

4. Click Next. In this next dialog box, you select the type of form: Columnar, Tabular, Datasheet, or Justified.

5. Click Justified and then click Next. You must now select the style of the form. The option will already be set at your last

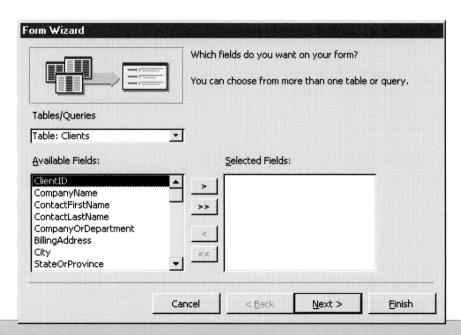

Figure 9.5: In the first Form Wizard dialog box, choose the fields that you want displayed

choice, either from Form Wizard or from Database Wizard. If you selected the International style the last time in Database Wizard, for example, that same style will be selected here. When you click on a style, a preview of it will appear in the panel to the left of the list.

6. Choose a style that you like, and then click Next. In this final dialog box, enter a form title, and select if you want to open the form, show it in Design view, or show help information.

7. Type **Clients Justified** and then click Finish to see the form (Figure 9.6).

8. Close the form when you're done admiring your handiwork.

If you create a form with fewer than all of the fields, as you just did, the form still works as explained in Chapter 2. You can still use the form to display information from the table, as well as to edit and add new records. Of course, you'll only be able to see, edit, or add the fields displayed in the form. When you add a new record, for example, fields not on the form will be blank. Because of this, you must add the primary key field to the form if you plan to use it to add records when the primary key is not an AutoNumber type. You must also include in your form any required fields.

When you're done examining your new form, close it. You do not have to save it because the Form Wizard has already done that for you.

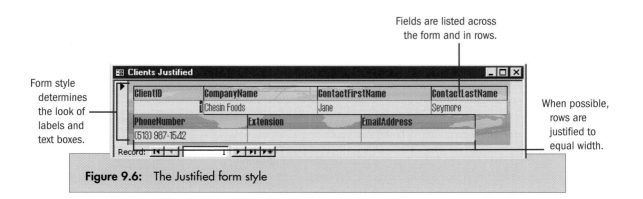

Fields are listed across the form and in rows.

Form style determines the look of labels and text boxes.

When possible, rows are justified to equal width.

Figure 9.6: The Justified form style

Creating Forms from Multiple Tables

Now for something really special. Let's create a form that takes advantage of the relationships between tables. Picture this: You want to review orders placed by clients. If you just open the Orders table, you'll see the overall order information but not the client's name (ID only) and none of the individual item details. That's not very nice. You'd also like to write the details of an order while viewing some information from the Clients and Orders table all on the same screen. This requires what's called a form/subform. The form refers to the "one" table, and the subform to the "many" table. In this form, we'll have two subforms—one for the Orders table and another for the Order Details table.

Note the nuances here. When comparing the Clients and Orders tables, Clients is on the "one" side of the relationship and Orders is on the "many" side. If you consider the Orders and Order Details tables, however, Orders is now on the "one" side and Order Details is on the "many" side.

Creating a form/subform is easy. In fact, it works the same as a simple form. The difference is that you select fields from multiple tables, and then select the style of the subforms. There are a number of steps involved, so let's do it step-by-step:

CAUTION

In order to create a form/subform, the tables must have a one-to-many relationship, with referential integrity enforced. If not, it's a no-no, and Access will display a message telling you so.

1. Click Forms in the Database window.
2. Click New.
3. Click Form Wizard.
4. Pull down the table list and select Clients.
5. Click OK to see the wizard dialog box where you select fields.
6. Click ClientID, and then click >.
7. Click CompanyName, and then click >.
8. Pull down the table list and select Table: Orders. The fields in the Orders table are now listed.
9. Add the OrderNumber, Date, ShipBy, and Rush fields to the list.
10. Pull down the table list and select Table: Order Details.
11. Add the ItemID and Quantity fields to the list.

12. Click Next. In this next dialog box (Figure 9.7), you select how you want to view the form.

The suggested layout will depend on the relationships that you've created between the tables. In Figure 9.7, the form will be divided into three distinct areas, as shown in the preview panel on the right. There'll be a separate area for the fields from each of the three tables. Three separate (but related) forms are on the same page. You can also decide to have fewer sections or distinct form areas. If you want to combine the first two tables into one section, for example, click By Orders. There would then be just two sections—the fields from both Clients and Orders are in one section and the fields from Order Details are in the other. We don't want to do that now, so leave By Clients as the selection.

You can also select to have subforms or linked forms. With subforms, all of the forms appear onscreen. If you select linked forms, then a button appears rather than the subforms. Just click the button when you want the subform information to appear.

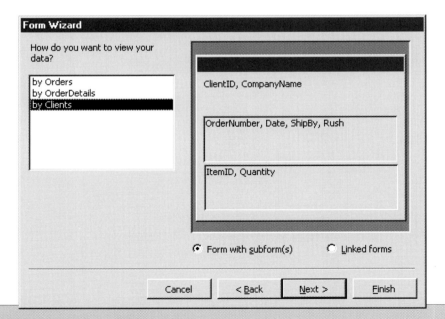

Figure 9.7: Choose how you want to organize your data

13. Click Next. You now must choose a look for each subform, either tabular or datasheet (Figure 9.8). Clicking an option will show how it appears in the preview area. The main form, by the way, is always columnar. Click the Tabular option for the second subform so you can see the difference between the two types.

14. Click Next. The box in which you can select a style appears.

15. Choose a style that suits your mood and then click Next. You can now name the form and each of the subforms. When you open the main form, all of the subforms appear as well. The subforms will also, however, appear listed separately in the Database window. You can also choose to open the form in Form view or Design view, and to show help information.

16. Type **Clients and Order Details** as the form name, and then click Finish to see the completed form (Figure 9.9).

You could have also added the Cost field from the Inventory database to see the cost of each item. However, unless you change the form in

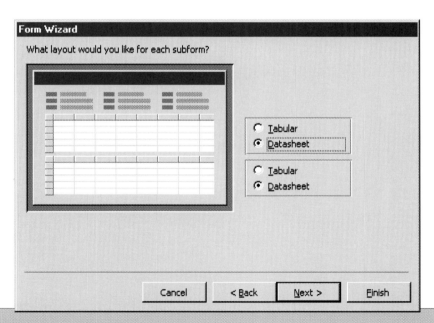

Figure 9.8: Select the appearance of each subform

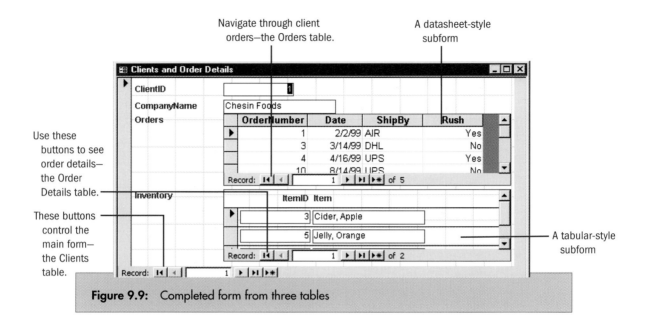

Figure 9.9: Completed form from three tables

Design view, a user could change the cost. In most cases, the cost is not changed when taking orders, so we left that field out for now.

Working with Subforms

There's an awful lot on your screen, but don't be intimidated. Take your time. There are actually three forms displayed, each representing one of three tables. Also notice that there are three sets (count 'em!) of navigation buttons. Each set controls one form, and thus the records in one table.

The buttons at the very bottom of the form control the main form from the records in the Clients table. As you select another client, the client information appears in the top of the form, and the orders appear in the Orders section. The details of the selected order appear in the Order Details section.

To see the details of another order, select it in the Orders section. To see the order for another client, change to that client record.

To add a new record, you first have to decide which table you want to add it to, and then choose one of the following:

- To add another client, for example, click the Add Record button at the bottom of the form. You can also click in any of the fields from the Clients table and then use the New Record button in the toolbar.
- To add an order, first display the client that is placing the order, and then click the New Record button in the Order subform (or, click an Order field and use the New Record button in the toolbar).
- To add details, make sure the focus is on the correct order as shown in the Orders section, and then click the New Record button in the Order Details section.

Use the same procedure to display or change information. Work your way from selecting the proper client, then the order, and then the order details. Because we did not include all of the fields in the form, you will only be able to see, edit, or add partial records.

Now on your own, play around with the form. Change records, add information, and experiment until you feel comfortable with how the form works. When you're done, close the form. The wizard has saved the form for you, and Access automatically saves each record that you create or modify.

You can apply a sort order and filter to each section of the form.

Emphasizing Information in Charts

Charts can be addictive, and like many things in life, they get overused. How many slick magazines and newspapers do you see with charts that are so fancy and junked-up that you can't make any sense out of them? A chart is supposed to make it easier to interpret information, and it can't when it's designed like a tie-dyed inkblot test.

With that pet peeve out of the way, we can now look at Chart Wizard. Chart Wizard is similar to Form Wizard. You get to select which fields

Chart Wizard produces a chart that you can customize in Design view. The capabilities are much like those available in Word and Excel.

you want to include and how you want the form to appear. The difference is that Chart Wizard presents your data in a graph.

Before jumping into a chart, you should understand some charting terminology. Look at Figure 9.10. This simple chart shows the number of dollars spent in each quarter of the year. The quarters are shown along the x-axis, which is represented by the horizontal line. The x-axis is sometimes called the *category axis*. Each bar in the chart represents the amount of money spent in one quarter. The amounts spent are shown in a scale along the y-axis, which is represented by the vertical line. The y-axis is sometimes called the *value axis*. When you create a chart, you tell Access which fields you want to chart, and which to use as the x-axis and the y-axis. The y-axis field, by the way, must contain numbers or currency amounts.

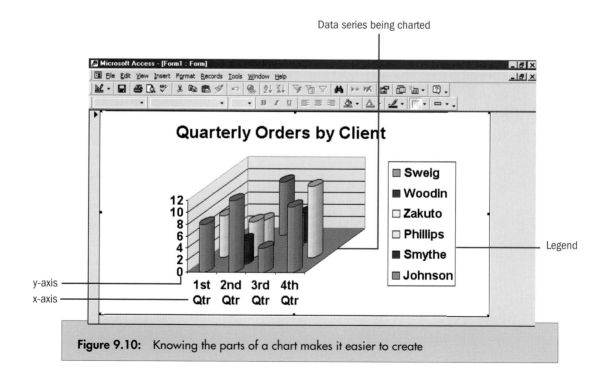

Figure 9.10:   Knowing the parts of a chart makes it easier to create

Now a friendly warning: It may take some trial and error to produce the chart that you have in mind. If your chart doesn't look right, just try making another, and then another, and so on until you get it right.

As an example, we will make a basic chart showing the number of orders placed by each client by the quarters of the year.

1. Click on Forms in the Objects list, select New, and then click Chart Wizard.

2. Pull down the table list at the bottom of the dialog box, choose Orders and then click OK to see the wizard box where you select fields.

3. Add the ClientID and the Date fields and then click Next. You now select the type of chart, as shown in Figure 9.11.

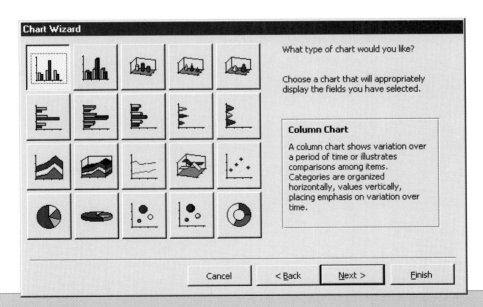

Figure 9.11: Choose the type of chart you want to create

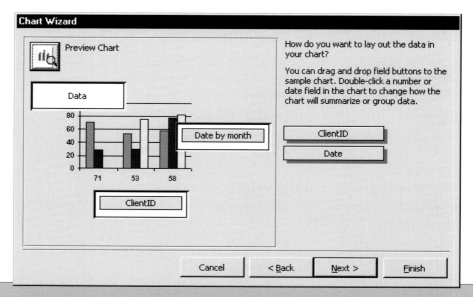

Figure 9.12: Designate the fields to use for the x- and y-axes

4. For this example, click Next to accept the default Column chart type. In the next dialog box (Figure 9.12), you designate how you want to chart the information.

As you move and adjust fields, the sample chart will change to reflect the new settings. However, don't trust what you see on the screen; it's just a rough sample of the type of chart that will be created.

Just as you double-clicked Date By Month to select another way to use it in the chart, you can also double-click the data item to select different ways to organize data.

The fields that you've selected will be listed on the right. Access tries to guess how you want to create the chart, and will select an x-axis and y-axis field for you. In this case, Access got a little confused. First, we want to count the number of times each client ordered in a month. So drag ClientID from the right side of the box to the Data box. It should read CountOfClientID.

Next we want to change how Access uses the other fields. We want to use the Date field to display orders by quarter, with the quarters along the x-axis. So, drag the Date field from the right to the box below the x-axis that now says ClientID; Access will display Date By

Month. To organize the data by quarters, double-click on the notation Date By Month below the x-axis to see this dialog box:

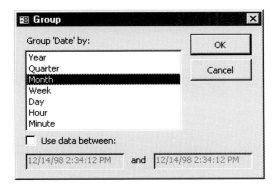

Select Quarter in the Group dialog box that appears and then click OK. Finally, drag the ClientID field from the right to the box indicating the legend—which now shows Date By Month. The client ID numbers will now be used for the legend to represent the series being charted.

Click on Preview Chart for a quick look at the chart so far. Click Close in the preview to return to Chart Wizard.

Now click Next. In the next Wizard, you enter a title for the chart, and select whether you want to include a legend. You can also choose to display the chart or modify it. Type **Chart of Orders** as the form name, and then select Finish to see the completed chart (Figure 9.13).

Click Save, type **Orders by Quarter**, and then click OK.

Modifying a Chart

If you've worked with charts in Excel or Word, then you'll feel right at home working with charts in Access—the techniques are about the same.

Click the Design View button to show the chart in Design view (we won't actually be dealing with that now—we're saving Design view for later). Now double-click on the chart. Windows displays the Microsoft

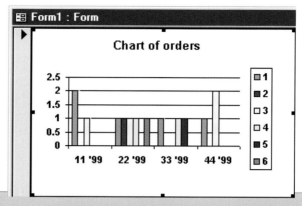

Figure 9.13: Your completed chart has more impact than a printed table

Graph application menu bar and toolbar, as shown in Figure 9.14. This is the program that actually created the chart for you.

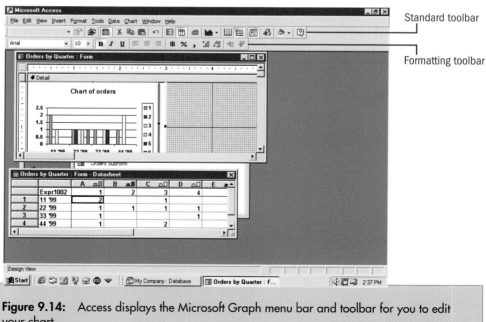

Figure 9.14: Access displays the Microsoft Graph menu bar and toolbar for you to edit your chart

You'll see the Chart window with your chart. Behind the chart is a datasheet (although it doesn't look like an Access datasheet) containing the charted information. The window also contains the Graph menu bar and two toolbars—the Standard toolbar and the Formatting toolbar. The Window and Help menu items contain the same options as those in a Document window. Table 9.1 shows the new functions available in the Microsoft Graph menus. Table 9.2 shows the functions of the Standard toolbar.

Menu Item	Functions
File	Returns to Access.
Edit	Imports data or a chart from a spreadsheet program, and performs editing techniques such as cut, copy, and paste.
View	Switches between the datasheet and graph, selects toolbars, and zooms the display.
Insert	Adds cells, titles, data labels, a legend, axis labels, gridlines, and trend lines.
Format	Formats the appearance of text and chart elements.
Tools	Displays options to select default colors, to allow drag-and-drop of cells, to move the insertion point to a new cell when you press ENTER, and to use AutoCorrect.
Data	Selects to display data series from row or column information, and to include or exclude specific rows or columns.
Chart	Changes the chart type, sets chart options, creates trend lines, and controls the 3-D perspective.

Table 9.1: Menu Options in Microsoft Graph

Toolbar Button	Button Name	Function
Chart Title ▾	Chart Objects	Pulls down the list and selects the part of the chart you want to edit.
	Format Object	Changes the format or properties of the selected object.
	Import File	Imports data from another document, table, or spreadsheet.
	View Datasheet	Toggles between the datasheet and the graph.
	Cut	Cuts.
	Copy	Copies.
	Paste	Pastes.
	Undo	Undoes previous action(s).
	By Row	Chooses data series from rows.
	By Column	Chooses data series from columns.
	Data Table	Inserts a copy of the datasheet into the graph.
	Chart Type	Selects the chart type.
	Category Axis Gridlines	Turns on or off vertical gridlines on the x-axis.
	Value Axis Gridlines	Turns on or off horizontal gridlines on the y-axis.
	Legend	Turns on or off the display of the legend.

Table 9.2: Microsoft Graph Standard Toolbar Buttons

Toolbar Button	Button Name	Function
	Drawing	Turns on or off the drawing toolbar to add text, objects, and custom drawings to the chart.
	Fill Color	Chooses a color for graph objects.
	Office Assistant	Gets context-sensitive help.

Table 9.2: Microsoft Graph Standard Toolbar Buttons *(continued)*

You use the buttons on the Formatting toolbar to format the appearance of text and numbers. In fact, its buttons will only be active when text or numbers are selected—and then only buttons that apply to the selected object. If you select a title, for example, the buttons that affect numbers will remain dimmed. Use the toolbar to select a font style and size, to change the alignment of text, pick a numeric format and number of decimal places, and to angle text upward and downward at a 45-degree angle.

Click the View Datasheet button to display the datasheet in the foreground. The datasheet is just like a spreadsheet, but the row headings appear in the column to the left of column A, and the column headings in the row above row 1.

While Access maintains a link between the table and the chart, Microsoft Graph does not. If you change the row or column headings, or the values in the datasheet shown in the Graph application, you'll see those changes reflected in the chart in the Chart window and while in Design view. But when you switch to Form view, the original data from the table will appear charted.

Bring the chart back to the foreground by clicking the View Datasheet button again. While you cannot change the information in the chart, you can use the toolbar and the menu bar options to change its appearance, as shown next.

 CAUTION
Because of some glitches in Access, your Chart window may appear different than shown here. The default chart may appear in the window, rather than the data and chart that you created. Changes you make to the chart type, titles, and other formats will still be applied to your chart when you return to Form or Report view.

DEFINITION

Handles:
Small boxes around a selected object used to change the object's size. Drag a handle to change the size of the object; drag the border between handles to change its position.

To change the appearance of any part of the chart, select it—either click on the part you want to edit, or pull down the Chart Object list in the toolbar and choose the object. When you point to a part of the chart with the mouse, by the way, the part's name will appear in a small ScreenTip.

As an example of changing a chart, let's edit the title, change the type of chart, and add gridlines. Click on the title of the chart. The title will appear surrounded by a frame with handles. Drag over the text in the title and type **Client Orders by Quarter**, then click elsewhere in the chart. Now, pull down the Chart Type button and select the area-type chart—the top button on the left side.

Finally, click the Category Axis Gridlines button to display vertical lines at the quarter indicators on the x-axis. Click outside of the chart area to return to Design view, and then click on Form view to see how the form now appears. The chart, shown next, displays the accumulated number of orders for all clients. Individual clients are represented by the area sections. Click Save to save the chart, and then close it to return to the Database window.

I f you wanted to use the quarters for the legend and the ClientID for the x-axis, click the ByColumn button.

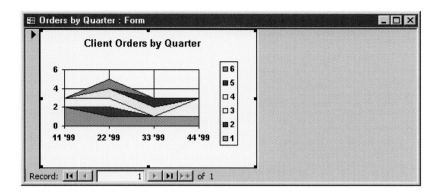

Now on Your Own

When you have some time, return to Design view and experiment with the menu bar and toolbar to learn more about creating graphs. Select the form in the Form page of the Database window, click Design, and then double-click the chart.

You can select or change the type of graph by selecting an option from the Chart Type list. When you point to a type in the list, its name appears. For each type of graph you can also choose from predefined formats. Choose Chart | Chart Type to display the dialog box shown in Figure 9.15.

The Standard Types tab of the dialog box offers commonly used chart types, as well as bars and columns of cones, cylinders, and pyramids. The Custom Types tab offers black-and-white styles, combination charts, and some highly decorative chart designs. As you pick a type in the Chart Type list, subtypes of it will appear in the Chart Sub-type list. To customize the rotation, elevation, and other aspects of a three-dimensional graph, choose 3-D View from the Chart menu to see its dialog box.

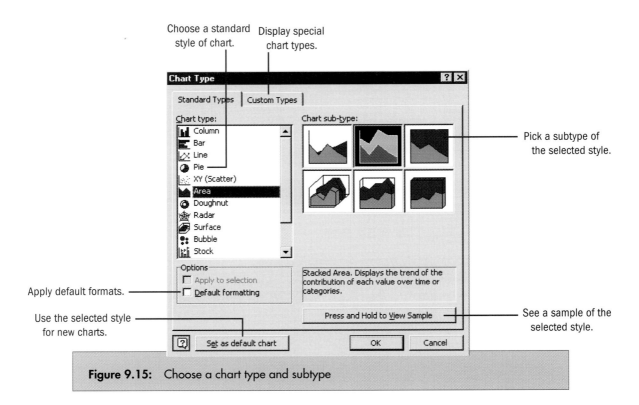

Figure 9.15: Choose a chart type and subtype

When you point to a section of the chart, its name appears in a ScreenTip. This makes it easier to select the part of the chart you want to edit.

You can format any part of the chart by selecting it and then choosing an option from the Format menu. You can also double-click on a part of the chart for its format options. To enter and customize the chart titles, change the type of axes and gridlines, choose the position of the legend, or add data labels and a data table, select Chart Options from the Chart menu.

Also experiment with the Chart Wizard, trying different arrangements of fields in the data, series, and axis positions.

Summary

Now that you can create your own forms, you can really customize your database. Use forms to enter, edit, and display information, and for sorting and filtering as you learned in Chapter 2. By adding selected fields to a form, you can even prevent other fields from being changed. While charts may not be appropriate for every table, take advantage of them if you want to graphically display data. Just make sure the chart makes a point.

While you can print out forms, they are really designed to view and change information on the screen. Reports, on the other hand, are meant to be printed and distributed. Reports can even help you analyze your information, as you will learn in the chapter to come.

CHAPTER 10

Creating Reports

INCLUDES

- Creating instant AutoReports
- Using Report Wizard
- Creating labels
- Using Snapshot Viewer

Create an Instant Report ➡ pp. 222–224

1. Select the table in the Database window.
2. Pull down the New Object button menu in the toolbar and click AutoReport.

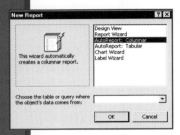

Select AutoReport Styles ➡ pp. 224–225

1. Click on the table in the Database window.
2. Pull down the New Object button menu in the toolbar and click Report.
3. Choose AutoReport: Columnar or AutoReport: Tabular, then click OK.
4. Save and close the report.

Use Report Wizard ➡ pp. 225–229

1. Display the Report page of the Database window, and then click New.
2. Click Report Wizard, then click OK.
3. Select the table and fields, then click Next.
4. If using fields from related tables, select overall grouping for sections, then click Next.
5. Select the field or fields to group by and grouping options, then click Next.
6. In the series of dialog boxes that appear, choose sort fields, layout options, and the overall style, clicking Next when you complete each box.
7. Enter a report title and select if you want to show the report in Print Preview or Design View, then click Finish to see the report.

Use Label Wizard ➡ pp. 229–233

1. Display the Reports page of the Database window and click New.
2. Select Label Wizard.
3. Select the table to use for the labels, and then click OK.
4. Choose a predefined format for your label size or create a custom label size, then click Next.
5. Select the font, font size, weight, and style to use for label text, and then click Next.
6. Arrange the layout of fields on the label prototype, and then click Next.
7. Select one or more fields for sorting, then click Next.
8. Type a report title, and then click Finish to see the labels in Print Preview.

E-mail a Snapshot Viewer Report ➡ pp. 234–235

1. Click the name of the report you want to use in the Database window.
2. Choose File | Export.
3. Pull down the Save As Type box and choose Snapshot Format.
4. Enter the filename and choose its location.
5. Click to place a check mark in the Autostart check box.
6. Click Save.
7. When Snapshot Viewer opens, select File | Send.
8. Enter the address of the recipient.
9. Click Send.

Maybe you don't want to admit it, but we're all just a little too neurotic to really trust a paperless world. We like to see a real signature on a contract and feel that grain between our fingers. Sure, we can do without the paper cuts and stapling our fingers while trying to separate pages for copying. Perhaps it's just instinctive, an unconscious reminder of the primordial forests of distant ancestors, but some of us just trust paper more than digital data.

Microsoft must feel the same way or at least be in synch with these feelings, because they've given us reports. Reports are meant to be printed, passed around, and bound in books. And they're so quick. You create reports just as you do forms. The only difference is that you use the AutoReport or Report options from the New Object list or select New from the Reports page of the Database window. If you've done forms, you can do reports.

As with forms and datasheets, the information you see when you preview (open) a report depends on what's actually in the table. Once you create a report, it will always show you the current contents of the underlying table. You only have to create a new report when you want a different layout or design.

Creating an Instant Report

Try it now. Start Access and open the My Company database. Then create a report as shown here:

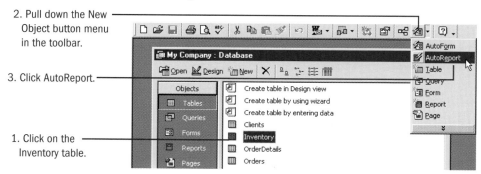

2. Pull down the New Object button menu in the toolbar.

3. Click AutoReport.

1. Click on the Inventory table.

Simple. AutoReport creates the columnar report (Figure 10.1). This means that all of the record's fields are listed in a column down the page. The report is rather sparse, with no heading, date, or page number, but it does show the contents of the table. Access will place one record after the next, but it will not divide a record between pages. If a record has more fields than can fit on one page, however, it will divide them between pages and start each record on a new page.

Now follow these steps:

1. Choose File | Save.

2. Type a name for your report—we'll use **Basic Inventory**—and then click OK.

3. Click the Close button on the toolbar to switch to Design view.

4. Pull down the View button menu to see the options Design View, Print Preview, and Layout Preview. Design View, as you know, lets you change the layout and design of the report. Print Preview shows you how the report will appear when printed. Layout Preview is only available for reports. Layout Preview collects just enough of the actual information to see a sample of how the report will appear. It's faster than Print Preview when you have a large table, but use it only for a quick

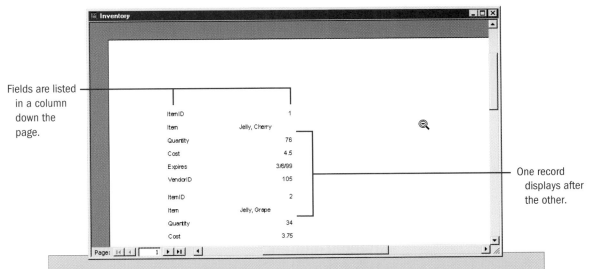

Figure 10.1: Create an instant columnar report with AutoReport

look at the report's structure and not to see what actually will be printed.

5. Finally, choose File | Close.

Creating Fancier Instant Reports

While the report you just created was rather plain-looking, you can create better-looking instant reports as well. Just use the New command from the Reports page of the Database window (or choose Report from the New Object button menu in the toolbar) to see this dialog box:

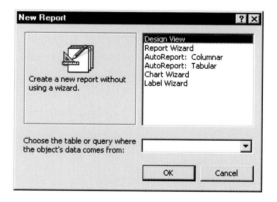

*C*hart Wizard works exactly the same for reports as it does for forms. Enough said.

You have two AutoReport options: Columnar and Tabular. Using AutoReport from the New Report menu takes a few more steps than using the New Object button and the reports take longer to generate, but it has a definite advantage. The reports are more formatted, as shown in Figure 10.2. The table name appears as the report heading, and the date and page number, along with the total number of pages, appear at the bottom of each page. In a tabular report, the fields are

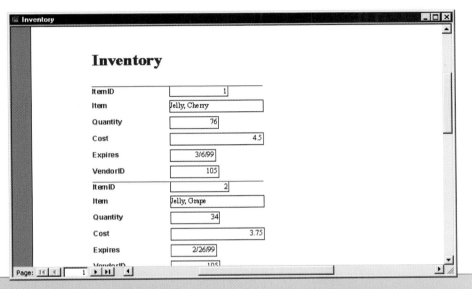

Figure 10.2: Use AutoReport from the New Report dialog box for better-looking instant output

listed across the top of the page, like column headings. The report will print in landscape orientation, and Access will try to print as many fields on a page as possible, even clipping some of the field names. Extra columns will print on another page.

Report Wizard

If you want more control over the design of your report without getting bogged down in report design, then use Report Wizard. Like Form Wizard, it lets you select fields and style options, and you can

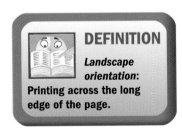

DEFINITION

Landscape orientation: Printing across the long edge of the page.

even create reports with fields from related tables. Start Report Wizard now by following these steps:

2. Click New.

3. Click Report Wizard.

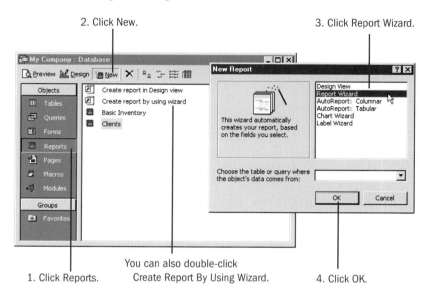

1. Click Reports.

You can also double-click
Create Report By Using Wizard.

4. Click OK.

In the first wizard dialog box, select the fields that you want to add to the report, including fields from related tables. From the Clients table, add the ClientID, CompanyName, BillingAddress, City, StateOrProvince, and PostalCode fields. From the Orders table, add the OrderNumber and Date fields. From the Order Details table, add the Quantity field. And from the Inventory table, add the Item and Cost fields, then click Next.

Since you have selected fields from multiple tables, the next Report Wizard dialog box (see Figure 10.3) then lets you choose their grouped arrangement, which is the same as grouping fields for forms and subforms. If you recall, this lets you select, if you want, the fields from each table listed separately or grouped together. In this case, the suggested grouping is ideal, so click Next.

The next dialog box lets you choose if you want to organize the information by any other groups. Click Next. When you do not group by a field, the records appear one after the other. Grouping by a

Client information
will appear first.

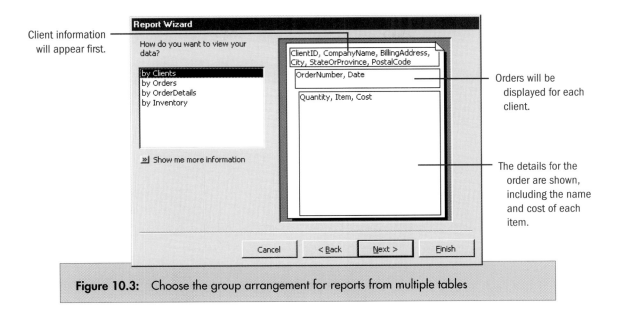

Orders will be
displayed for each
client.

The details for the
order are shown,
including the name
and cost of each
item.

Figure 10.3: Choose the group arrangement for reports from multiple tables

field lets you divide the report into sections—not grouped by tables but instead by the values in the selected field.

You can group by more than one field. For example, if you are interested in when clients placed orders, you could first group by ClientID (so all of a client's orders are listed together), and then by date (so they are in date order for each client). You could also group first by date and then by contact for each date. It all depends on how you want to view the records. In addition to selecting the fields for grouping, you can also select grouping options. By default, dates are grouped by month, but for all other fields each unique field value is another group—each ClientID, each Last Name, and so on. This is called *normal grouping*. Grouping Options let you change what is considered a group.

With a date field, for example, you can also select to group by year, quarter, day, or some other interval. You can also select normal grouping to use each unique date. For numeric and currency fields you can select normal, or by 10s, 50s, and so on. Text fields can be grouped normally, by the first letter of each value (such as As, Bs, and so on, for an index-type listing) or by some number of initial characters.

For a sample of grouping by the first character, add data to the Contact Management database and then preview the Alphabetical Contact Listing report. Preview the Weekly Call Summary report to see dates grouped by week. (This report has a special feature that lets you designate the range of dates you want to include—enter the dates **1/1/95** and **12/31/95**.)

Click Next to see the Report Wizard dialog box that lets you sort on up to four fields. This same box lets you choose summary options, so you can calculate and display the sum, average, minimum, or maximum values for each group. You can also decide to show the details and summary (such as information about each specific order, as well as the count of orders), show just summary information only (just the count for each client), or calculate the percentage of the total for each sum. Choose a sort order, if you want it, and then click Next.

Another Report Wizard dialog box lets you choose the layout for the details in the report, including portrait or landscape orientation, and lets you adjust field width so all fields fit on a page. Select a layout that suits your mood and then click Next. In the next wizard dialog box, you select the overall style of the report. The style determines the background color, the font used for report headings and text, and the design of lines separating report sections. Take your pick and then click Next. You can now enter a report title, and choose if you want it to appear in Print Preview or Design View. Type **Client Orders** as the report title, and then click Finish to see the report in Print Preview (see Figure 10.4).

The report includes all of the information, although it could not be used to print invoices. The extended price has not been calculated, nor

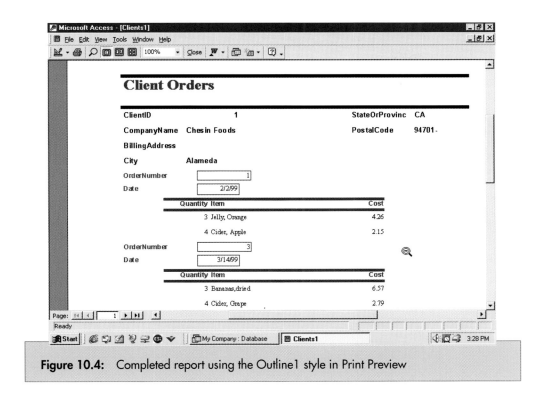

Figure 10.4: Completed report using the Outline1 style in Print Preview

the totals for each order. We'll take care of that later. Choose File |
Close to return to the Database window.

Label Wizard

If you need to print mailing labels from your table, then you'll love
Label Wizard. As with all wizards, you select options from a series of
dialog boxes. In this case, you select the label format and the
arrangement of fields on the label.

Use the Label Wizard for name badges, shelf labels, and other labeling tasks, in addition to mailing labels.

The best way to learn the Label Wizard is to use it. So let's create mailing labels for the people in the Clients table. Start as shown here:

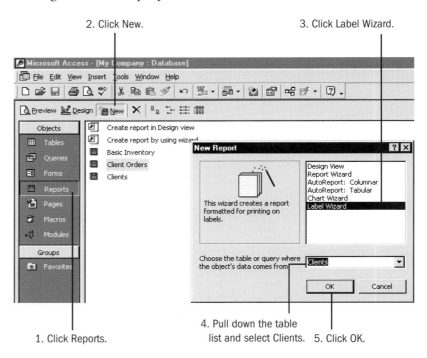

In the first wizard dialog box (see Figure 10.5), you must select a definition that matches the labels that you are using. We're going to use the Avery 5096 label, so select Avery from the Filter by Manufacturer list, click English in the Unit of Measure section, and click 5096 in the Product Number list now. But if you want a different form, select the manufacturer, the label type (either sheet feed or continuous), choose the unit of measure, and then scroll the list to select the specific form. For now, click Next.

If none of the predefined labels are correct, click Customize. You'll see a dialog box where you can define your own custom label sizes. To create a new size, click the New button in that dialog box. Another box appears where you enter the specifications for your label, including its type, size, number across the page, and details about its spacing on the page and in relation to other labels.

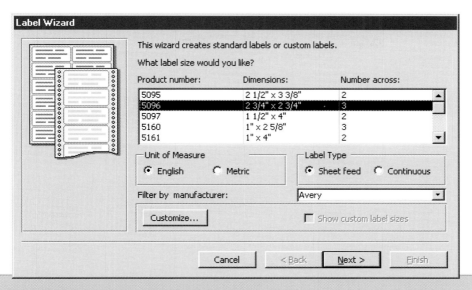

Figure 10.5: Choose a predefined label format, or create your own

The next wizard dialog box lets you choose the font, font size, weight, style, and color for the label text. The default is Arial, 8 point, light. Click on the Font Name list in the dialog box, scroll the list of fonts, and select Times New Roman. Make your choices from the options and then click Next.

Now you must arrange the fields on the label using the dialog box shown in Figure 10.6. Since we're creating a mailing label, we want a standard address format. You add a field to the label in much the same way you add fields to forms and reports. Double-click ContactFirstName in the Available Fields list, or click it once and then click the > button. Access moves the field to the Prototype label area and surrounds it in braces.

After you move a field to the prototype, the next field in the list is automatically selected. Before adding the ContactLastName field, however, press the SPACEBAR. This will insert a space between the names in the label. Double-click ContactLastName to add it to the label, and then press ENTER to move to the next line in the prototype.

CAUTION
If you select a large font size, your information may not fit on the labels. For standard address labels, stick with 12 points or less.

DEFINITION
Prototype: A model that represents the final product, but which is not the final product itself.

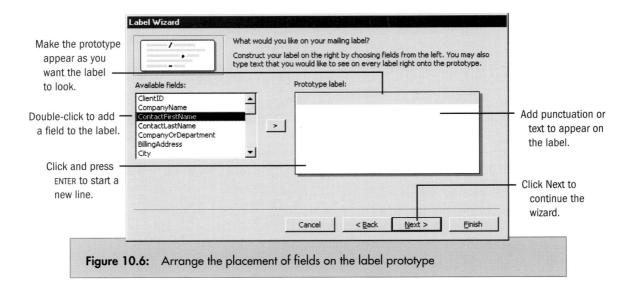

Figure 10.6: Arrange the placement of fields on the label prototype

Make the prototype appear as you want the label to look.

Double-click to add a field to the label.

Click and press ENTER *to start a new line.*

Add punctuation or text to appear on the label.

Click Next to continue the wizard.

There is no < button to remove a field from the prototype. To remove a field, click it and then press DEL.

Now add the BillingAddress field to the prototype and press ENTER, then add the City field. Type a comma and a space after the City field, add the StateOrProvince field, type two spaces, and then add the PostalCode field. The completed prototype will look like this:

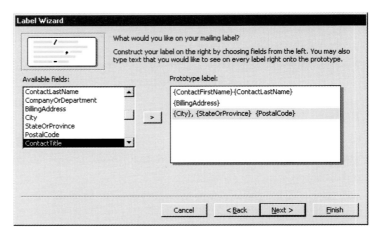

Click Next. The next dialog box lets you select one or more fields to sort the labels by. You can use any of the fields in the table, even those not on the label itself. Since we want to take advantage of bulk rates, double-click on the PostalCode field to add it to the Sort By list, and then click Next.

The final wizard dialog box asks if you want to see the labels in Print Preview or Design View. Leave the option set to the default to see the labels as they will look when printed. Type **Labels** for the report name, and then click Finish to see the labels as shown in Figure 10.7.

Choose File | Close to return to the Database window. When you're ready to print labels, just select the report, get your labels ready in the printer, and click the Print button.

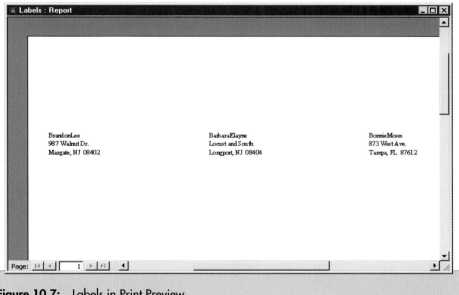

Figure 10.7: Labels in Print Preview

Creating Reports with Snapshot Viewer

If Snapshot Viewer is not already installed on your system, it will install when you create your first snapshot report.

While reports are basically designed to be printed, they can also be viewed on screen. But what if you want to share a report with a person who does not have Access? Easy. The answer is Snapshot Viewer.

Snapshot Viewer is a handy little program that lets anyone view an Access report—complete with its layout, graphics, and embedded objects. If a user who gets your report doesn't have Snapshot Viewer, he or she can quickly download it over the Internet. In fact, Snapshot Viewer can be installed so users can view your reports directly from their Internet browser.

To save a report to be viewed by Snapshot Viewer, follow these steps:

1. Click the name of the report you want to use in the Database window.
2. Choose File | Export.
3. Pull down the Save As Type box and choose Snapshot Format.
4. Enter the filename and choose its location.
5. Disable the Autostart check box if you do not want to view the snapshot after it is saved.
6. Click Save.

If you did not disable the Autostart check box, the report appears in Snapshot Viewer, as shown in Figure 10.8.

A person who has Snapshot Viewer can now read your report by opening it with Snapshot Viewer on his or her own computer.

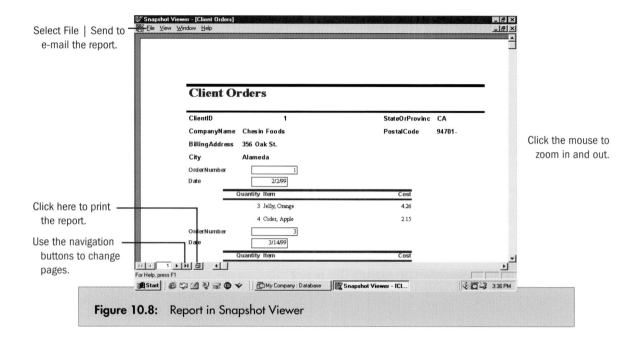

Select File | Send to e-mail the report.

Click the mouse to zoom in and out.

Click here to print the report.

Use the navigation buttons to change pages.

Figure 10.8: Report in Snapshot Viewer

Summary

When you need a hard copy of your information, there is nothing like a report. Even those created with AutoReport are pretty handy to have around. By using Report Wizard, you can customize your reports even more, especially when you want to print information from more than one table. And when you want to address envelopes, don't forget about the Label Wizard. It is a great time-saver.

Recording information into a database program and displaying it in forms and reports is nice, but what good is it? You could do the same with a good typist and file clerk. The real important work of a database program is to help you find specific information when you need it, and to help make important decisions. You'll start learning how to perform these wonders with queries in Chapter 11.

Finding and Changing Information with Queries

INCLUDES

- Creating a quick query with the Simple Query Wizard
- Selecting records with queries
- Creating a parameter query
- Calculating with queries
- Summarizing data with queries
- Establishing query properties
- Creating crosstab queries
- Converting filters and queries
- Performing actions with queries

Create a Quick Query with the Simple Query Wizard ➡ pp. 243–245

1. Display the Queries page of the Database window, and then click New.
2. Select Simple Query Wizard, and then click OK.
3. For each field you want in the result set, choose the table or query containing the field, and then double-click the field name.
4. Click Next.
5. To summarize information in groups when using fields from more than one table, choose Summary.
6. Click Summary Options.
7. Select the Count Records In option to report the number of items in each group.
8. Select the operator for each field.
9. Click OK and then Next.
10. If you included a date field in the query, specify how to group the dates, and then click Next.
11. Enter a title for the query and click Finish.

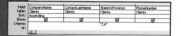

Select Records with Queries ➡ pp. 246–250

1. Display the Queries page of the Database window, and then click New.
2. Select Design View, and then click OK.
3. Double-click each table containing fields you want to include.
4. Click Close.
5. Double-click each field you want to include in the query.
6. For each field you want to sort by, click the Sort row, and select Ascending or Descending.
7. Enter any conditions in the appropriate Criteria row.
8. Click Run to see the result set.
9. Click View to return to Design view.
10. Save and close the query.

Create a Parameter Query ➡ pp. 251–254

1. Create a query that includes the fields, sorts, and criteria desired.
2. In the Criteria row for each field that you want to enter as a parameter, type a prompt in square brackets.
3. If desired, use multiple parameters with the BETWEEN...AND or OR operators.
4. Run the query.
5. Enter the values desired for each parameter.

Calculate a Value with Fields ➡ pp. 254–257

1. Create a query that includes the fields, sorts, and criteria desired.
2. In the Field row for each calculated field you want to create, enter the formula for the calculation.
3. Precede the formula with a column name (header) and a colon.
4. Enclose field names in square brackets.
5. Qualify ambiguous fields with the table name in the format, [Table name]![Field name].
6. Run the query.

Summarize Information ➡ pp. 257–258

1. Create a query that includes the fields, sorts, and criteria desired.
2. Delete any fields not needed to select unique records or for summarizing information.
3. Click the Totals button to add the Total row to the grid.
4. At Group By, set those fields that will determine unique records.
5. For each field to be summarized, pull down the Total list and select the operator.
6. Run the query.

Set Query Properties ➡ pp. 258–259

1. Create a query that includes the fields, sorts, and criteria desired.
2. Enter the number of records to be displayed in the Top Values box in the toolbar.
3. Click anywhere in the gray area around the field list boxes.
4. Click the Properties button.
5. Set the query properties.

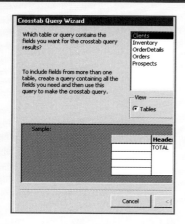

Create a Crosstab Query ➡ p. 259

1. To create a crosstab query from fields in a related table, create and save a query that includes those fields.
2. Start a new query from the Database window.
3. Choose Crosstab Query Wizard.
4. Choose the table or query to use as the basis for the crosstab, and then click Next.
5. Choose the field to use for row headings, and then click Next.
6. Choose the field to use for column headings, and then click Next.
7. Choose the fields and operators to summarize information, and then click Next.
8. Enter a name for the query, and then click Finish.

Convert Between Filters and Queries ➡ p. 263

1. Display a Filter By Form or Advanced Filter/Sort window.
2. To convert a query to a filter, choose File | Load From Query and select the query. To convert the filter to a query, choose File | Save As Query and enter a query name.

Make a New Table ➡ pp. 264–265

1. Create a query containing the fields you want in the new table.
2. Choose Query | Make-Table Query.
3. In the Table Name text box, enter the name of the new table, and then click OK.
4. Run the query.
5. Click Yes at the message.

Append Records to a Table ➡ pp. 265–266

Create a query that contains the fields you want to append to another table.
2. Choose Query | Append.
3. In the Table Name text box, enter the name of the destination table, or select the table from the list, and then click OK.
4. In the Append To row, amend any field name in the destination table that does not have a matching field name in the source table.
5. Run the query.
6. Click OK at the prompt.

Delete Records with a Query → pp. 266–267

1. Start a new query for the table you want to delete records from.
2. Choose Query | Delete.
3. Double-click the asterisk from the field list, or drag the individual fields needed for criteria.
4. Enter the criteria under the field names.
5. Click View to confirm that the correct records are selected.
6. Click View to return to Design view.
7. Run the query, and then click Yes at the prompt.

Update Records with a Query → pp. 267–268

1. Create a query containing the fields you want updated.
2. Double-click any individual field names that you'll need for criteria.
3. Enter the criteria under the field names.
4. Choose Query | Update Query.
5. In the Update To row, enter formulas that indicate how you want to change the values in the fields.
6. Run the query.
7. Click OK at the prompt.

Queries are the fastest way to get information out of a database. After all, having thousands of records stored on your disk is not the reason to have a database program; doing something with the darn stuff is. Sure, you can get information using forms and reports, and even use filters to select which records you want to appear. However, you'll get the job done much faster with queries.

What's a Query?

DEFINITION

Query:
A question you ask to find information in the database.

You can use a query whenever you find yourself thinking, "I need to know," or when you're asking who, what, when, where, and how questions. Who owes me money? What is Bob's telephone number? When was my fourth divorce granted? Where's my copy of the *Star Wars* video? How much do I still owe the IRS? A query lets you see just the specific fields and records you're interested in, when you're not interested in seeing it all. You can also perform calculations on fields and summarize information in groups, and you can even group together fields from multiple tables and other queries.

The output of a query is a special datasheet called a *result set,* because it shows the results of the query, or a *dynaset,* because there is a dynamic link between the result set and the underlying table. Whatever it is called, the results are the fields you asked for, and the records that meet any conditions that you establish. But it is still a datasheet of the table, so any changes you make to the information in the result set are actually made to the table.

There are several ways to create a query. Using the Simple Query Wizard, you follow a series of dialog boxes to specify the fields you want to use and the type of results you want. You can also create a query, in Design view, manually. Three other wizards that you can use are described in Table 11.1. They're relatively intuitive to use, so except for the Crosstab Query Wizard (which will be explained later in the "Creating a Crosstab Query" section), we won't bother going over them in this chapter.

Wizard	Function
Crosstab Query Wizard	Analyzes information like a spreadsheet. You select the fields to use for the row and column headings and the fields to summarize in the body of the spreadsheet.
Find Duplicate Query Wizard	Finds the records that have values in common, including duplicate records.
Find Unmatched Query Wizard	Locates records that have no matching values, such as clients who have not placed an order and, therefore, whose number is not matched in the Orders table.

Table 11.1:   Additional Query Wizards

Quick Queries with the Simple Query Wizard

The Simple Query Wizard is a way to create a query without worrying about how queries actually work. It is also great when you want to make some even not-so-simple queries that summarize information.

As with other wizards, you select the fields you want to include—even from related tables—and you tell Access how you want the information presented. For example, to analyze client orders in terms of inventory, you'd need to use fields from at least two tables.

To start the wizard, use the steps shown here:

The main limitation of Simple Query Wizard is that you cannot use it to select specific records, unless you first create the query and then edit it in Design view.

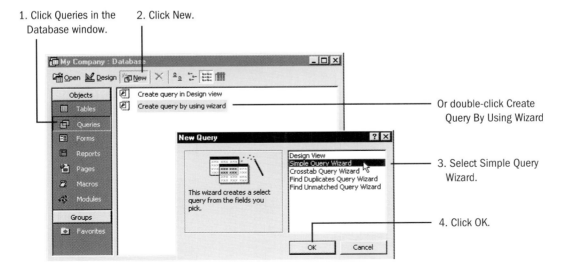

1. Click Queries in the Database window.

2. Click New.

Or double-click Create Query By Using Wizard

3. Select Simple Query Wizard.

4. Click OK.

SHORTCUT You can also start a new query by choosing Query from the New Object toolbar button. Any table selected at the time will be used as the basis for the query.

The first wizard dialog box will look very familiar—it lets you select fields from one or more tables, just as you learned in previous chapters when creating a form and report. To analyze client orders in terms of inventory, select the Clients table (in the Tables/Queries list) and then double-click the ClientID and CompanyName fields to add them to the query. Then, select the Order Details table and add the Quantity field. After you select the fields and click Next, Access displays a dialog box for you to choose how you want to display the records, as shown in Figure 11.1.

If you select to see all of the records, the result set lists a row for each item ordered. In our example, we're not interested in the details, just the summary by client. So click Summary, and then click the Summary Options button to choose how you want the information analyzed.

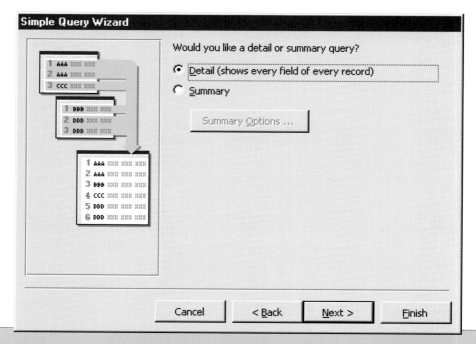

Figure 11.1: Choose to see the details of the records or just summarize their data

A dialog box appears listing the numeric and currency fields in the query—in this case, just Quantity—and the options Sum, Avg, Min, and Max for each field. To calculate the total quantity of items ordered, click Sum, and to average the number of items per order, click Avg. You should also click the check box labeled Count Records In Order Details for a total count, and then you can click OK to return to the wizard dialog box. Click Next. The final wizard dialog box lets you enter a query title and select to display the results or the design. Type **Item Analysis** in the title text box and then click Finish. The results of our sample query, which we've called Item Analysis, are shown next. The query results show one row for each client, reporting the total number of items ordered, the average number of items per order, and the number of orders for all invoices.

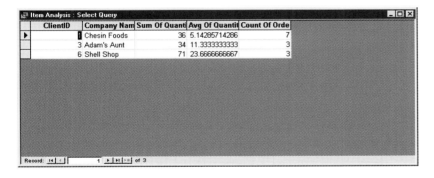

When you've finished looking at the results, close the Query window. You do not have to save the query, because the Wizard automatically saves it for you.

Running a Query

As with a form or report, you can open a saved query at any time. Opening a query runs the query, showing the selected records in a result set. To run a query, follow these steps:

I f you include a date field in the query, a wizard dialog box appears asking how you want to group the dates. These options are Unique like date/time, Day, Month, Quarter, and Year.

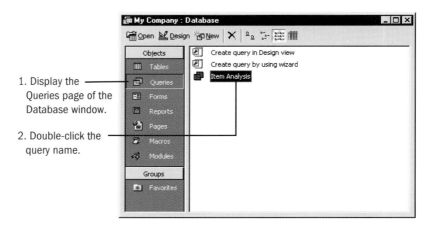

1. Display the Queries page of the Database window.

2. Double-click the query name.

Selecting Records with Queries

In the Simple Query Wizard dialog boxes, you can choose fields and perform mathematical operations, but you can't enter criteria as you can in a filter. What if, for example, you're planning a beach vacation and you'd like to mix a little business with pleasure (or the other way around, if you're planning on deducting the trip as a business expense)? You don't want to list every client in the result set, just those in California, or New Jersey, or Florida, or wherever you're planning to go.

Look at the Tables/Queries page of the Options dialog box to see what default values you can set for queries.

Rather than use the Simple Query Wizard, create the query in Design view. To do this, click New in the Queries page of the Database window, select Design View, and then click OK. Access displays the Query window with the Show Table dialog box:

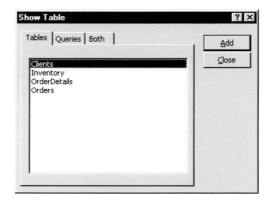

In this dialog box, you can choose the tables you want to use for the query. You can select a single table or related tables. For our example, we want to query the Clients table, so click Clients and then Add (or double-click Clients), and then close the box. The Query window will appear with the table, much like the Advanced Filter/Sort grid you learned about in Chapter 3, as shown here. (We told you that learning about the grid would come in handy.)

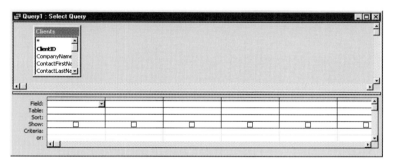

Choosing Fields to Display

After you add the tables to the Query window, you have to add the fields that you want to use for the query. To add a field to the grid, double-click it or drag it to the first blank column in the field row. (You can widen the field list box to display the field's full names.) For our example, we want to display clients in a specific state, so double-click CompanyName in the Clients table. Then, in the same way, add the ContactLastName, the StateOrProvince, and the PhoneNumber fields (in that order). Notice that the Table row of the grid shows the table from where the field information is coming. This will become more useful when you're using fields from related tables.

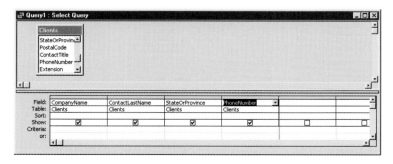

SHORTCUT

You can drag columns to change their order in the query, but it's faster just to insert them in the order in which you want them listed.

Sorting Records

You should also sort the result set in a way that makes the information more useful. To make it easier to find a specific client, for example, click in the Sort row of the CompanyName field, pull down the list, and select Ascending. Your other sorting options are Descending and (not sorted)—the parentheses are Access's idea, not ours. This will sort the result set by client names. However, you do not have to use a sort or any criteria if you want to see all of the records in their original order.

Selecting Records with Criteria

Filters and queries not only look alike but also can be interchanged. Refer to "Filters and Queries," later in this chapter.

To list clients in a specific state, you need to enter a criterion. To do this, click the Criteria row in the column for the field and type the value you want to use. For example, to list clients in California, click in the Criteria row under StateOrProvince and then type **CA**:

Field:	CompanyName	ContactLastName	StateOrProvince	PhoneNumber		
Table:	Clients	Clients	Clients	Clients		
Sort:	Ascending					
Show:	☑	☑	☑	☑	☐	☐
Criteria:			CA			
or:						

Criteria work the same way in queries as you learned to use them for filters. (Review Chapter 3 for information on criteria.) Here's a recap:

- Enter a specific value to test for equality.
- Use operators to test for values (<, >, <=, =<, <>).
- Use AND or OR operators for compound conditions.
- Use Is Null to test for blank fields, Is Not Null for fields with contents.
- Use In to determine if the value is in a set of values.
- Use BETWEEN...AND to test for a range.
- Criteria for multiple fields are treated as an AND condition.
- Use the Or row in the grid to create OR conditions for a field or between multiple fields.

From Design view, you display the result set by clicking on either the View or Run button. Click View now to see the result set. Notice that Access lists the company name, contact last name, state, and telephone number of clients in California. Click View again to return to Design view. You can always click View to toggle back and forth between the Design and Datasheet views. (To modify an existing query, select it in the Queries page and then click Design.)

Now consider the Show row. When the check box in the row (we'll call it the Show box) is checked, the field in that column of the grid will appear in the result set. Since all of the clients listed are in California, you really don't need to include the state in the result set; but you can't delete the field from the query, because you need it in the grid for the criteria. To use the field for the query but not show it in the result set, deselect its Show box to remove the check mark in the Show row. If you do that and run the query, the StateOrProvince field is not shown in the result set but it is still used to limit the list by its content.

When you open a query, by the way, Access will delete all fields with the Show box deselected if they are not used for sorting, criteria, or parameters. If they are being used, Access will move the fields to the end of the grid, following the last displayed field.

If you have created the query that we've discussed, save it with the database. Choose File | Save, type **California Clients**, and click OK.

Using All Fields

If you want to use all, or a majority of the fields in a query, you don't have to bother with moving them individually. To add all of the fields to the grid, double-click the table name on the top of the field list box to select all fields, and then drag the selection to the Field row. All of the fields will be inserted, one per column. You can then select a sort order and set criteria in as many fields as required.

You can also include all of the fields by dragging the asterisk from the top of the field list into the grid. In this case, the individual fields

View   Run

SHORTCUT
Do you like the Simple Query Wizard, but wish it could select specific records? Use the wizard to create the query, then open it in Design view and add the criteria yourself.

To delete a field from the query, click the gray bar above its field name in the grid and then press DEL.

do not appear in the grid, just the name of the table and an asterisk (like Clients.*) appears in one of the columns. When you run the query, however, all of the fields appear in the result set.

You cannot designate a sort or criteria for the column using an asterisk, because it does not represent any individual field. But if you need to, there's a quick solution. In addition to the asterisk, drag any individual field that you want to use for a sort order or criteria, and then make your selections or entries for it. Deselect its Show box so the field will not appear twice in the result set (once from the asterisk and again from the individual column). For example, here is a query that displays all of the fields from the Clients table, but only those clients from California, sorted by last name:

SHORTCUT
If you do not want to include some fields, just deselect their Show boxes. If you decide to display the fields after you run the query, just select their Show boxes again.

Field:	Clients.*		ContactLastName	StateOrProvince				
Table:	Clients		Clients	Clients				
Sort:			Ascending					
Show:	☑		☐	☐	☐	☐	☐	☐
Criteria:				"CA"				
or:								

Adding Tables to a Query

A query can include fields from more than one table, even if you only select one table originally. To add a table, follow the instructions you see in Figure 11.2.

If you have already closed the query, click California Clients in the Queries page and then click Design. Add the Orders table. If the tables are related, Access will show a line between the related fields. For example, if you add the Orders table to the California Clients query, a line appears showing the one-to-many relationship:

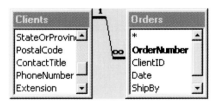

You can now use fields from both tables. For example, if you want to see the dates on which clients placed orders, just double-click the Date field in the Orders table. In fact, add the Date field to the query now.

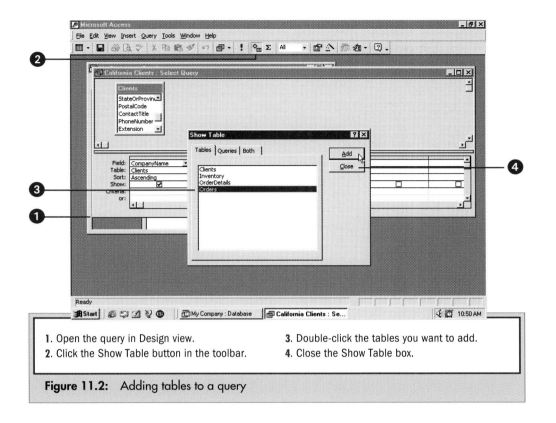

1. Open the query in Design view.
2. Click the Show Table button in the toolbar.
3. Double-click the tables you want to add.
4. Close the Show Table box.

Figure 11.2: Adding tables to a query

All-Purpose Parameter Queries

Entering specific criteria into a query really limits it. If you change your mind and decide to call on clients while vacationing on the fair beaches of New Jersey, for example, you can't just run the same query—it will always show clients in California. Instead of using specific criteria, you can enter a parameter.

As an example, you could make the California Clients query more useful by changing it so you can select the state at the time you run the query. In Design view, delete any text in the Criteria row for the StateOrProvince field, and then enter the parameter prompt, [**Enter the State**] directly in the grid. You could also enter the prompt using the Zoom Box by pressing SHIFT-F2 (you don't have to display the Zoom Box to enter any long criteria or prompts; you could just type it

If you did not establish formal relationships, Access will relate the tables in the query if the added table contains a field name that matches the primary key in the first table.

in the column). The parameter serves as a prompt, letting you know what you have to enter when you run the query, and it must be surrounded by square brackets.

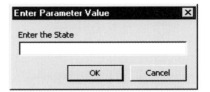

When you run the modified query (either from the Query window or from the Database window), Access displays this dialog box:

If you type **NJ** and then click OK, Access lists clients only in New Jersey.

Using Multiple Parameters

You should strive to create queries that are as flexible as possible. Whenever you can, use parameters instead of hard coding the criteria into the query. This way, you can use a query as a general solution rather than a specific one. The previous query, for example, can be run (opened) to locate clients in any particular state, not just the one entered in the Criteria row. Many beginning Access users forget about parameters and end up with long lists of queries that could easily be reduced to just a few.

For even greater flexibility in selecting records, use more than one parameter—as many as you need to select records. As an example,

---

EXPERT ADVICE

Leave the Show box selected for the parameter field. Showing the field will remind you what criteria you've entered, especially if you plan to print the results.

suppose you want to list clients in a specific state who have placed orders during a certain time period. You will need three parameters: the name of the desired state, a starting date, and an ending date of orders. The query we modified previously already has a parameter for the state. Now enter the following criteria in the Date field: **BETWEEN [Enter the starting date] AND [Enter the ending date]**.

Now when you run the query, three prompt boxes appear. You can enter **NJ** in the first, then **1/1/97** for the starting date in the second box, and **6/1/97** for the ending date in the third prompt box.

There are other ways to use two parameters in one field. The BETWEEN... AND syntax, for example, can be used to test for a numeric or currency range, as in BETWEEN [Enter low salary range] AND [Enter high salary range], to list employees in a certain range of income.

You can also use multiple parameters to create an OR condition. When you run the query that includes the parameter in the StateOrProvince field, you can only enter one state abbreviation when the parameter prompt appears; you cannot type, for example, CA or PA. If you know you want to test for two values, you can enter a parameter like this: **[Enter the first state] OR [Enter the second state]**. You'll see two prompts, and Access will use them for an OR condition.

Changing Parameter Order

If you run the previous query, Access first requests the state and then the dates. That's because the parameters are in that order, from left to right, in the query grid. You can change the order that parameters are asked for in two ways. In the first way, you change the order of the fields in the grid by dragging their columns, just as you do in a datasheet. This also changes the order in which the fields appear in the result set. If you want to change the order in which parameters are asked for, but not their order in the result set, then use the Parameters box.

To display the box shown here, first make sure you are working in Design view, and then choose Query | Parameters:

You might also need to set the order if you use a parameter in a field that is not shown, since Access will move it to the end of the table.

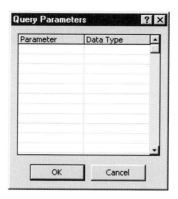

Type each of the parameters in the order you want them to appear. Type the exact same thing you entered in the square brackets, but don't include the brackets. For each, pull down the Data Type list and select the same type as the field.

Now click OK. When you run the query, the parameters will be asked for, in the same order as in the list.

Calculating Values with Fields

So far, you've used queries to select and display data from your table. There's a lot of other information that a table can give you. This information can be calculated from the values that are stored in the table. For example, the Order Details table contains a field called Quantity, and the Inventory table has a field called Cost. Quantity is how many of the item the client orders and Cost is the price of that item. To calculate the extended price, you multiply the values in the two fields. (You'll also need to calculate the extended price to determine later the total price of the order.)

Use the example in Figure 11.3 to create a query that can serve as the basis for an inventory report. No fields are used from the Inventory table but it is included so its fields are available to perform the calculation of the extended price.

To perform a calculation, you enter an expression (a formula) in the Field row. In our example, enter **Extended: [Order Details]![Quantity]*[Cost]** in the empty column in the Field row next to the ItemID field. The notation, Extended:, designates the text to use for the column heading. In other words, enter the heading name followed by a colon. If you do not specify a heading, Access will create a rather cryptic one for you. Enter the field names exactly as they are in the table, in square brackets. The exclamation point is used to separate the name of the table from the field. The asterisk is used to indicate a multiplication operation.

f Access displays a parameter dialog box or reports an error instead of performing the calculation, then carefully check the expression. Make sure you typed the table and field names exactly as they are, including spaces.

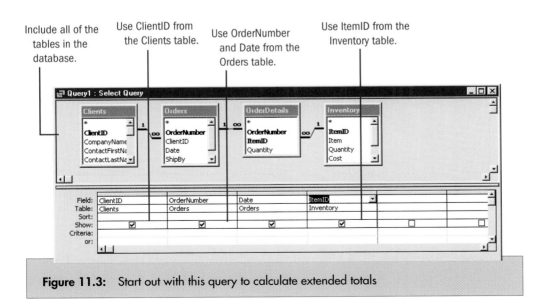

Include all of the tables in the database.

Use ClientID from the Clients table.

Use OrderNumber and Date from the Orders table.

Use ItemID from the Inventory table.

Figure 11.3: Start out with this query to calculate extended totals

You can create complex calculation expressions using built-in functions by clicking on the Build button to display the Expression Builder box. When you have time, open one of your queries and try it out.

If a field name is only in one of the tables, you do not have to use the table name. However, two of our tables have a field called Quantity. If you had used only the field names in this operation, Access would slap your hands and display an error reporting an ambiguous field name. We don't want to upset Access, so indicate which field to use in the notation by including the table name, an exclamation point, and then the field name, as follows: [Order Details]![Quantity]. In this case, you're using the Quantity field from the Order Details table, not from the Inventory table.

Run the query, and you see the extended cost of each item in the invoice. (When you add another field to the grid, Access automatically selects its Show box.) Save and close the query, typing **Order Summary** when prompted by Access to name the query.

Setting Properties

Access will display field values using the same format they have in the table. When it shows information from a currency field, for example, the values will appear formatted as currency in the result set. When you create a calculated field, however, you should set its properties to determine how you want it to appear.

To set the field's properties, click in any row of the calculated field, click the right mouse button, and select Properties from the shortcut menu. You can also click in the field and then click the Properties button in the toolbar. You'll see this dialog box:

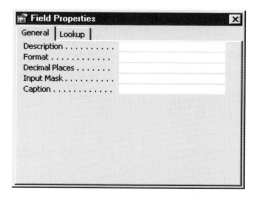

Most of the properties are used for advanced functions. The Input Mask property determines the format to enter if the field contains a parameter. To set the format, pull down the Format list and select the format you want to use, and then close the dialog box.

Summarizing Information

The Simple Query Wizard lets you summarize information by group. You may also want to summarize information in queries that you create in Design view. For example, we just looked at a query that listed the extended amount for each item in an order. Rather than be concerned with the details, however, you may be more interested to see the total value for each order. In order to summarize information, you need to add another row to the grid and tell Access which fields to use for the group and what type of math to perform.

Open the Order Summary query in Design view by clicking it and then clicking the Design button. To add the row used for summarization, click the Totals button to display a row labeled Total, as shown next. By default, all of the fields are set at Group By. If you want to calculate the totals of invoices, you'll have to group by fields that will result in the individual orders, such as ClientID and OrderNumber, because they represent unique orders.

Σ

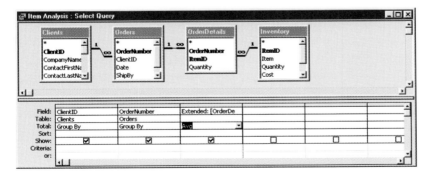

We're also no longer interested in the individual items, so you can delete the Date and the Item fields. Click the gray bar above the column to select these fields, and press DEL to delete them. In the fields that you're not grouping by, you designate the type of summary to create. For example, to display the total for each invoice, click in the Total row for the calculated field, pull down the list, and select Sum. When you run the query, Access will display the total of the calculated fields for each order.

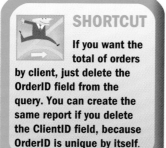

SHORTCUT

If you want the total of orders by client, just delete the OrderID field from the query. You can create the same report if you delete the ClientID field, because OrderID is unique by itself.

The Total list contains a number of options other than Sum. You can choose from other mathematical and statistical operations, use the Where option, or create an expression. Select the Where option when you want to specify a criterion to form the groups. For example, if you only want to include New Jersey clients, add the StateOrProvince field to the grid, choose Where as the operator, and enter **NJ** in the Criteria row. (When you select Where, Access automatically deselects the field's Show box.)

The Where operator determines which records to use for the groups. You may also want to determine which group results are shown. For instance, suppose you only want to list an order if its total is over $500. You do this in the Criteria row for the calculated field by entering >500 in the Criteria row.

Query Properties

There are other ways to control which records or groups are reported. You may have noticed the text box in the Query toolbar with All as its selection. This is the Top Values box, as shown next. By default, Access lists all of the records that meet your criteria. When you're sorting your records, however, you may only be interested in certain ones, such as the top five largest orders or the ten lowest-ranked students.

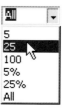

To specify a number of records to display, enter the number in the Top Values text box, or pull down the list and choose from the available options.

You can also control the output using Query properties. To display the Query properties, click anywhere in the gray area around the field list boxes and click the Properties button (or right-click and choose Properties from the shortcut menu) to see this dialog box:

```
Query Properties                              ×
 General
 Description . . . . . . . . . .
 Output All Fields . . . . . .   No
 Top Values . . . . . . . . . .  25
 Unique Values . . . . . . . .   No
 Unique Records . . . . . . .    Yes
 Run Permissions . . . . . .     User's
 Source Database . . . . . .     (current)
 Source Connect Str . . . .
 Record Locks . . . . . . . .    No Locks
 Recordset Type . . . . . .      Dynaset
 ODBC Timeout . . . . . . .      60
 Filter . . . . . . . . . . . . .
 Order By . . . . . . . . . . .
```

The two other most useful properties are Unique Values and Unique Records. While no two entire records in a table should be alike, there may be a combination of fields used in a query that may result in duplicate rows in the result set. When Unique Values is set at No, Access will display all of the records, even if the values in the fields are the same. When set at Yes, only one of each row appears in the result set.

The Unique Records property is similar, but it takes into account all of the fields, even those not used in the query. When set at Yes, duplicate records are not used for the query.

To show as much data as possible, set both the Unique Values and Unique Records properties to No.

We've finished with the Query Properties dialog box, so close it now and then close the Query window.

Creating a Crosstab Query

While the other Query Wizards are rather straightforward and intuitive, we'd like to briefly cover the Crosstab Query Wizard. A crosstab (an

EXPERT ADVICE

While you can create a crosstab query manually in Design view, it pays to use the Crosstab Query Wizard.

abbreviation of cross tabulation) analyzes information based on two or more fields from one or more tables. For example, suppose you're interested in the ordering habits of clients. You want to see what products your clients order, as well as the totals for each item. This means looking at the data in two ways, by client and by the item:

ClientID	Total Of Quant	Bananas,dried	Cider, Apple	Cider, Grape	Coffee Beans	Jelly, Cherry	Jelly
1	36	3	4		6	12	
3	34			12	12	10	
6	71					13	

Unfortunately, the Crosstab Query Wizard can only use fields from one table or query and not from related tables. To use fields from related tables in a crosstab, you should first create a regular query that contains those fields. To analyze client orders, for example, let's start by creating a query in Design view, as shown in Figure 11-4. Add all four tables, and use the ClientID field from the Clients table, the Quantity fields from the Order Details table, and the Item field from the Inventory table. You need to use the Orders table even though no

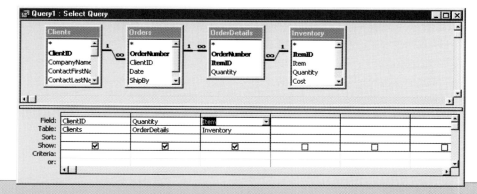

Figure 11.4: Create this query to prepare for the crosstab

fields from it are being used because it links the other tables. This simple query will show the item, and quantity of each item, for all orders. Save that query, typing in the name **For The Crosstab**.

Now create the crosstab using these steps:

1. Click New in the Queries page of the Database window, and double-click Crosstab Query Wizard. The first wizard dialog box asks what table or query you want to use for the crosstab fields.

2. If just the tables are listed, click the Queries option button to list the queries in the database. Click the For The Crosstab query you created, and then click Next.

3. In the second wizard dialog box, designate the field you want to use for the row headings. If you are analyzing client orders, for example, double-click ClientID and then Next.

4. The next wizard dialog box asks what field to use for the column headings. For our example, use the Item field to get this second dimension in the analysis.

5. The next wizard dialog box, shown next, asks which field to use for the summaries and the type of operator to use. It uses average by default. To total the quantity, for example, select Sum in the Function list, and make sure the Yes, Include Row Sum check box is enabled; then click Next.

You can select up to three fields, but too many makes the crosstab more difficult to interpret.

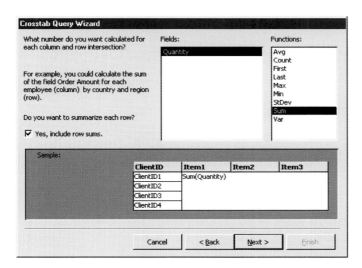

6. The last wizard dialog box is the old standard—it asks for the name (we've called ours **Stock Flow**) and whether you want to view it or show it in Design view. Click Finish to see the Crosstab result set. When you finish reviewing the data, switch to Design view.

Figure 11.5 shows the sample crosstab query in Design view. As you can see, a crosstab query is a special type of total query, with an additional row called Crosstab.

In the Crosstab row, pull down the list that appears and designate how the field is being used. The options are Row Heading, Column Heading, Value, and (not shown). You must have at least one row and column heading and one value field. Selecting (not shown) uses the field for sorting or criteria but does not include it in the result set. The Row Heading and Column Heading fields are used for groups, and the Value field must use a summary operator.

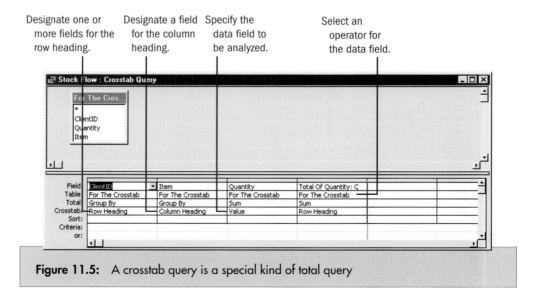

Figure 11.5: A crosstab query is a special kind of total query

Filters and Queries

Filters and queries do similar work. They both use a grid arrangement
to determine what records appear and how they are sorted. And once
you create one, you can quickly use it as the other. When a Filter By
Form or Advanced Filter/Sort window is displayed, use these buttons
in the toolbar:

 Load From Query lets you use the specifications from an existing
query in the current filter.

 Save As Query saves the filter specification as a query. You can
then open or change the query as if it were created in Design view.

You can also choose Load From
Query and Save As Query from
the File menu.

Taking Action with Queries

Sometimes you want to perform an action that affects more than one
record, such as deleting records that are no longer needed, or
increasing prices by a certain percentage across the board. Rather than
wasting time changing one record at a time, you can deal with them
all at once with an action query. An action query doesn't just select
data, it does something with it. It deletes records, changes information
in your table, creates a new table, or adds records to another table.

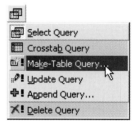

You begin an action query like any other—in the Query window, after
you've added the tables containing the fields you want to use. You then
choose the type of action to perform from the Query menu, or from the
pull-down menu of the Query Type button on the toolbar.

You can only perform the action by clicking on the Run button or by
selecting Query | Run—you cannot perform the action query by clicking
on the View button to display the datasheet. So before running an action
query, you should click the View button to display the records that will
be deleted, copied, appended, or updated, depending on the type of
action you're performing. When you're certain that the correct records
will be affected, return to Design view and run the query.

The names of action queries in the Database window are preceded by an icon representing the type.

You may find it even safer to design and run the query as a select query first (make sure you choose Select as the query type) to confirm the records. Then select the action type and complete the design before running it. This way you're certain that you won't run the query by mistake. To stop an action query after you start it, press CTRL-Break.

Making a New Table

When you want to create a new table with information from another, create a Make-Table query. For example, suppose you want to combine fields from several related tables. You can create a new table without having to retype the same information, and without cutting and pasting individual records from one table to another.

To make a new table, create a query containing the fields that you want to copy to a new table. (Double-click the asterisk if you want to move all of the fields.) They can be fields from a single table, or several related tables, but you can only have one AutoNumber field. Enter any criteria you'll need to select the records you want to copy, and deselect the Show box for fields that you want to use for criteria or sorting, but which you do not want to add to the new table. Click the View button to confirm that the correct records are selected. Now change to Query Design view, and choose Query | Make-Table Query to see this dialog box:

SHORTCUT

If all you want to do is copy the entire table, just use the Copy and Paste commands from the shortcut menu in the Datasheet window.

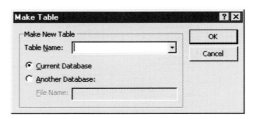

In the Table Name text box, enter the name of the new table you want to create. Click OK to return to the Query Design window; then click the Run button to perform the action. You'll see a dialog box reporting the number of records pasted into the new table. Click Yes to make the table, and then close the query without saving it. The new table will not have the key or indexes from the original table, it will not inherit the field's properties, and it will not have any relationships established. So, after creating the table, open it in Design view and create any keys, indexes, or set any properties desired.

DEFINITION

Inherit: Receive characteristics from the source of the objects. Properties assigned to a field will not be inherited in the newly made table.

Appending Records to a Table

A Make-Table query adds records to a new table. An Append query adds records to another, already existing table. Information from one table is placed in a corresponding field in the other, but you can append fields even if the records do not have the same number of fields and the same field names. For example, suppose you have a Clients table and a Prospects table. Prospects become clients once they place an order. You can add a prospect to the client table, even though the field is called CompanyName in one table and ProspectName in the other. You just tell Access to append information from the ProspectName field to the CompanyName field.

To append records to a table, create a query that selects the records you want to append and that includes the fields you want to add. You don't have to add all of the fields if you don't want to. Next, pull down the Query Type list and select Append Query to see a box similar to that shown for Make-Table queries. In the Table Name text box, enter the name of the table to which you want to append the records. Select the database in which to store the table in either the Current Database or Another Database, and then click OK. You'll now see a new row in the grid, titled Append To, and the Show row disappears.

You use the Append To row to indicate where each field in the grid should be inserted into the destination table. If any field names are the same in both, the names will automatically appear in the Append To row. For example, if the CompanyName field is in both tables, then the data from the field CompanyName in the source table will be added to the CompanyName field in the destination table. If field names are not the same or you want to change those inserted by Access, enter the field names in the Append To row. If you pull down the list, you'll see the fields in the destination table. In this query, for example, I'm appending a number of fields that do not have exact matching names:

Field:	ProspectName	ContactLastName	Address	City	State	
Table:	Prospects	Prospects	Prospects	Prospects	Prospects	
Sort:						
Append To:	CompanyName	ContactLastName	BillingAddress	City	StateOrProvince	
Criteria:						
or:						

Both tables have fields called ContactLastName and City, so these are copied from one table to the same field in the other table. The other field names differ, so the field ProspectName will be copied to the field called CompanyName, Address to BillingAddress, and State to StateOrProvince. You can also combine text fields to copy them into the other table. In this example, the ContactFirstName and ContactLastName fields are combined and copied into a field called Contact, as shown here:

Field:	ProspectName	Expr1: [ContactFirstName]+' '+[ContactLastName]				
Table:	Prospects					
Sort:						
Append To:	CompanyName	Contact				
Criteria:						
or:						

Fields in the destination table to which no data are being appended will not be affected and will be blank.

You cannot append fields that will create duplicate keys—this will also generate a hand-slapping error message. In fact, if the destination table has an AutoNumber field, don't even bother appending fields into it. If you do, the fields will retain their existing numbers. If you do not append the fields, the fields will be renumbered to fit into the new table. Click the View button to confirm that the correct records will be appended. Return to Design view and run the query. You'll see a dialog box reporting the number of rows that will be appended. Select Yes to append the records.

Deleting Records with a Query

A Delete query will let you delete records based on selection criteria. To create a Delete query, first create a query that selects the records you want to delete, and then pull down the Query Type list and select Delete Query. The Sort and Show rows in the grid will be replaced by one row labeled Delete. Next, drag any fields to the grid that you'll need for criteria. The entire record will be deleted no matter how few fields are in the grid. Enter the criteria under the field names, then click the View button to ensure that the correct records will be deleted. Return to Design view and run the query. A dialog box will appear, reporting the number of rows that will be deleted. Click Yes to delete the records.

Deleting Related Records

Using a Delete query with related tables offers a new challenge. For example, if a customer cancels an order, you want to delete the record in the Orders table, as well as the related records in the Order Details table. When referential integrity is enforced, you cannot use a single query to delete records from a one table that has related records in a many table. That's a no-no and will result in an error message. But all is not lost. The trick is to use two queries; you delete the many records first, then the one records.

In the Query window, add the one and the many tables. Select the Delete query type, and then double-click the asterisk from the many table. Next, drag any fields from the one table that you need to use for criteria, and enter the criteria. Click the Query View button to confirm the records, return to Design view, and run the query.

You now can delete the records from the one table. In Design view, click the field list of the many table and press DEL. Just the criteria fields for the one table should remain in the grid. Now, run the query to delete the records.

Updating Records with a Query

Use an Update query to make changes to the values in a table. For example, suppose you have to increase the cost of all items in your inventory table by five percent. Rather than manually calculate and change each of the records in the inventory table, you can change them all (or just selected records) in one step using a query.

To update records, add the fields that are needed to select records and the fields you want to update, to the grid. Pull down the Query

Type list and select Update Query to see a new row, the Update To row, which replaces the Sort and Show rows.

In the Update To row, enter formulas that indicate how you want to change the values in the fields. For example, to increase values by five percent in a field called Cost, enter the formula [**Cost**]*1.05:

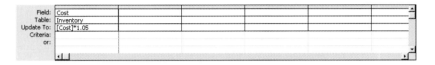

Use the View button to make sure just the correct records will be changed, and then run the query. A dialog box will appear reporting the number of rows that will be updated—select OK.

Summary

By creating and using queries, you can quickly access all sorts of information from your database without having to first create a special form or report. That's the beauty of a query. You can get information on an ad hoc basis, whenever you need it, and with almost any combination of fields, even from multiple tables. Use Select queries to display information, and use Action queries to do something with the information. Just be cautious using Delete and Update queries. Make sure they do exactly what you want.

Well, you've been working with all of the bits and pieces of an Access database. It's now time to work with the whole thing. In Chapter 12, you'll learn how to protect your database with passwords and encryption, how to analyze and improve their performance, and how to share information between databases.

Refining Databases and Tables

INCLUDES

- Using passwords
- Encrypting, compacting, and repairing databases
- Splitting databases
- Using objects from other databases
- Reading database properties
- Analyzing tables and databases

Protect Data with Passwords ➥ pp. 273–275

1. Choose File | Open.
2. Select the database, pull down the Open list, and choose Open Exclusive.
3. Select Tools | Security | Set Database Password.
4. In the dialog box that appears, type your secret password.
5. In the Verify box, type the same password again.
6. Click OK.
7. To remove a password, select Tools | Security | Unset Database Password, enter the password, and then click OK.

Encrypt or Decrypt a Database ➥ pp. 275–276

1. Close all databases.
2. Select Tools | Security | Encrypt/Decrypt Database.
3. Select the database that you want to encrypt or decrypt, and click OK.
4. To complete encryption, enter a name and select a location where you want to store the database, and click Save.

Compact and Repair a Database ➥ pp. 276–278

1. Open the database.
2. Select Tools | Database Utilities.
3. Click Compact and Repair Database.

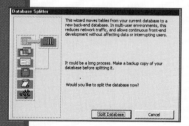

Split a Database ➥ pp. 278–279

1. Open the database.
2. Select Tools | Database Utilities | Database Splitter.
3. Click Split Database.
4. Type the name of a new database where you want to store the tables.
5. Click Split.
6. Click OK to close the message box that appears.

Import Objects from Other Databases ➡ pp. 279–281

1. Open the database you want to add objects to.
2. Select File | Get External Data | Import.
3. Double-click the database containing the object you want to import.
4. Click all of the objects you want to import.
5. If necessary, click Options and enable the desired option.
6. Click OK.

Link a Table ➡ pp. 279–281

1. Open the database to which you want to add a linked table.
2. Select File | Get External Data | Link Tables.
3. Double-click the database containing the object you want to link.
4. Click all of the tables you want to link.
5. Click OK.

Copy an Object to Another Database ➡ pp. 282–283

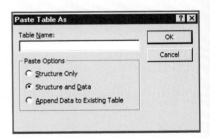

1. Open the database containing the object you want to copy.
2. Right-click the object and choose Copy from the shortcut menu.
3. Open the other database and display any page of the Database window.
4. Right-click the mouse and click Paste.
5. Enter an object name and select Paste Options, if given.
6. Click OK.

Read Database Properties ➡ pp. 284–285

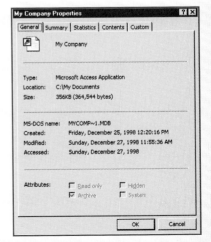

1. Open the database.
2. Select File | Database Properties.
3. Click Cancel when you finish reviewing the properties.

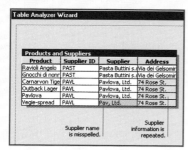

Analyze a Table ➡ pp. 285–287

1. Open the database.
2. Select Tools | Analyze | Table.
3. Read the first wizard box and click Next.
4. Read the second wizard box and click Next.
5. Double-click the table to be analyzed.
6. Select Yes, Let The Wizard Decide, and then click Next.
7. Adjust the suggested layout of fields, as desired.
8. Double-click a proposed table's title bar, type a name for the table, and then click OK. Repeat for each table and then click Next.
9. Confirm the selection of keys or set new keys, and then click Next.
10. Select to have Access create a query, then click Finish.

Analyze Database Performance ➡ pp. 287–289

1. Open the database that you want to optimize.
2. Select Tools | Analyze | Performance.
3. Click the All Object Types tab.
4. Click the Select All button, and then click OK.
5. Read each suggestion, recommendation, idea, and their suggestion notes.
6. Select all of the recommendations and suggestions you want Access to perform.
7. Click Optimize.
8. If a warning appears regarding side effects, click Yes to continue.
9. Enter any query or other object name that you are prompted for.
10. Read the ideas and make notes about how to implement them.
11. Close the Performance Analyzer box.
12. Implement the ideas, if desired.

We all know that it's easy to get caught up with the minutiae in life. And even though a database is only as strong as its weakest link, it pays to take a step back and get a wide-angle view. Make some time to think about security against unwanted prying eyes and Net surfers, and to find ways to make your database generally more efficient. In this chapter, you'll learn how to secure your database against intrusion, how to fine-tune your database by compacting and repairing it, and how to use Access to analyze performance.

Protecting Data with Passwords

The subject of passwords can bring to mind the cheap plastic decoder rings of childhood, invisible ink, and Agent Maxwell Smart speaking into his shoe. Data security used to be easy—you locked your file cabinet and hired a snarling dog or an equally snarling, but less sociable, security guard. Then along came computers and hackers and security has become a science on par with quantum physics.

Passwords, like locks on doors and windows, can only protect you from the casual thief. Access lets you set two types of passwords. What's imaginatively called the *database password* controls who will be able to open your database. A more complex type of password, called the *security account password*, controls users when they log on to a network workgroup. Security account passwords, and the user-level security that they provide, are best left to database or network administrators who have the time for that stuff. They can use something called the Security Wizard from the Tools menu, although even they shouldn't run the wizard until they've first taken some other steps (that network administrators like to keep to themselves).

CAUTION

Don't forget your password—you'll lock yourself out without it. If you don't trust your memory, write down the password and store it in your sock drawer.

Now for the rest of us. To set a database password, you have to first open the database using the Open Exclusive option. So follow these steps:

1. If the database is already open, close it.
2. Click Open in the toolbar.
3. In the Open dialog box, click the database.
4. Pull down the list next to the Open button and choose Open Exclusive.

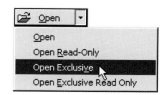

5. Select Tools | Security | Set Database Password.

6. In the Set Database Password box, type your secret password. Keep in mind that passwords are case-sensitive, so keep an eye on the CAPS LOCK key. As you type your password, only a series of asterisks will appear, protecting you from prying eyes. (Talk about paranoid.)
7. In the Verify box, type the same password again.
8. Click OK.

Now, whenever you or anyone else opens the database, a dialog box will appear asking for the password. Type the secret password—using the same case (upper/lower) with which you created it—and then click OK.

You should not use a database password if you are planning on synchronizing a replica database. You won't be able to synchronize it.

When you get tired of typing the password every time you open the database, remove it. To do so, open the database using the Open Exclusive option (of course, you'll have to enter the password to open it), then select Tools | Security | Unset Database Password—you'll see this option only if you're using a password. Type the password, and click OK.

Encrypting a Database

Psst. Over here, in the shadows. Oremay ecretsay tuffsay. Pass it around.

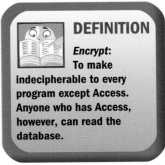

DEFINITION

Encrypt: To make indecipherable to every program except Access. Anyone who has Access, however, can read the database.

There's one major flaw with database passwords. You don't necessarily have to open a database to see what's in it. You can open the database into most word processing programs, for example. You'll have to slosh through thousands of garbage characters, but eventually you'll be able to read exactly what's in the tables. There are even special programs that are designed to extract information from the database and to convert it to some other form. Fortunately for us, Bill Gates must have owned one of those decoder rings as a child because he lets us encrypt the database.

Encrypting sounds very protective, but it is unfortunately rather ho-hum. While no one will be able to read the table information with a word processing program, everyone who has Access can get into it as easily as you can. So encryption, by itself, is practically useless. You have to both encrypt the database and use a password for any sort of real protection.

To encrypt a database, follow these steps:

1. Close any database that you're working on, but remain in Access. You cannot encrypt when a database is open. If you're on a network, call around and make sure no one else is using the database. If people are using the database, tell them to close it, or wait until they're done.

2. Next, select Tools | Security | Encrypt/Decrypt Database.

3. In the dialog box that appears, select the database that you want to encrypt, and click OK.

CAUTION

If you give the database a different name or save it in another location when you encrypt it, you will actually have two sets of the same information. Be careful that you, or someone else, knows which database to use.

4. In the next dialog box that appears, enter a name and select where you want to store the database, and then select Save.

If you use the same name and location as the original (non-encrypted) database, Access will replace it with the encrypted version. If you use a different name or location, Access makes an encrypted copy of your database. In either case, during the process you'll need enough hard disk space to store the original file and the encrypted copy. You decrypt a database following the exact same steps as for encrypting a database.

Just remember, encrypting the database by itself does not provide any protection against a thief who also has Access.

Compacting and Repairing a Database

When you encrypt a database, Access also compacts it.

Database files can be very large. If you've already got a lot of stuff on your hard disk, there might not be enough space to store the entire database in one piece. If this happens, Windows saves the bits and pieces of the database wherever it can. When you open the database, Windows collects the bits and pieces together. The situation gets worse as you add and delete records, tables, and other objects. So after a time, you've got database scattered all over the hard-disk landscape. Compacting (also known as *defragmentation*) draws all of the pieces together and stores them all, or as much as possible, in one place. This makes Access run a little faster and you a little happier.

Microsoft Access builds a pretty solid database, but things can still go wrong. During all of the bumping and grinding of your hard disk, something can happen to the database file as it is etched into electrons. When Access opens, encrypts, or decrypts a database, it will usually report if it detects any problem with the database and will ask if you want to repair it. But this self-diagnosis doesn't always work. If your database starts acting strange, then try repairing it yourself before spending money on technical support.

If the database cannot be repaired, try using a backup copy. If that doesn't work, call for support!

Access lets you compact and repair a database all at the same time. The following illustration shows how.

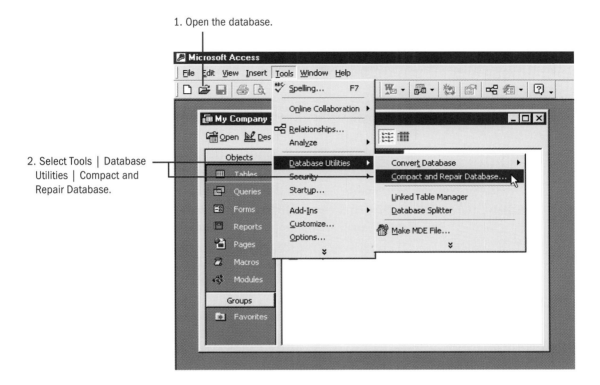

1. Open the database.

2. Select Tools | Database Utilities | Compact and Repair Database.

You can also compact and repair a database without opening it. Close the open database, and then choose Tools | Database Utilities | Compact and Repair Database. In the dialog box that appears, select the database you want to compact and repair, and then click Compact. Next, enter the name and select the location where you want to store the resulting file. As with encrypting, you can give the same name and location as the original, or you can use a different name or location to make a compacted copy. If you do want to compact it to the same name, make a copy of it first in another location.

Compacting a database has a nice side benefit if you use an AutoNumber field. Normally, Access doesn't recycle AutoNumber values. If you delete a record, its number will not be assigned to a new record. Compacting changes this, to a degree. If you've deleted records from the end of a table, Access will reset the AutoNumber value to one higher than the last undeleted record, so new records begin AutoNumbering from that point.

Splitting a Database

The critical part of your database is the information in the tables. Forms, reports, queries, macros, and modules are the icing on top of the biscotti. The people who use your database don't necessarily need to use, or want to use, the same forms, reports, or queries. If everyone stored their own personalized forms and reports in the database, your Database window would be cluttered like the Champs-Elysées after Bastille Day.

You can let everyone have their own forms and reports by storing the tables in a separate database. This way, each user can modify his or her own objects without changing the interface of another.

Here's how. First, make a backup copy of the database, just in case. Next, follow these steps:

1. Open the database, and select Tools | Database Utilities | Database Splitter to see the first of two wizard boxes. This box just tells you what the splitter does and that it may take a long time.

2. Click Split Database.

3. In the dialog box that appears, type the name of a new database where you want to store the tables and then click Split. Access does its thing and then displays a message that the database has been split.

4. Click OK to remove the message.

In the Database window, you'll see arrows pointing to the tables to indicate that they are linked, as shown next.

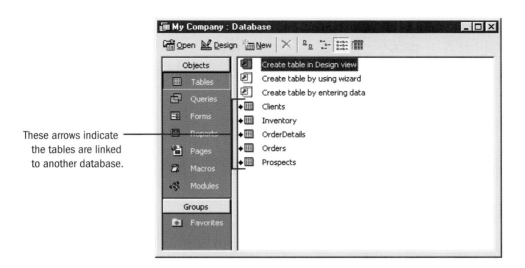

These arrows indicate the tables are linked to another database.

You use the database exactly the same as before. Adding, editing, or deleting records changes the tables, just as before, except that the tables are actually part of a different database.

If you want to link the tables with another database so that you can create a different set of forms or reports, use the Get External Data command that you will learn about next. You would also use that command if you want to unsplit the databases, placing the tables back with the forms and other objects.

DEFINITION

Linked:
A connection that allows one database to access tables stored in another database. The data remains in its original format.

Using Objects from Other Databases

Recycling is admirable. It can save the environment and save money, and those logos are way cool. You can also save time by recycling tables, forms, reports, and other database objects. For instance, suppose you spend mega-time creating a perfect database. There's a table or some other object in it that you'd like to use either wholly or in part in another database. Why re-create it, when you can just borrow it?

CAUTION

If you need to transport the split database—or one with links to other tables—on a floppy disk, copy both the one containing the tables and the one with the forms, reports, and other objects. If you copy just the original database, where will it get its information?

DEFINITION

Import:
To make a copy of a database object in another database. The original object is unchanged and will be unaffected if you change the copy.

You can also import or link tables by selecting Import Table or Link Table from the New Table dialog box.

SHORTCUT

You can choose Import and Link Tables from the shortcut menu that appears when you right-click in the Database window when no object is selected.

The Get External Data command lets you import any part of a database or create a link to a database table. Open the database you want to add objects to, then select File | Get External Data. You have two choices:

- If you want to copy the object from one database to another, click Import.
- If you want to create a link to the table, click Link Tables.

In the dialog box that appears, double-click the database containing the object you want to import or link. A Database window appears where you select the object itself, as in Figure 12.1. If you are linking a table, the window only contains the Tables page.

Now click as many of the objects as you want to import or link. Clicking on one object does not remove the highlight from another. To deselect an object, click it again. You can also use the Select All and Deselect All buttons. Before actually importing any object, you might want to check out your options. Clicking the Options button expands the dialog box to show these choices (the options do not appear if you are linking a table):

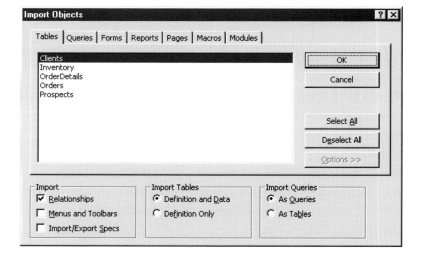

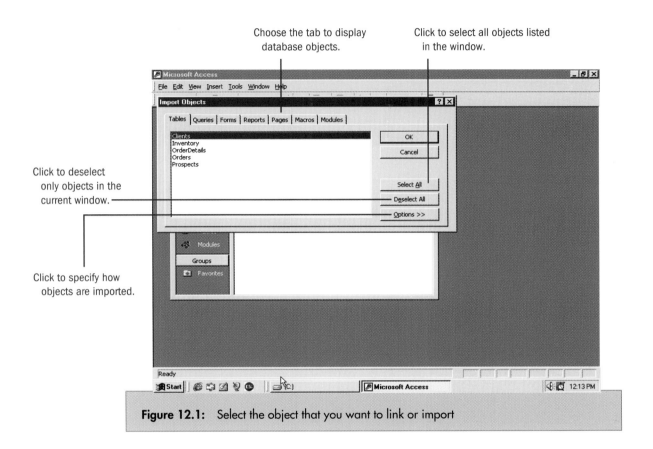

Choose the tab to display
database objects.

Click to select all objects listed
in the window.

Click to deselect
only objects in the
current window.

Click to specify how
objects are imported.

Figure 12.1:   Select the object that you want to link or import

The options in the Import section let you also import relationships
between tables, any custom toolbars and menus that you've created,
and specifications for importing and exporting objects. In the Import
Tables section, choose to import the definition and the data, or just
the definition alone. Select just the definition when you want to create
a new table using the same specifications but without the information.
In the Import Queries section, select to import the queries as queries
or as tables. Importing a query as a table is a good way to create a table
using fields from related tables in the other database.

Once you've selected the object and the options, click OK. The
objects will be added to the appropriate pages of the Database window.

Copying Objects

The Get External Data command brings objects into the open database. You can go the other way around—from the open database to another—and you can make a copy of an object in its own database.

To make a copy of an object to the same database, click the object you want to copy in the Database window, and then choose File | Save As to see this dialog box:

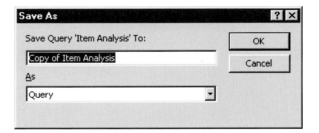

Type the name you want to give the object, then pull down the As drop-down list and choose the type of object you want to create. The As list will be dimmed for certain types of objects, such as reports, that cannot be converted into other types. Click OK to complete the process.

To place a copy of an object in another database, follow these steps:

1. Click the object you want to copy in the Database window.

2. Choose File | Export.

3. In the Export dialog box that appears, choose the database where you want to place the object, and then click Save to see the following dialog box. The Export Tables options are only available if you are exporting a table.

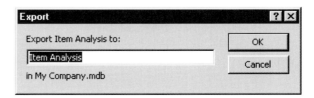

4. Enter a name for the object, if you want to rename it.

5. If you are exporting a table, choose if you want to export the table definition (the design) and the data within the table, or just the definition.

6. Click OK.

You can also use the Clipboard to copy objects, using either the Cut, Copy, and Paste buttons on the toolbar, or the shortcut menu that appears when you click the right mouse button. For example, to copy an object, click it in the Database window and then click the Copy button. This is a pain, because you then have to open the other database and click the Paste button. But it does offer one advantage; if you copy a table, you'll see this dialog box when you choose Paste:

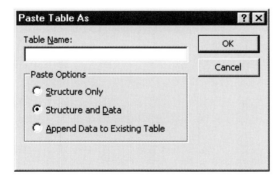

You can choose to paste just the structure of the table (its field definitions), or the structure and the data. If you want to append the information to another table having the same structure, type the name of the existing table and select Append Data to Existing Table. (If you copied an object other than a table, a box will appear for you to enter a new name.)

SHORTCUT
Cut, copy, paste, rename, or delete a selected object by clicking the right mouse button on it and choosing an option from the shortcut menu that appears.

Unsplitting a Database

If you split a database and then change your mind, you can unsplit it. Open the database that contains the forms, reports, and other objects, and display the Tables page. Delete all of the linked objects (the ones with the arrow pointing to them) by right-clicking the object and choosing Delete from the shortcut menu. Next, select File | Get

External Data | Import to import all of the tables from the original database you created with the Database Splitter, and then click OK.

Database Properties

Every object is associated with a series of properties that describe the object and give you information about it. After you open a database, select File | Database Properties. You'll see a dialog box with five tabbed pages, as shown in Figure 12.2. Some of the information on the pages is redundant, and some of it is nice but relatively useless. So we'll just recap what you'll find.

The General page contains the name, type, location, size, and file attributes of the database. It also includes its MS-DOS name and the dates and times the database was created, last modified, and last accessed. The MS-DOS name is useful if you have to copy, delete, or otherwise manipulate the database file in DOS and not in Windows.

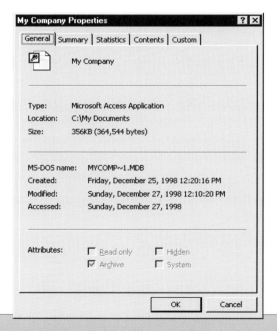

Figure 12.2: Every object is associated with this series of properties

The Summary page lists the title, subject, author, manager, company, category, keywords, and comments. You can use the information on this page to locate databases.

The Statistics page shows the dates and times the database was created, last modified, accessed, and printed. It also shows who last saved the database, the revision number, and total editing time. Revision Number reports how many times the database has been saved and whether you made any changes to it or not. Total Editing Time shows the length of the editing session, or how long the file was open, even if you did not edit it (as long as you saved it).

The Contents page lists the tables, queries, forms, reports, macros, and modules in the database. It's the same thing you see when looking at the Database window, just all together in a list format.

The Custom page lets you define your own properties—a rather advanced function for database gurus.

Table Analyzer

Serious database people worry all the time if their tables are normalized. They're not concerned about IQ, social behavior, or the regular stuff that we humans care about. Normalization is a series of rules to avoid duplicated information, mistakes, and problems, and it deserves serious consideration at a certain level.

We're really too busy to worry about normalization, but we can take some quick steps to check the health of tables. Table Analyzer looks at a table to help fix one common mistake made by entry-level database creators—making a table that contains duplicate information, which really should be divided into two or more related tables. The Analyzer Wizard isn't 100 percent automatic, and it needs a little help and input from you, but you can't mess anything up. It never changes your tables. It just creates new tables that you can use in their place. Here's how to use Table Analyzer:

1. Open the database containing the table you want to check.
2. Pull down the Analyze list in the toolbar and click Analyze Table, or choose Tools | Analyze | Table. If you did not yet

install the Table Analyzer feature, a box appears asking if you want to install it. Insert your Office or Access CD into your computer and click Yes.

3. The first wizard box is purely FYI, letting you see examples of how duplicated information wastes space and can result in errors. Click Next for another FYI box.

4. In the next dialog box, read how dividing the tables into two or more tables can help. Click Next.

5. Select the table that you want to analyze (at this point, you can also opt to deselect the Show Introductory Pages option for the next time you run the wizard). After you select the table, click Next.

6. You now have two choices to arrange your fields in the table:
   - Yes, Let The Wizard Decide.
   - No, I Want To Decide.

7. Make your selection and then click Next.

   If you choose to make the decision yourself, a box will appear so you can create additional tables and move fields around as you want. However, since it's much easier to have the wizard decide for you, rather than doing it yourself, we won't look at doint it yourself in detail.

   If you choose to let the wizard decide, Access spends a moment performing an analysis. If no corrections are needed, Access recommends not splitting the table. If corrections are needed, Access shows a suggested table layout, like the one shown in Figure 12.3.

8. If you do not like the layout, drag fields from one table to another. You can also select buttons to rename the table, undo your action, and display tips. When you're done, click Next.

9. You are then asked to confirm the keys. The wizard asks if the boldface fields uniquely identify the records. You can use the buttons to set a key or have Access add a key for you. When you're happy, click Next.

The wizard's suggested
table layout

Click to name the
suggested tables.

Drag fields from
table to table if
you want a
different layout.

The line shows the
relationship
between tables.

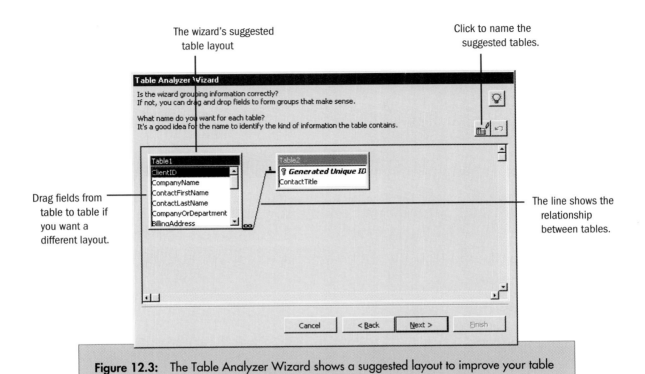

Figure 12.3: The Table Analyzer Wizard shows a suggested layout to improve your table

The final wizard box asks if it should create a query that looks like the original table. Keep in mind that the wizard creates a whole new set of tables, leaving your original unchanged, and that all of your forms, reports, and queries will still look for fields in the original table. If you tell the wizard to create a query for you, it will rename the original table, so forms, reports, and other queries get information from the new query instead. You won't have to modify the other objects, because they are fooled into thinking they're still working with the original table.

Performance Analyzer

On some computers, Access can run a little slow. We think even Microsoft wouldn't mind admitting that. Getting Access to run faster might mean adding memory or fine-tuning the Windows environment. If you don't have the money or the fortitude for these

DEFINITION

Optimize:
Adjust parts of the database to achieve optimal performance. Optimization speeds access to your information and prevents some database errors.

solutions, then try to optimize the database. This too can be daunting, but you're not entirely on your own.

Open the database that you want to optimize and select Tools | Analyze | Performance. You can also pull down the Analyze list in the toolbar and click Analyze Performance. You'll see a dialog box like the one shown here:

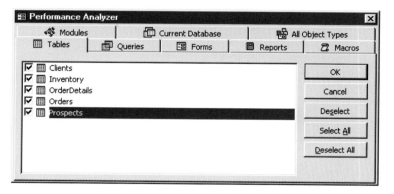

To put an idea into play, click it, read the Analysis notes, and then do it yourself.

You have to select the objects you want Access to check. You can select any combination of objects, combining different types in the same analysis. When you've selected the desired objects from the tabs of the dialog box, click OK.

Access checks the objects and then displays a dialog box like the one in Figure 12.4, showing some ways to optimize the database. Icons next to each item indicate the type of suggested change. Click each suggestion to read more about it in the Suggestion Notes box.

To have Access perform a recommended or suggested change, click the Optimize button—it will become active when you click a recommendation or suggestion. If optimizing will create any side effects, a dialog box appears asking if you want to continue. Click No, and read the suggestion notes first to make sure you understand the side effects. Then, if desired, click Optimize to continue. You may be asked to enter the name of queries or other objects that Access creates. When it is done, Access places a check mark next to each of the items that it analyzed, and you can close the Performance Analyzer dialog box.

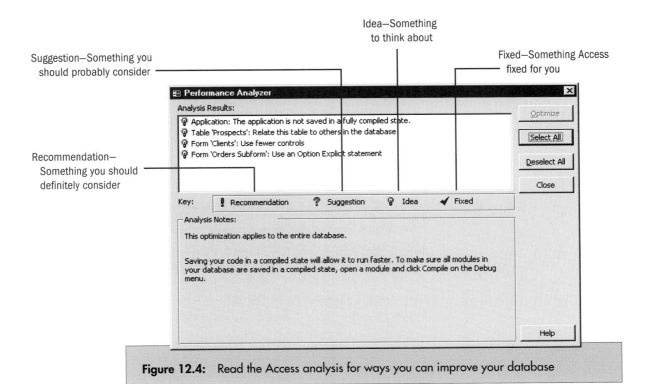

Idea—Something
to think about

Suggestion—Something you
should probably consider

Fixed—Something Access
fixed for you

Recommendation—
Something you should
definitely consider

Figure 12.4: Read the Access analysis for ways you can improve your database

Summary

Consider the techniques that you've learned in this chapter as a database toolkit. You may not need to use them often, but they can sure come in handy. Combine a password with data encryption to safeguard your work—just don't forget that password! Splitting a database, or adding links to other tables, can also help. Linking, or even importing information, can save you from retyping a lot of information, something none of us has time for. Use the table and performance analyzers often to make sure your databases are up to par.

Just as you can fine-tune the performance and structure of a database, you can fine-tune and customize forms and reports. In the next chapter, you'll learn how to create eye-catching forms and reports, and how to use Access's OLE data types to store pictures, sounds, and other objects in your tables.

CHAPTER 13

Creating Custom Forms and OLE Fields

INCLUDES

- Changing the size and position of controls
- Adding text and fields
- Adding OLE objects to forms and reports

Create a Form in Design View ➥ pp. 294–297

1. Select New in the Forms page of the Database window.
2. Choose Design View.
3. Select the table or query that you want to use as the basis for a form.
4. Click OK.
5. Add fields, labels, and controls as desired.

To customize an existing form, click the form in the Database window and then click Design.

Change the Form or Section Size ➥ p. 295

- To change the size of a section, point to the top of the section bar, and drag up or down.
- To change the size of the form, drag a border of the form.

Use AutoFormat ➥ pp. 298–299

1. While in Design view, click the AutoFormat button.
2. Click the style you want to add.
3. Click Options and deselect items to be omitted from the format.
4. Click OK.

Change the Size and Position of a Control ➥ pp. 299–300

1. Click the control to be modified.
2. To resize the control, drag any of the small sizing handles surrounding the control, or select Format | Size and choose an option.
3. To move the control, drag the large handle to move that control only, or drag the control border to move the control and its associated label or text box.

Add Text to a Form ➥ p. 301

1. Click the Label button.
2. Click or drag where you want to type text.
3. Type the text.
4. If necessary, press SHIFT-ENTER to start a new line.
5. Press ENTER or click elsewhere on the form to stop entering text.

Add a Field to a Form ➥ p. 302

1. Click the Field List button to display a list of available fields.
2. Drag the field name down onto the form.

Create an OLE Object Field Type ➥ pp. 303–304

1. Open the table in Design view.
2. Click in the first blank row.
3. Enter a field name.
4. Pull down the Data Type list and select OLE Object.
5. Save the table.

Insert an OLE Object ➥ p. 303

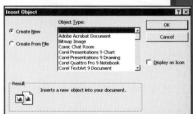

1. Click in the table or form field.
2. Choose Insert | Object.
3. To create a new object, click Create New, then double-click the object type. Create the object and then close the application.
4. To use an existing object, click the Create from File option, enter the path and name of the file, and then click OK.

Forms are great because you can use them to enter, edit, or just review information in your database. And besides, they are easy to create. However, don't expect the Form Wizard to do everything. If you really want to supercharge a form, you'll need to work in Design view. Here is where you can create a new form from scratch, or edit one that you've already created (or that's been created for you by the Database Wizard). Just let me warn you ahead of time: There are a lot of options when it comes to form design, more than a truly busy person can worry about. In fact, designing forms is an art and science all in itself, worthy of several chapters, if not its own book. In this chapter I'll show you how to customize the look of the form and the way it works. After that, you'll have to experiment on your own—when you have the time, that is.

You can make reports and data pages just as pretty as forms. Most of the techniques are the same; things just get a little more complicated. Don't worry, be happy.

Opening a Form in Design View

If the toolbox is not displayed, click the Toolbox button, or choose View | Toolbox.

You can create an entirely new form in Design view, although it is easier to customize an existing form because it will already include fields, labels, headings, and maybe some other design elements. To start a new form from scratch, select New in the Forms page and then choose Design View from the New Form dialog box. Select the table or query that you want to use as the basis for the form and then click OK.

To customize a form, you must display it in Design view. Click the form name in the Database window and then click Design. If the form is already displayed, just pull down the Form View button and select Design View.

EXPERT ADVICE

Creating a form from scratch is a real challenge, but it can be done. It is faster to create a form using Form Wizard or AutoForm and then customize it in Design view.

The Design window is shown in Figure 13.1. Use the rulers to help align and place controls on the form. Use the form selector box on the left of the ruler to select the entire form. Most of the buttons on the first toolbar are old familiar faces. You'll learn about the others later. The toolbox is a collection of buttons for commands that add and edit objects on your form. See Table 13.1 for a description of the toolbox buttons.

The form itself can contain up to five sections. The gray bars containing the section names are called *section selectors*. To select the entire section, click its selector. To change the spacing of a section, drag the appropriate section selector up or down.

You can display a page header and footer, and a form header and footer, by selecting them from the View menu. The Detail section

To change the size of the form itself, point to the line where the form ends and darker background of the window starts, and then drag.

The Form Header prints once, at the very top of the first form.

The Page Header prints on the top of every page.

Form Selector

Standard toolbar

Formatting toolbar

Toolbox

Rulers

The Detail section displays records.

The Form Footer appears once, at the bottom of the form.

The Page Footer prints on the bottom of every page.

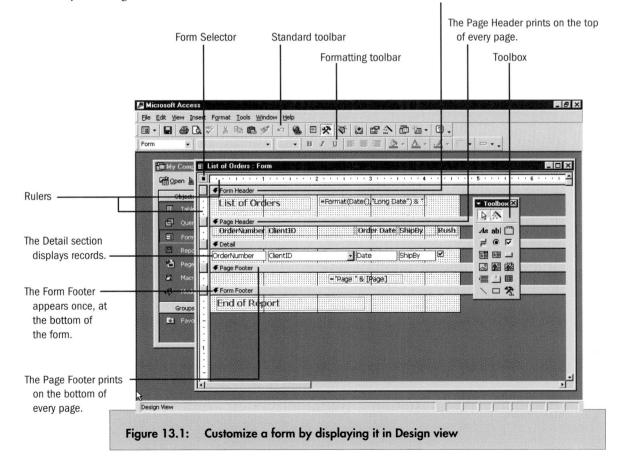

Figure 13.1: Customize a form by displaying it in Design view

Tool	Name	Function
	Select Objects	Enables object (control) selecting prior to moving, sizing, or editing them.
	Control Wizard	Turns Control Wizards on and off. When selected, automatically runs a wizard when you insert an option group, combo or list box, command button, or subform/subreport.
Aa	Label	Creates a label box to enter descriptive text.
ab|	Text Box	Creates a text box to enter, edit, or display data from the forms record source.
	Option Group	Creates a group where you can place related check boxes, option buttons, or toggle buttons in an option group. Only one button in an option group can be selected at a time.
	Toggle Button	Creates a toggle button to select an On or Off value. You can insert a toggle button in an option group.
	Option Button	Creates an option button to use by itself or in an option group.
	Checkbox	Creates a check box to use by itself or in a group.
	Combo Box	Creates a combo box. A combo box enables you to select a value from a list or you can enter a value in the box at the top of the list.
	List Box	Creates a list box. A list box enables you to select a value from a list.
	Command Button	Runs a macro or performs an Access command that you specify.
	Image	Inserts a graphic image onto the form.
	Unbound Object Frame	Creates a box where you can insert an unbound object.
	Bound Object Frame	Inserts a box for a bound object, one that is associated with data from the table, and thus changes as you move from record to record.
	Page Break	Inserts a page break. A page break marks the start of a new page on a form that has multiple screens, or a printed form that has more than one page.

Table 13.1: Forms Toolbox

Tool	Name	Function
	Tab Control	Creates forms with tabbed pages, similar to a Windows dialog box.
	Subform/Subreport	Embeds another form or report in the original form.
	Line	Draws a line.
	Rectangle	Draws a rectangle.
	More Controls	Displays ActiveX and other controls.

Table 13.1: Forms Toolbox *(continued)*

contains controls, including sets of labels and text boxes. A label is descriptive text telling you what to enter into the text box. The text box will contain the actual contents of the field. In many cases in Design view, the label will contain the same text that you see in the box—both will have the field name—but that doesn't always have to be the case. You can change the label, perhaps changing ClientID to Client Number, to make it easier for the uninitiated to fill out the form.

Access Controls

We've been calling the things on the form *objects*. That's fudging it a little, because Access has a special name for them—*controls*. So, to satisfy the purists (and Microsoft), I'll start referring to them as controls from now on. They're called controls simply because they control some object that appears on the form. The semantics are a little silly, but Microsoft does control the world.

There are a number of controls that you can add to a form, classified in three main categories: bound controls, unbound controls, or calculated controls.

- A *bound control* gets its content from a table or query, so its contents will change each time you display a different record. It is thus bound, or connected to, something else. The most common type of bound control is a text box that displays the contents of a field.

- An *unbound control* is not connected to any data, so its contents will be the same no matter what record is displayed. Typical unbound controls are the labels next to field text boxes, lines, boxes, and pictures.

- A *calculated control* shows the results of a calculation or an expression. You would use a calculated control, for example, to create a client's full name by combining the FirstName and LastName fields.

Formatting the Entire Form

If any text boxes are selected when you click the AutoFormat button, only those boxes will be affected by the font, color, and border formats.

One of the quickest and most effective changes you can make is to change the overall look of the form. When you create a form with Form Wizard, you can select an overall style, such as International, Clouds, and so on. Remember? Well, you can select from the same styles when you create your own form, and you can change the style already applied to a completed form.

To apply or change the style, click the AutoFormat button. You'll see a dialog box listing the styles. Each style includes a background picture, as well as the font, color, and border styles of text and text boxes. To control which aspects of the style are applied to boxes, click the Options button to expand the box with these choices:

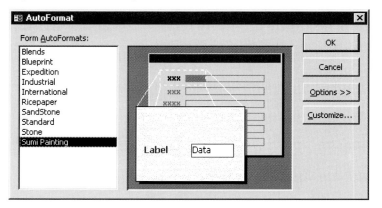

Deselect the styles that you do not want to apply. The box also contains a Customize button. Click the style you want to customize, and then click the Customize button to see these options:

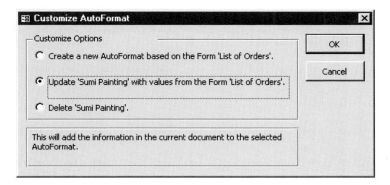

You can create an entirely new style based on the design of the current form. You can also update the style selected in the AutoFormat list so it conforms to the background picture and formats of your current form. And you can delete the style from the list.

Changing the Size and Position of Controls

You can customize your form by changing the size and position of its controls, and by adding new controls. To change the size and position of a control, such as a label or text box, you have to select it first. It's easy, but it requires a bit of explanation because the selection handles are a little different than what we're used to seeing in Windows. You also have to keep in mind that there's a connection between a text box and its label.

To select a text box or label, click it with the mouse. In the corners of the box, handles will appear, with one larger handle in the upper-left corner. The corresponding control—the label for the text box, for instance—will have a similar large handle in its upper-left corner. Use the handles to change the position or size of the control as shown in Figure 13.2.

CAUTION

Before clicking wildly to select controls, make sure the select button in the toolbar appears pressed down. If not, clicking in the form may cause some other strange and wondrous things to occur.

Drag the border of a control to move both
related controls, the label and the text box.

Drag the large handle
to move an
individual control,
the label or text box
(but not both).

Drag the smaller
handles to change
the control size.

Figure 13.2: Changing the position and size of a control

SHORTCUT

**You can also
select a control
by choosing it from the
Object list in the Formatting
toolbar. To select multiple
controls, click the ruler to
the left of or above them.
Clicking on the ruler on the
left side, for example, will
select all controls opposite
the position where you
clicked.**

To select more than one control, hold down the SHIFT key as you click each. You can also drag the mouse around controls, forming a rectangle that will select the controls within it. By default, you do not have to draw the box all the way around a control to select it—as long as the box touches any part of the control, it will be selected when you release the mouse button.

When you change the size or position of a control, watch the horizontal and vertical rulers. Access will display a highlighted area showing the control's size and position.

You can also change the size of controls using the Size command from the Format menu.

SHORTCUT

**To delete a
control, select
it and press DEL. If you
select and delete a text
box, the corresponding
label will also be deleted.
Deleting the label, however,
will not delete the text box.**

Adding Text

To add your own text to forms, headers, or footers, use the Label button. In this example, text was added to the Header section to identify the form, and in the Detail section to give instructions:

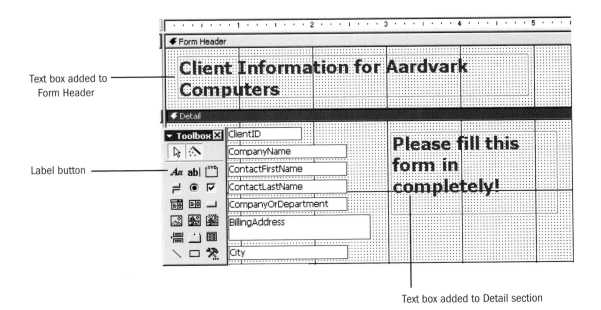

Text box added to Form Header

Label button

Text box added to Detail section

Click the Label button, then click where you want to type text, and type. Of course, you can use the Formatting toolbar to change its appearance. To format text, the label should be selected, but the insertion point should not be visible in the text box.

The label text will appear in a box. As you type, Access will wrap lines if the text reaches the right boundary of the label. To end one line and start a new one, press SHIFT-ENTER. Press ENTER or click elsewhere on the form to stop entering text. By default, the box holding text is transparent. Use the Back Color and Fore Color buttons to change the color of the box and its text. You can select the box to change its position or size. Edit the text in the box as you would any other.

To change a label, click it and then edit it as you would any text. Do not change the text in a text box unless you want to use the box for another field. You can create a box of a certain size before typing by clicking on the Label button and then dragging the mouse to form the box.

Adding Controls

You can also add other fields to the form from the underlying table or query using the Field list. For example, suppose you used Form Wizard to create a form containing selected fields from a table. If you later decide you want to include another field, you can add it in Design view.

Click the Field List button to display a list of the fields in the table or query used for the form. Drag the field down onto the form. When you release the mouse, the label and text box for the field will appear. This is a bound control because it is linked to the field in the table.

To insert a calculated control, you need to insert an unbound text box. This is a box that begins its life without any information from the table. Click the Text Box button and then click where you want it to appear on the form. Now you have to enter an expression to perform the calculation. You can enter the expression directly in the text box on the form, or in the Control Source property that you'll learn about later. Expressions start with the = sign and field names are surrounded in square brackets. For example, to enter the extended value of inventory, you would enter the formula =**[Quantity]*****[Cost]**.

You can use similar techniques to add text fields together (called *concatenating fields*), such as combining the first and last name fields to create a full name. You use the ampersand (&) between field names and you must be explicit about where to add spaces and other punctuation marks. Here's an example of concatenating:

> =[FirstName] " " [LastName]

The quotation marks with the space between them tells Access to insert a space in that position, between the LastName and FirstName fields.

To calculate and display a grand total, use the Sum function, like this:

=sum([Quantity]*[Cost]).

Displaying Graphics in OLE Fields

One of the data types that you can choose for a field is OLE Object. We haven't talked much about it earlier because it is a special data type, with some special considerations. An OLE Object field can store a document created by some other application.

For example, suppose you run an executive placement agency, and you use Access to maintain a database of your clients. You also use Microsoft Word to maintain a résumé for each client. When scanning your records for a suitable candidate, you'd like to move quickly from Access to the candidate's résumé in Word. That's easy. Just store the résumés in an OLE Object field, and then display them in Word by double-clicking on the field in an Access table or form.

Do you run a world-famous modeling agency? Use an OLE Object type to store each model's portrait. Are you a real-estate agent? Use an OLE Object type to store photographs of each property. Are you an accountant? Use an OLE Object type to store Excel worksheets. Are you a musician? Use an OLE Object type to store that next hit single. Just double-click the field to see the portrait, property, or worksheet, or to play that recording.

Before you can insert an OLE object in a table, form, or report, you have to create an OLE Object field in the table. To create an OLE Object field, select OLE Object when you are defining the field in Design view. Then, to add the objects to the table, click in the field and choose Insert | Object, or right-click the field and choose Insert Object from the shortcut menu that appears. Access will display the dialog box shown next. The dialog box has two main options—Create New and Create from File.

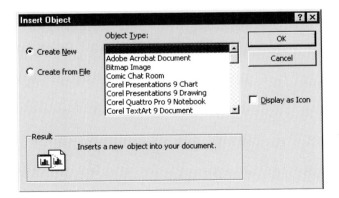

Use Create New when you have not already created the object that you want to add. Scroll the Object Type list and double-click the type of object you want to create. Windows will open the application used

Use the Link option to connect the object file to the table. Your database will then always contain the most up-to-date version of the object. Use the Display as Icon check box to display an icon that represents the object rather than the entire object itself.

to create that type of object. If you choose Microsoft Excel Worksheet, for example, Windows will start Excel. Create the file and then close the application to return to Access.

If you have already created the object, click Create from File in the Insert Object dialog box. You can then type the path and name of the object file, or select Browse to locate it on your disk.

Even though you'll probably use the same type of object for each record, it is not required. Records can contain Word documents, Excel worksheets, graphic images, sound or video files, or any other type of object. Note that Access indicates the type of object in the datasheet. To actually display or edit the object, double-click the field. Windows will open the application you used to create the object, and it will display it in the application's window, ready to be edited.

Summary

There is a lot that you can do to create customized forms and reports. You've learned the basics in this chapter, such as changing the size and position of controls, and adding text and fields. You've also learned how to use the OLE Object type. If you have graphic or sound files on hand, try adding an OLE Object type to a table and practice using this powerful feature.

Use what you've learned in this book to create and manage your databases. If you run into trouble, have questions, or just forget how to do something, go back to the chapter and refresh your memory. Whenever possible, take advantage of Access wizards and other automated features—such as AutoFormat and Format Painter—to save yourself time.

Index